À LA MODE

À LA MODE

120 RECIPES
· IN ·
60 PAIRINGS

PIES, TARTS, CAKES, CRISPS, AND MORE
TOPPED WITH ICE CREAM,
GELATO, FROZEN CUSTARD, AND MORE

BRUCE WEINSTEIN &
MARK SCARBROUGH

—◆—

PHOTOGRAPHS BY ERIC MEDSKER

ST. MARTIN'S GRIFFIN
NEW YORK

À la Mode. Copyright © 2016 by
Bruce Weinstein and Mark Scarbrough.
Photographs © 2016 by Eric Medsker.
All rights reserved. Printed in China. For
information, address St. Martin's Press,
175 Fifth Avenue, New York, N.Y. 10010.

www.stmartins.com

Book design by Jan Derevjanik

The Library of Congress
Cataloging-in-Publication Data
is available upon request.

ISBN 978-1-250-07213-9
(trade paperback)

ISBN 978-1-250-08553-5 (e-book)

Our books may be purchased in bulk
for promotional, educational, or business
use. Please contact your local bookseller
or the Macmillan Corporate and Premium
Sales Department at 1-800-221-7945,
extension 5442, or by e-mail at
MacmillanSpecialMarkets@macmillan.com.

First Edition: June 2016

10 9 8 7 6 5 4 3 2 1

CONTENTS

INTRODUCTION

—◆—

AN INVITATION TO OUR HOMECOMING

Sixteen years ago we wrote our first ice cream book. It was a wonderful opportunity, but we didn't quit our day jobs. Then the book sold hundreds of thousands of copies on QVC, at big-box retailers, in bookstores, and even on this newfangled thing called Amazon. We soon realized what we'd dreamed: we launched a food-writing career that has spun out into more than two dozen books on peanut butter, ham, goat, pressure cookers, boozy blender drinks, and more—and that's not counting the ones ghost-written for celebrities. No wonder our pants don't fit.

We've circled back and are having another go at ice cream. Mind you, we've been making the stuff all along, even on some really great tours for National Ice Cream Month (July). You haven't lived until you've stood outside in the San Diego heat with a table of sundaes and tried to make them last long enough for the host to get off the set and do a TV segment with you on the patio. Some things don't go well by design.

We've learned other things, too. We've got some new tricks for the steps that come before the ice cream machine. Like most Americans, we've gone nuts for frozen custard. And we're into purer flavors.

But there's another reason these ice creams are simpler this time around. This book is not a collection of frozen dessert recipes. Instead, it explores sublime pairings: an ice cream, gelato, or sherbet *plus* the dessert it was designed to accompany. We don't have to mention Bacon Maple Walnut Pie with Malt Frozen Custard more than once, do we?

Everything's à la mode! Which means everything is about balance. We think of these recipes as sets of rhymed couplets. (Sorry, one of us was an English major. He still can't help himself.) They are not only linked on the page but also constructed to complete each other. Some will seem obvious: Steamed Holiday Pudding and Frozen Hard Sauce. Others have to be experienced to be understood like Apricot Brandy Slab Pie alongside Chai Frozen Custard with a Lemon Curd Swirl.

As you'll see, we may love ice cream, but it's not necessarily the starting point in this book. Each pairing begins with a baked good—a pie or cake, brownies or scones, a layer cake or a jelly roll—and then includes the frozen treat as its partner on the plate or in the bowl. Or maybe you couldn't wait that long and you're snarfing at the counter. We won't judge.

You end up with 120 recipes in sixty pairings. That said, the dessert and ice cream recipes are presented separately. You might want to make one without the other. You could make our Bourbon Peach Pie and buy vanilla ice cream or you could make our Cherry Cheesecake Ice Cream and enjoy it right out of the machine on a warm summer day.

These pairings are grouped into sections, based not on the ice creams, but on the desserts that are their soul mates. Although each section opener offers some baking tips and tricks for what's ahead, there's plenty of help throughout: our best "pro tips" as well as serving suggestions and make-ahead guidelines.

Before we get to all that, let's look at how to make frozen desserts in general. We'd like to lay down some of our time-tested tricks for the smoothest, creamiest treats around.

ICE CREAM BASICS

ICE CREAM KNOW-HOW

———— ◆ ————

You love it from the first bite: that creamy richness, both sweet and cold. It's smooth, too, if sometimes with a slight chew, a good textural contrast before the frozen treat softens. There may be nuts or bits of fruit. They're second fiddles. The point is the feel, the melt, the slight shudder—and the second bite.

Ice cream is the best afternoon treat, the perfect dessert, and the go-to late-night snack. It's the antidote to a hot day. It's also apparently the antidote to a winter storm. Come to New England. You'll find our supermarket freezers bare before a "snowpocalypse."

Still, there's nothing like homemade. Sure, premium ice creams have gotten smoother and creamier over the last few decades, but you can't beat the home-churned stuff. How do you make it to capture all it promises? Let's hold that question for a minute while we discuss the current state of ice cream in these United States.

WHY MOST ICE CREAM ISN'T ICE CREAM ANYMORE

Back in the late '80s a couple of ice cream stands in Wisconsin (we're looking at you, Michael's and Culver's) started cranking out a cross between ice cream and gelato, something they called "frozen custard." For years, most Americans had been making custard-based ice creams in hand-cranked machines on their back porches. However, these Badger State concoctions were different: the custards were made not just with milk (as in gelato), or even with milk plus a little cream (as in the American standby), but with a heavy pour of cream. What's more, they weren't made with just a few egg yolks (again, as was sometimes the case with the American standby) but with gobs of them (as in gelato).

More cream, more egg yolks, a richer custard—naturally, the mere notion flashed across the country (probably after it took a nap). In its wake, all frozen treats, even the likes of sherbet, have undergone what we call a *frozen-custard-ization*; they've become creamier, thicker, and sweeter. Even sorbet has gotten into the act. Pastry chefs now violate its no-dairy prime directive to create buttermilk or goat cheese sorbet (by which we take it that they're still "sorbets" since they contain no cream, if other dairy).

Know it or not, we've all been happily frozen-custard-ized.

THE LAY OF OUR LAND

As you can see, ice cream and its ilk have gotten richer while the definition of what's what has gotten murkier. So before we get rolling, here's what we mean by the terms.

ICE CREAM · a churned, frozen, *mostly cream*-based dessert *without eggs*. Some are not thickened (like the Italian classic *fior di latte*); others include flour, cornstarch, or potato starch. Even melted chocolate adds a slight chew. Most are made from a mix of cream and milk, sometimes in equal measure. Or all that was true before that vaunted frozen-custard-ization. Still, we stick by the old definition, although we bend it when there are only a couple of egg yolks in a recipe, not really enough to set the mix up into a puddinglike custard but just to enrich it. We'll call that "ice cream" although it's a "light" frozen custard.

GELATO · a churned, frozen, *milk*-based dessert made *with eggs* (usually just the yolks). This Italian staple uses lots of eggs, sometimes six or eight yolks per quart. They're the primary thickener (unless other liquids like brandy have been added, at which point even all those eggs need help). But there's a "but"—Italian whole milk production includes up to 6 percent butterfat; American, 3.25 percent. More cream has been left in Italian whole milk. We Americans then must compensate by adding a touch of cream (say, ¼ cup) to a gelato recipe to get that *eccessivamente* soft, creamy texture.

FROZEN CUSTARD · the crown prince of churned, frozen desserts. Consider it an egg-rich gelato with *lots* of cream—but never *only* cream or it would get unpleasantly rich. Frozen custard is instead made with a mix of cream and milk, although distinctly weighted to the former.

SHERBET · a frozen, churned, milk-and-sweetened-fruit-puree combination. It was probably a Persian concoction that got popular across medieval and Renaissance Europe as trade routes increased. It was made by pouring mare's milk over fruit and shaved ice. Modern sherbet is actually an American revamp of the classic, using a sweetened fruit puree, rather than fresh fruit. (And no mare's milk!) However, because of that frozen-custard-ization, sherbets these days almost always include gelatin (or another thickener) to make them even creamier.

SORBET · a churned, frozen, sweetened fruit puree, no dairy or eggs in the mix. These days, that standard definition has slipped quite a bit. Witness our one sorbet in this book. It doesn't include dairy or eggs; it also substitutes peanut butter for the fruit.

FROZEN YOGURT · just what it seems—churned, frozen yogurt. However, we always add a little cream. Why not? We want an ultrasoft texture that keeps that yogurt zip intact.

SEMIFREDDO · a frozen loaf of utter bliss, not churned, instead built from three components. Despite pale imitations in Italian-American restaurants, a semifreddo is actually a mix of pastry-chef favorites: a zabaglione (a thickened egg-yolk sauce), a Swiss meringue (a cooked egg-white-and-sugar mix, like Marshmallow Fluff), and whipped cream. It's complicated to make. You'll dirty every bowl you own. It's also one of our passions. We've included two here plus a "semifreddo-ish" version of Bavarian cream, a traditional sauce.

THE PROBLEM WITH AIR

First, here's the rule: churn frozen treats as little as possible.

Now here's the explanation. Ice creams, gelati, and the rest are frozen foams: air is churned into a liquid, even a thickened liquid, which in turn freezes around those bubbles to create a pleasingly light texture. In fact, ice cream's famed creaminess is a result of the churned-in air, not the thickened custard. If you don't believe us, try setting a small bowl of chocolate pudding in your freezer overnight and then sample the results.

In industry parlance, the amount of churned-in air is the "overrun"—that is, how much the volume of the final ice cream "runs over" the original volume of the custard. Standard, store-brand ice cream can have a 100 percent (or more!) overrun. That means the ice cream is at least double the volume of its starting mixture. Or to put it another way, it's at least half air. Thus, it turns foamy as it melts: all that air comes out of suspension. A premium ice cream is denser: maybe a 50 percent overrun, or a creamier 30 percent overrun, or even a ridiculous 15 percent overrun.

We do indeed want some air in the mix (otherwise we're eating a block of frozen pudding) but we don't want too much (otherwise we're eating foamy nothingness). With home ice cream machines, the bulk of the air is churned in once the custard starts to firm up. After all, an ice-cream machine's dasher is not moving as fast as, say, the beaters of an electric mixer; the dasher can hardly put much air into a still-liquid custard. It adds more as the custard freezes. And again, we want to churn in just enough air for a great texture, not so much as to make the ice cream foamy.

To churn less, everything must be cold. If the insert to your ice-cream maker needs to be *frozen*, it must, indeed, be frozen. It should frost when you take it out of the freezer (unless you live in zero-humidity Nevada). Nothing should slosh inside. If you're using a machine with a built-in compressor, follow the manufacturer's instructions: some require the compressor to run for a bit before freezing; others are plug-and-play. And if you're churning by hand (the old-school way), you need to follow the manufacturer's instructions, adding salt to the chipped ice around the canister to drop the freezing point below 32°F.

No matter which machine you've got, put its dasher and lid in your freezer for an hour or two before you make ice cream. The colder they are, the less air you'll churn in (and so the lower the overrun). Or store the lid and dasher in your freezer so they're ready when you are.

In like manner, chill the custard or other ice cream mix before freezing it in the machine. In fact, most of these mixes can be made at least a day in advance and stored overnight in the refrigerator. As a bonus, their flavors will mellow and balance. So plan ahead.

While we're at it, read the instruction booklet for your machine. Refresh your memory by looking it up online if you've lost the original. Clean *and dry* the parts that will touch food.

But what if you're ready for ice cream *now* and don't have four hours to chill the custard? Fill a very large bowl about halfway with ice, add a little water, then pour the custard into a medium bowl. Set this in the ice bath and chill, stirring occasionally, for about 30 minutes, replenishing the ice as necessary.

All of the above about overrun and air leads us to two final points:

1 · If you're going to eat a frozen dessert right out of the machine, enjoy it slightly underfrozen, when it's still a bit soft. It'll be creamier and richer with a lower overrun.

2 · If you're going to make the frozen dessert and store it in your freezer for a while, keep churning it to get a little more air into it, until it's firmer and the dasher has a hard time pulling through it, until it pulls away from the sides of the canister. In this case, it will be firm enough that it won't trap many ice crystals as it becomes more solid in your freezer. You'll end up with creamier ice cream when you finally enjoy it.

170°F: A MORE IMPORTANT NUMBER THAN 32°F

Before we ever get to the ice-cream machine, how do you know when a custard is, well, a custard—when it has thickened to the right point to make the creamiest ice cream or gelato? What we're about to tell you is one of the most innovative features of this book. (And a food geek's dream come true.)

There's a long-standing culinary trope about custards, invoked once all the eggs, dairy, and possible thickeners are in the saucepan over the heat: cook them until they can coat the back of a wooden spoon. In other words, dip a wooden spoon in them, run your finger along its back, and watch the line you make; it should have distinct edges that do not run when you tilt the spoon this way and that.

Great. But there are two problems. First, that's a pretty subjective cue. What if your notion of a firm line isn't ours? And second, reading that explanation takes about as long as doing it—and the custard is over the heat at a delicate point while you're adjudicating lines. You should be stirring; you could scramble the eggs.

We advocate a more scientific approach. Either use a (cleaned and dried!) instant-read meat thermometer or invest in a laser thermometer to take the custard's temperature as you stir it (thereby keeping hot and cold spots even throughout). Yes, eggs start to curdle (that is, scramble) at about 160°F *at sea level*. They are fully scrambled at 170°F *at sea level*. However, there are various protective barriers in all these custards: fats (the cream, egg yolks, sometimes even butter) and/or other thickeners (flour, cornstarch, etc.). We can push these custards to 175°F, maybe 178°F in some cases—but that's the outer limit, the breaking point. So we feel the best custards for gelato and the like should be cooked to 170°F *at sea level*. We want it as close to curdling as possible for the thickest gelato or frozen custard from the machine.

You must stir. Do not whisk. Use a wooden spoon. In fact, search cookware stores and sites for a wooden spoon with a small point off of one side, specifically designed to get into the crook of a saucepan. And keep the heat low. Be patient. We say it takes a range of timing: 4 to 7 minutes or 5 to 9 minutes or the like. Even such wide time markers can be misleading based on how much heat the "low" setting on your stove puts out or the rate at which you stir.

With a thermometer in hand, you'll never be wrong. Unless you don't live *at sea level* (or within 2,000 feet of it). At 3,500 feet above sea level, cook the custard—stirring constantly—until it's at 167°F. At 5,000 feet, until it's at 165°F. And at 8,000 feet, until it's at 159°F. Split the difference at other elevations.

YOLKS AND WHITES

You're about to use a lot of egg yolks (as well as some whites), and you're about to get messy.

First rule of thumb: Crack an egg against a flat countertop, never the rim of the bowl. You're less likely to drive bits of shell inside. Residual contaminants can lurk on the shell. Its shards can also puncture the yolk.

To separate eggs, go with the pastry chef–approved method. (You squeamish, swallow hard.) Wash and dry your hands. Set a bowl in the sink or on the countertop. Crack the egg out of its shell and into one palm. Put your hand over the bowl. Spread your fingers slightly and tip your hand so that the white runs between your fingers and into the bowl below, cupping the yolk in your palm. Now put the separated yolk in a second bowl. Then soldier on to get as many yolks and/or whites as you need.

Unused egg whites can be frozen in a sealed glass or plastic container. Or put one white in each slot of a plastic ice cube tray, then freeze them hard. Unmold them and seal in a plastic bag. Date it so you know their freshness. Use within 1 year. They should be used only for dishes in which they're thoroughly cooked (like cakes and quick breads).

Unused egg yolks are more difficult. Whisk in ⅛ teaspoon salt for each large egg yolk, then freeze in a sealed glass or plastic container for up to 4 months. Again, use them only in dishes in which they're thoroughly cooked.

In either case, thaw them in the refrigerator overnight. As a general rule, 2 tablespoons thawed frozen egg white = the white of 1 large egg; 1 tablespoon thawed frozen egg yolk = the yolk of 1 large egg. Use frozen yolks within 4 hours of thawing.

the motor, the churning speed, and the surface area exposed to the ambient environment. We have two built-in-compressor machines, exactly the same make, year, and model number. One will make 4 cups (a quart) on the nose; the other, sometimes 4½ cups from the same recipe. Yours may make a full quart, a little more, or even a little less, depending not only on the speed and torque but also on the temperature of the custard when it goes in as well as the temperature of the dasher and even the machine's lid.

STORING ICE CREAM

If you're not going to eat a frozen dessert right out of the machine (whatsamattawichew?), spoon it into a glass or plastic container, seal it tightly, and store it against the floor of your freezer (or otherwise against the coldest part in newer-fangled appliances).

We suggest storage lengths for every frozen dessert in the book. Our numbers are subjective but based on the custard's thickness, its overrun capacity, the sugar level, the presence of mix-ins, and/or the effectiveness of its thickeners. Some frozen custards have never lasted more than a few days in our house. Who are we kidding? More than a few hours. We're looking at you, Salt Caramel. No matter, self-defrosting freezers are the enemies of ice cream. Their temperature rises to just above freezing on a set cycle, thereby melting any ice crystals in the unit but also melting any stored ice cream a bit—and then refreezing it, now with its own crystals in tow. Sad to say, most ice creams won't keep their pristine texture. If you intend to keep the ice cream or gelato more than a week (seriously?), press plastic wrap directly against its surface once it's frozen hard, then seal the container and store it in the coldest part of your freezer. However, always set the custard out on the countertop for a few minutes to soften it up. The flavors will be more pronounced; the texture, more irresistible.

"HOW MUCH?" SEEMS LIKE SUCH A SIMPLE QUESTION

Most of these recipes make a quart (or 4 cups). Some make a little more (say, 5 cups); a few, a little less, based on egg/cream ratios that ended up compromised if the overall volume was increased. (Interested in adding half an egg yolk? We thought not.)

Some older canister-insert machines make *exactly* 1 quart, no room to spare. If you've got one of these, pour in the custard or ice cream mix to its requisite fill line and freeze away. Cover the remainder of the custard mix (or what you have) and store it in the refrigerator to freeze in a second batch later in the day or even tomorrow.

In the end, different machines will add different amounts of air based on the torque of

A HALF-DOZEN TIPS FOR MAKING PERFECT ICE CREAM

Now that you know the problems of overrun and the best temperature for the set of custards, let's nail down a few more ways to get great results.

1 · USE ROOM-TEMPERATURE EGGS AND EGG YOLKS.

They will thicken more quickly when beaten with sugar or when stirred over the heat. You want to keep the custard as thick and rich as possible *before* it hits the ice-cream machine. You can get your eggs at room temperature in two ways. One, crack them out of their shells, separating the yolks from the whites if necessary, and set them in a small bowl on the countertop for 15 minutes. Or two, submerge the eggs *in their shells* in a bowl of warm (not hot!) tap water for 5 minutes.

2 · IN ALMOST ALL CASES, BEAT THE ROOM-TEMPERATURE EGGS AND THE SUGAR TO THE "RIBBON STAGE."

Such cookbook terminology is a long-standing marker of the desired consistency. You'll know you've hit it when the mixture's color lightens considerably because of all that added air *and* the mixture slides from the turned-off beaters in thick, fairly wide ribbons (not thin dribbles), ribbons that lie on top of the mixture in the bowl below before slowly dissolving. You want to reach the ribbon stage to make sure the sugar has dissolved enough that it won't revert to a granular form when heated *and* to make sure there's enough air in the mixture to provide a fluffy, light consistency to the ice cream. If you have a stand mixer, use the whisk attachment (not the paddle).

3 · WHEN YOU BLEND HOT INGREDIENTS, REMOVE THE CENTER KNOB FROM THE BLENDER'S LID.

Doing so will mitigate a pressure buildup inside the canister. You'll avoid a spray of hot liquid all over you and your cabinets. That said, lay a clean kitchen towel over the small opening.

4 · TEMPER THE EGGS CAREFULLY.

When asked to do so, start by beating some of the hot milk or cream mixture into the eggs until smooth, then beat this combined mixture into the remaining milk or cream mixture in the saucepan. You can't shortchange this step but you can prolong it. We're not trying to beat in air; we're just trying to get the eggs adjusted to the heat. The whole tempering process start to finish should take you about a minute (provided all your equipment's out and ready to go).

5 · WATCH ELECTRIC CORDS AROUND HEATING ELEMENTS.

In general, when you're using an electric mixer to beat things in a saucepan, take the pan off the heat (put it on a hot pad on your countertop, if necessary) so the cord isn't near an open flame or a heating element. That said, you must sometimes beat over the heat—for example, when you're making a zabaglione or a Swiss meringue for a semifreddo. Pull the cord back; always note where it is.

6 · STRAIN THE HOT CUSTARD BEFORE CHILLING IT.

Pass it through a fine-mesh sieve unless it has bits of fruit, nuts, or such in the mix. Remember: you've worked to get the custard to the edge of the point at which the eggs would scramble. There may be hot spots in the pan—or spots you missed with your wooden spoon—in which case there may be a few tiny bits of scrambled egg. A fine-mesh sieve will take care of the problem. But if you don't have one, don't worry. To improvise, line a standard colander with cheesecloth. Or go commando and skip this step. Skim through the custard, off the heat, to make sure there are as few eggy bits in it as possible. If a few remain, spoon them out. Even if you miss some, they won't ruin the dessert once it's churned and frozen.

PIES & TARTS

THERE'S BEEN A PIE RENAISSANCE. Not so long ago, a home-made crust was a sign of early onset insanity—or of too much time on your hands (often the same thing). Then mavens like Allison Kave rekindled the craft. Now only the brave admit to premade crusts.

We love rolling them out! Listen, when two men are joined in one career, it's nice to find something testosterone-free. There's a Zen quiet about pies. Sure, some pastry chefs may try to turn them into tattooed free-for-alls. But it's really about the gentle swoosh and click of floured hands and a rolling pin, the peace of a warm kitchen.

Pies and ice creams might seem like a natural combo, but it ain't necessarily so. While cream, meringue, and ice-box pies would be too cloying with a scoop of ice cream, many others are not calibrated to match up. The standard strawberry-rhubarb pie is too darn sweet. You know you're in trouble when the vanilla ice cream feels like the savory bit.

As you'll see, an *à la mode* pairing needs a balance between its partners. Many herbal notes in a pie prove a bad match (but strangely, not the same ones in an ice cream). Bitterness among the undertones works in your favor (hello, caramel and chocolate). Sour notes need to be ramped up; overall sweetness, toned down (unless you mean to go over the top).

You'll find lots of classic American pies here, all with a twist in the flavors to better match the frozen desserts: bourbon with peaches, vanilla with rhubarb, or bacon with walnuts. You'll also find a handful of fancier creations, including one that can only be described as peanut brittle morphed into a tart. And we've got one old-fashioned treat, a slab pie—the biggest newton cookie you've ever seen.

· SPECIAL INGREDIENTS ·

Let's clarify three items you'll see in this section—not in every recipe, but time and again.

1 · **INSTANT TAPIOCA.** We don't mean the giant pearls found in Asian bubble teas or the somewhat smaller pearls used to make the 1950s cafeteria pudding. Rather, we mean the ground tapioca (thus, "instant") found in the baking aisle. It's a time-worn pie ingredient, probably more familiar to your grandmother than to you: the dehydrated starch from the cassava root creates a richer, less gooey filling than flour alone and less jiggly than cornstarch. In most cases, we like a mix of instant tapioca and flour for a "spreadable" set.

2 · **SOLID VEGETABLE SHORTENING.** Most of our crusts are a combination of butter and shortening. The latter needn't be loaded with trans fats. Look for expeller-pressed vegetable shortening, sold in sticks like butter, often in the dairy case. Skip any added, artificial flavorings; buy the plain stuff; and use it in your crusts as you would butter. Store it in the refrigerator.

3 · **VINEGAR.** We usually add a dash of acid to crusts for two reasons. One, we like the slight bump of sour it gives to the crust, a better foil to the sweet filling, especially since we're often working with butter/shortening combo crusts. And two, we add it to help snap the glutens a bit and make the crust crisper. True, a quarter teaspoon of cider vinegar is not going to stop that mass of gluten in its tracks. But in butter/shortening combo crusts, it does raise the pH just a tad and so prevents some—certainly not all—of the glutens from turning doughy.

· MAKING CRUSTS ·

We'll have plenty of tips in the individual recipes where they'll be most helpful. But here are the basic instructions for rolling out pie and tart crusts.

1 · **START WITH A GLASS PIE PLATE.** Yes, the hipster kids love the old metal plates. But you'll end up with a crisper, browner crust in glass because there's less insulation. If you must bake a pie crust in a metal pan, you may need to add 5 minutes or so to the baking time to get the filling bubbling—which means the fluted edge or the topping can begin to burn. Lay a piece of aluminum foil on top if you notice any scorching. By contrast, tarts are always baked in a metal pan with a removable bottom. Their crusts are generally thicker and cakier; they don't need the extra zap of heat the glass plate provides.

2 · **KEEP THE FAT COLD.** The butter and even any expeller-pressed shortening should be right out of the fridge. Cold fat will hold its shape and not "melt" into the flour at room temperature. Cold fat will also yield tiny globs throughout the dough—which will then lead to more tender crusts with more flaky bits.

3 · **WORK IN THE FAT WITH A PASTRY CUTTER OR A FORK.** Press the fat through the tines and into the flour mixture, repeatedly cleaning off the cutter or the fork before going at it from different directions. The final mixture should look like coarse sand grains that have been coated in flour.

4 · **ADD AS LITTLE LIQUID AS POSSIBLE.** Start with the smallest amount stated; add more only as necessary. If you accidentally add too much water to a dough and it turns sticky, you can add a little extra flour. But be careful: the crust can become tough when the ratios fall apart.

5 · USE COLD WATER. It will keep the fat from melting so quickly in the dough.

6 · WORK ON WAX PAPER. It's an old-guard pastry secret. Sprinkle some water droplets on your work surface to keep the wax paper from slipping around, then set a large sheet on top. Always dust it with flour unless otherwise directed.

7 · GATHER THE DOUGH INTO A BALL, SET IT ON THE WAX PAPER, PRESS IT INTO A DISK, AND DUST WITH FLOUR. To mitigate some of the stress on the glutens during rolling, gently press the pie crust dough into a flattened, round disk, 1 to 1½ inches thick. Unless told not to, sprinkle the disk with flour.

8 · ROLL A CRUST FROM THE MIDDLE OUT, NOT FROM SIDE TO SIDE. For an even thickness and better shape, set the rolling pin right in the center of the dough disk and push out to an edge; then turn the pin a bit, set it at the center again, and make another push to the edge, and so on, always working from the middle out, around and around the crust. Yes, you'll make *many* more strokes. But you'll end up with better texture *and* shape.

All pie and tart crusts have a bit of overhang once they're in the pie plate.

9 · MEASURE ACCURATELY. Hold the pie plate over the crust occasionally to see what size you've got. Better yet, measure with a clean ruler. You want a little excess so you can shape it to the plate without worrying about perfection from the get-go. If you're working with a tart pan, simply press the edge into the already fluted sides.

10 · PEEL UP THE WAX PAPER WITH THE CRUST ON IT, INVERT IT OVER THE PIE PLATE, AND SET IT DOWN INSIDE. Set it down into the plate, position it at the center, then gently peel off the wax paper, leaving the crust in the plate. Press it gently to conform to the plate's or tart pan's shape.

11 · FIX THE EDGE. You can trim off any overhang with a small knife. Or you can make a thicker edge (some recipes require you to leave it very thick). In any case, do something about that unadorned edge.

- Press the tines of a fork all the way around the perimeter of the pie, making lots of little, parallel indentations on the lip.

- Or turn a flatware spoon upside down and press it around the crust, making little half-moons (extra points if you make two sets, one inside the other).

- Or do something fancier: take the thumb and forefinger of your nondominant hand and set these on the inside lip of the crust; push them out while pushing in-between them with the forefinger of your dominant hand (like putting an "I" inside a "U"). Work your way around the crust, making these indentations at the rim.

- Or go all out and roll the trimmed bits from the crust into long strands, then braid these like rope before pressing them onto the crust around the rim of the pie plate.

12 · FINALLY, ONLY COVER A BAKED PIE OR TART ONCE IT HAS COOLED TO ROOM TEMPERATURE. Steam is a crust's natural enemy. That pie or tart can sit out for several hours before it needs to be covered. Don't rush the process or you'll end up with a gummy slice.

You're now ready to make lots of pies and tarts to go with creamy, rich ice creams, gelati, and frozen custards. We'll start basic and move to greater innovation. Peach, blueberry, apple-cranberry, rhubarb—they're all here. But did someone mention Camembert in an ice cream or fresh fennel in a pie? Just you wait.

BOURBON PEACH PIE
◆
VANILLA BEAN GELATO

How do we make a peach pie *more* Southern? We add bourbon! And make it good bourbon. Don't use the $75 stuff but instead a decent bottle of aged-in-wood, molasses-scented spirit. Peach pie deserves it. And so does this vanilla gelato. It's ridiculously luxurious, thanks to its nine egg yolks. Listen, we need a pie topper that can stand up to the bourbon.

BOURBON PEACH PIE
· YIELD: ONE 9-INCH PIE ·
◆

Our pie is very juicy. Choose firm, sweet-smelling peaches. Stir the filling as little as possible to keep the fruit from breaking down. Even so, depending on the moisture content of the peaches, the filling may drip over the crust into the oven. If you're worried, put a rack at the lowest level under the pie, then lay a large sheet of aluminum foil on that rack to save on cleanup. However, the extra insulation may slow down the baking enough that you'll need to add 5 or 10 minutes, which means the top crust may begin to burn slightly at the edges. If so, lay strips of aluminum foil around the rim of the pie as it finishes baking. Or throw caution to the wind and plan on cleaning up the oven if the peaches were too soft.

FOR THE CRUST

2½ cups all-purpose flour, plus additional for dusting

½ teaspoon salt

12 tablespoons (1½ sticks) cold unsalted butter, cut into small bits

¼ cup (4 tablespoons) solid vegetable shortening

At least 5 tablespoons very cold water

½ teaspoon apple cider vinegar

FOR THE FILLING

6 cups thinly sliced, pitted, and peeled, ripe but not squishy peaches (7 to 8 medium peaches)

⅓ cup packed dark brown sugar

¼ cup bourbon

¼ cup granulated white sugar

2 tablespoons cornstarch

1½ tablespoons instant tapioca

¼ teaspoon ground cinnamon

¼ teaspoon salt

OVEN RACK · center | **OVEN TEMPERATURE** · 350°F

TO MAKE THE CRUST

1 · Whisk the flour and salt in a large bowl, then cut in the butter and shortening with a pastry cutter or a fork until the mixture resembles coarsely ground, dry (but white) cornmeal.

2 · Stir 5 tablespoons of cold water and the vinegar in a small bowl or cup, then add to the flour mixture. Stir with a fork until a soft but coherent dough forms, stirring in more cold water in 1-teaspoon increments as needed. Divide the dough into two balls, one slightly larger than the other (about a 60/40 split).

3 · Dust the larger ball with flour and roll it into an 11-inch circle, following the instructions starting on page 22. Center and set the crust into a 9-inch pie plate; do not trim the excess. Lay clean kitchen towels over both the crust in the pie plate and the smaller dough ball.

TO MAKE THE FILLING

4 · Gently stir the peaches, brown sugar, bourbon, granulated white sugar, cornstarch, tapioca, cinnamon, and salt in a clean large bowl until

blended. Set aside, undisturbed, for 10 minutes. Pour and scrape into the prepared crust.

TO FINISH UP

5 · Roll the smaller ball of dough into a 10-inch circle, using the same technique as in step 3. Center and set it on top of the pie. Now trim any excess crust and crimp the crusts together around the perimeter so no filling can leak out. If desired, flute or decorate the sealed edge. Make 4 slits in the top crust to release steam as the filling cooks.

6 · Bake until the filling is bubbling through the slits and the crust is lightly browned, about 50 minutes. Cool on a wire rack at room temperature for at least 1 hour or to room temperature. Slice into wedges to serve. Store tightly covered with plastic wrap on the counter for 1 day or in the refrigerator for 3 days.

PRO TIP · Buy freestone peaches, not cling.

VANILLA BEAN GELATO
· YIELD: ABOUT I QUART ·

Here's our bulked-up version of vanilla gelato. Although we don't often do so, we divided the sugar so that only ½ cup gets beaten in with the egg yolks. We discovered that too much sugar weighed down the yolks; we had a hard time getting the mixture to the ribbon stage. In the end, it's all about texture: velvety and smooth.

2⅓ cups whole milk

¼ cup heavy cream

I vanilla bean, split lengthwise

I cup granulated white sugar

9 large egg yolks, at room temperature

¼ teaspoon salt

TO MAKE THE CUSTARD

1 · Stir the milk, cream, vanilla bean, and ½ cup of the sugar in a large saucepan over medium heat until the sugar has dissolved. Warm, undisturbed, until small bubbles fizz around the inside perimeter of the pan. Cover and set aside at room temperature for 30 minutes.

2 · Fish out the vanilla bean, set it on a cutting board, and run a small paring knife along the cut surface to extract the tiny, black seeds. Reserve the pod (see Pro Tip) and stir the scraped-out seeds back into the milk mixture. Set over low heat and warm again until those bubbles fizz around the interior perimeter.

3 · Meanwhile, beat the egg yolks, salt, and the remaining ½ cup sugar in a large bowl with an electric mixer at medium-high speed until quite thick and pale yellow, until wide ribbons fall off the turned-off beaters, about 5 minutes.

4 · Beat about half the hot milk mixture at medium speed into the egg yolk mixture in a slow, steady stream, then beat this combined mixture into the remaining hot milk mixture in the pan. Set the pan over low heat and cook, stirring constantly, until the custard thickly coats the back of a wooden spoon and the temperature registers 170°F, 5 to 9 minutes.

5 · Strain the mixture through a fine-mesh sieve into a bowl, then refrigerate for at least 4 hours or up to 2 days, covering once the custard is cold.

TO FREEZE IT

6 · Prepare an ice-cream machine. Stir the cold custard, then freeze it in the machine according to the manufacturer's instructions, until you can scoop up a small mound with edges that do not instantly start to melt. Store in a sealed container in the freezer for up to 1 month.

À LA MODE IT · To send the proper shudders down your spine, either the pie should be warm or the gelato should be fresh from the machine. If you've made both the pie and the gelato earlier in the day, set the whole pie, uncovered, in a 250°F oven for 10 minutes, just to warm it up.

PRO TIP · Dry the scraped-out vanilla bean pod halves at room temperature for a day, then bury them in 3 cups white granulated sugar in a sealed glass jar. Set in a cool, dark pantry for about I month. Remove the pod halves and you've got vanilla sugar, great in cookies or on oatmeal.

BLUEBERRY PIE

— ⬦ —

MARZIPAN GELATO

Although raspberries and almonds are a classic combo, blueberries and almonds may be a bit of a surprise. They're a gentler pairing, not as in-your-face. In fact, blueberries and almonds (or marzipan, as the case may be) are pretty mellow. So we've added a little orange zest, a surprise accent we find irresistible with blueberries. It brings the right balance to the flavors, a subtle citrus spark that keeps the dominant pair from becoming slackers in this fine American combo.

BLUEBERRY PIE

· YIELD: ONE 9-INCH PIE ·

— · ⬦ · —

Don't even think about using frozen blueberries. The pie will get too soupy. In fact, when you mix this filling together, the fresh blueberries won't start to break down the way, say, peaches will—which means the dry ingredients like the sugar and flour will fall to the bottom of the bowl. We're actually stirring them together to get the dry ingredients well blended; the blueberries are tagalongs to pick up bits of cinnamon or what have you. As you pour the filling into the crust, layer the blueberries with the dry mix so you don't end up with a film of undissolved sugar and flour on top of the pie.

FOR THE CRUST

2 1/2 cups all-purpose flour, plus additional for dusting

1 teaspoon salt

3/4 cup (12 tablespoons) solid vegetable shortening

3 tablespoons cold unsalted butter, cut into small bits

At least 6 tablespoons very cold water

1 teaspoon apple cider vinegar

FOR THE FILLING

5 cups fresh blueberries

2/3 cup granulated white sugar

2 tablespoons all-purpose flour

1 1/2 tablespoons instant tapioca

1 teaspoon finely grated orange zest

1/4 teaspoon salt

1/8 teaspoon ground cloves

OVEN RACK · center | OVEN TEMPERATURE · 350°F

TO MAKE THE CRUST

1 · Mix the flour and salt in a large bowl, then cut in the shortening and butter with a pastry cutter or a fork until the mixture resembles coarse, dry sand.

2 · Stir 6 tablespoons of cold water and the vinegar in a small bowl or cup, then pour it into the flour mixture. Stir with a fork until a pliable but not sticky dough forms, adding more cold water in 1-teaspoon increments as necessary. Divide the dough into two balls, one slightly larger than the other (about a 60/40 split). Dust the larger with flour and roll it into an 11-inch circle following the instructions on page 22. Center and set the crust into a 9-inch pie plate; do not trim the excess. Lay clean kitchen towels over both the crust in the pie plate and the second ball of dough.

TO MAKE THE FILLING

3 · Mix the blueberries, sugar, flour, tapioca, orange zest, salt, and the cloves in a large bowl. Pour into the prepared crust.

4 · Roll the remaining ball of dough into a 10-inch circle, using the same technique as for the first one. Center it on top of the pie. Trim any excess dough. Crimp and seal the top and bottom crust together so that no bit of filling can leak out. If desired, flute the edge or work some magic on it with the tines of a fork. Make 4 slits in the top of the crust to let heat and steam escape as the pie bakes.

5 · Bake the pie until the filling is bubbling through the slits, until the crust is lightly browned and flaky, 45 to 50 minutes. Cool the pie on a wire rack for at least 1 hour or to room temperature before slicing into wedges to serve. Store tightly covered in plastic wrap in the refrigerator for up to 2 days.

PRO TIP · You need more water to make this crust than the one in the previous recipe because there's less butter here. Or to put it another way, solid vegetable shortening has less water content than butter. Anytime you alter the butter/shortening ratio in a crust, you must account for the difference in the moisture content of the fats used.

MARZIPAN GELATO
· YIELD: 1 VERY FULL QUART ·

Marzipan is ground almond paste (see Pro Tip below). It is sometimes shaped into little candies—*which you don't want in this recipe!* Those cute little watermelon slices or bunny rabbits are often painted or dyed. You don't need pink or brown gelato. (The candies are also quite expensive.) Instead, look for tubes of plain marzipan in the baking aisle or order it online. This gelato is made in a food processor to grind that marzipan as smoothly as possible. If you want a really smooth gelato, use a turbo blender. Yes, you'll also add more air and end up with a foamier mixture. Set it aside for 15 minutes to help the foam dissipate before you heat it in the pan.

2½ cups whole milk

¼ cup heavy cream

One 7-ounce tube marzipan

⅔ cup granulated white sugar

4 large egg yolks, at room temperature

½ teaspoon almond extract

½ teaspoon salt

TO MAKE THE CUSTARD

1 · Heat the milk and cream in a medium saucepan set over medium heat until small bubbles fizz around the inside perimeter of the pan. Meanwhile, process the marzipan, sugar, and egg yolks in a large food processor until smooth, scraping down the inside of the canister a couple of times.

2 · With the machine running, pour in the hot milk mixture through the feed tube in a slow, steady stream and process until smooth. Pour this mixture back into the saucepan; set it over low heat. Cook, stirring constantly, until the mixture thickly coats the back of a wooden spoon, until the temperature registers 170°F, 4 to 7 minutes.

3 · Strain the mixture through a fine-mesh sieve into a medium bowl or container and chill in the refrigerator for at least 4 hours or up to 1 day, covering after the mixture is cold.

TO FREEZE IT

4 · Prepare an ice-cream machine. Stir the almond extract and salt into the cold custard until smooth. Freeze it in the machine according to the manufacturer's instructions, until you can spoon up a small mound with edges that do not immediately begin to melt. Store in a sealed container in the freezer for up to 1 month.

À LA MODE IT · The real decision is a slice of warm pie or a scoop of freshly made gelato. The reason? The flavors of the gelato will be better if they're not locked tight in a hard-frozen ball. Either the pie should melt it a bit or the gelato should be somewhat soft to begin with.

PRO TIP · Almond paste is a mixture of ground almonds and sugar; marzipan is a mixture of ground almonds and sugar *or* honey, as well as almond oil and/or almond extract. In truth, either will do, although marzipan tends to be more finely ground and so creates a creamier gelato.

APPLE-CRANBERRY STREUSEL PIE

—◆—

HONEY CAMEMBERT ICE CREAM

Sharp cheddar with apple pie is a New England tradition, so we set out to match them up. We quickly discovered the cheesy ice cream overpowered the pie. So we gave the latter the oomph of tart cranberries, another New England tradition. Now it overpowered the ice cream! Then we swapped out the cheddar for Camembert, a surprising addition that brought a sophisticated but sharp finish. And the streusel topping made it all work, a down-home crunch to balance the uptown ice cream. Our work paid off: this matchup is better than the sum of its parts.

APPLE-CRANBERRY STREUSEL PIE

· YIELD: ONE 9-INCH PIE ·

—◆—

The best pie crusts are made with a mix of solid vegetable shortening and butter. If they're made with only shortening, the crusts get crunchy, almost like crackers; if with only butter, they get thick and even go boggy at the center. So we mix the two for cakier or crunchier results, based on what pairs best with the filling. Here, we wanted a slightly cakier crust to match the buttery crumble on top of the pie.

FOR THE CRUST

I cup all-purpose flour, plus additional for dusting

¼ teaspoon salt

10 tablespoons (I stick plus 2 tablespoons) cold unsalted butter, cut into small bits

1½ tablespoons solid vegetable shortening

At least 3 tablespoons very cold water

½ teaspoon apple cider vinegar

FOR THE FILLING

5 cups sliced, peeled, and cored, medium-tart baking apples, such as Empire, Rome, or Northern Spy (about 5 medium)

I cup fresh or frozen cranberries (do not thaw)

⅔ cup white granulated sugar

2 tablespoons instant tapioca

2 tablespoons all-purpose flour

FOR THE STREUSEL

8 tablespoons (I stick) unsalted butter, cut into small bits

½ cup all-purpose flour

¼ cup packed dark brown sugar

2 tablespoons white granulated sugar

½ teaspoon ground cinnamon

¼ teaspoon salt

OVEN RACK · center | **OVEN TEMPERATURE** · 375°F

TO MAKE THE CRUST

1 · Mix the flour and salt in a small bowl, then cut in the butter and shortening with a pastry cutter or a fork until the mixture resembles coarse cornmeal.

2 · Stir 3 tablespoons of cold water and the vinegar in a small bowl or cup. Add it to the flour mixture and stir with a fork until a soft, pliable, smooth dough forms, adding more cold water in ½-tablespoon increments as needed. Gather the dough into a ball, dust it with flour, and roll it into an 11-inch circle, following the instructions that begin on page 22. Center and set the crust into a 9-inch pie plate. Trim and crimp the edge, fluting it or otherwise creating a decorative pattern at the rim if desired.

TO MAKE THE FILLING

3 · Mix the apples, cranberries, white sugar, tapioca, and flour in a large bowl. Set aside for 10 minutes while you make the streusel.

TO MAKE THE STREUSEL

4 · Process the butter, flour, brown sugar, white sugar, cinnamon, and salt in a food processor until crumbly, like coarsely ground cracker crumbs.

TO PUT IT ALL TOGETHER

5 · Pour and scrape every drop of the filling into the prepared crust. Crumble and sprinkle the streusel evenly over the filling.

6 · Bake the pie for 20 minutes. Reduce the oven temperature to 350°F and continue baking until the streusel is lightly browned and the filling is bubbling underneath, about 40 minutes more. If the streusel starts to brown too deeply, drape a sheet of aluminum foil loosely over the pie to protect it. Cool the pie on a wire rack for at least 1 hour or to room temperature before slicing into wedges. Store tightly covered with plastic wrap on the countertop for up to 2 days.

PRO TIP · The streusel topping in the food processor will be at the right consistency when a small bit squeezed between your fingers holds its shape. When you sprinkle it over the pie, squeeze some, crumble some, then squeeze some more and crumble some more, making slightly larger and smaller bits across the pie, like a collection of very small pebbles mixed with coarse sand.

HONEY CAMEMBERT ICE CREAM

· YIELD: 1 FULL QUART ·

——·◈·——

Don't buy the ripest, runniest Camembert in the case. Chances are, it has collapsed in the middle because it's a little long in the tooth, now with unpleasant ammonia accents. Instead, look for a firm, taut wheel with that characteristic, tangy aroma. Don't worry: it will mellow in the frozen custard to create a sublime contrast for the pie. And choose a bright, floral honey.

1½ cups heavy cream

1¼ cups whole milk

⅔ cup mildly flavored honey, such as wildflower honey

3 large egg yolks, at room temperature

8 ounces Camembert, at room temperature and rind sliced off

¼ teaspoon salt

TO MAKE THE ICE CREAM

1 · Heat the cream and milk in a large saucepan set over medium heat until tiny bubbles fizz around the inside perimeter of the pan. Meanwhile, beat the honey, egg yolks, and salt with an electric mixer at medium speed until thick and pale yellow, until thick ribbons slide from the turned-off beaters, about 4 minutes.

2 · Beat about half the hot milk mixture into the egg yolk mixture in a small, steady stream. Then beat this combined mixture into the remaining hot milk mixture in the pan until smooth. Set the pan over low heat and cook, stirring constantly, until the custard thickly coats the back of a wooden spoon and the temperature registers 170°F, 4 to 7 minutes.

3 · Set the cheese in a medium bowl, pour the hot custard on top, and whisk until the cheese dissolves into the custard. Strain the mixture through a fine-mesh sieve into a second medium bowl, then refrigerate for at least 4 hours or up to 1 day, covering the custard once it has cooled.

TO FREEZE IT

4 · Prepare an ice-cream maker. Stir the cold custard. Freeze it in the machine according to the manufacturer's instructions, until you can scoop up a mound with edges that do not instantly melt. Store in a sealed container in the freezer for up to 2 weeks.

À LA MODE IT · Because you worked to get a crunchy, crumbly topping on the pie, set a scoop of the ice cream to the side of a slice, rather than on top.

STRAWBERRY-ALMOND CRUMB PIE

BANANA-NOUGATINE ICE CREAM

Here's a better strawberry pie. We didn't worry about keeping the strawberries whole but gave them an almond crunchy top to match their natural sweetness—and took it all over the top by crushing up a classic French almond candy into banana ice cream as the pairing. In the end, this one's all about contrasts: the sweet strawberries with the slightly bitter caramel, the oat-filled topping with the slightly chewy ice cream, and the sweetness of maple syrup with the pop of a liqueur.

STRAWBERRY-ALMOND CRUMB PIE

· YIELD: ONE 9-INCH PIE ·

If you like crisps as well as pies, this dessert may be the best of all possible worlds: as if you've baked a crisp inside a pie shell—that is, a more jamlike filling underneath an oat-and-almond topping. Don't slice the strawberries too thin or they'll get watery. Cut larger ones into ¼-inch-thick slices; quarter or even halve smaller strawberries.

FOR THE CRUST

I cup all-purpose flour, plus additional for dusting

I tablespoon finely chopped slivered almonds

½ teaspoon salt

I tablespoon cold unsalted butter

¼ cup almond oil

At least 2 tablespoons very cold water

¼ teaspoon distilled white vinegar

¼ teaspoon almond extract

FOR THE FILLING

6 cups hulled and sliced or quartered strawberries

½ cup granulated white sugar

3 tablespoons all-purpose flour

3 tablespoons instant tapioca

½ teaspoon ground cinnamon

¼ teaspoon salt

FOR THE ALMOND-CRUMB TOPPING

I cup all-purpose flour

½ cup rolled oats (do not use steel-cut or quick-cooking)

⅓ cup almond oil

¼ cup dark amber or even Grade B maple syrup

¼ cup packed light brown sugar

¼ cup sliced almonds

½ teaspoon ground cinnamon

OVEN RACK · center | OVEN TEMPERATURE · 350°F

TO MAKE THE CRUST

1 · Mix the flour, almonds, and salt in a large bowl. Cut in the butter with a pastry cutter or a fork until uniform throughout, then stir in the almond oil with a fork until the mixture resembles somewhat damp, coarse meal.

2 · Stir 2 tablespoons of cold water, the vinegar, and almond extract in a small cup or bowl. Add it to the flour mixture and stir until a soft, smooth, and slightly sticky dough forms, adding more cold water in 1-teaspoon increments as necessary. Gather the dough into a ball, dust it with flour, and roll it into an 11-inch crust, using the instructions on page 22. Center and set the crust into a 9-inch pie plate. Trim and flute the edge. Lay a clean kitchen towel over the pie plate.

TO MAKE THE FILLING

3 · Mix the strawberries, white sugar, flour, tapioca, cinnamon, and salt in a large bowl. Set aside for 10 minutes. Stir, then pour into the prepared crust.

TO MAKE THE CRUMB TOPPING

4 · Mix the flour, oats, almond oil, maple syrup, brown sugar, sliced almonds, and cinnamon in a clean, large bowl until you can crumble bits between your fingers; then do so over the pie, covering the filling evenly.

TO FINISH IT UP

5 · Bake the pie until the topping is lightly browned and the filling is bubbling, 50 minutes to 1 hour. If the topping begins to brown too deeply, tent the pie loosely with aluminum foil but remove the foil for the final few minutes of baking to make sure the topping dries out. Cool the pie on a wire rack for at least 1½ hours or to room temperature before slicing into somewhat wet, messy wedges to serve. Store tightly wrapped in plastic wrap on the countertop for up to 1 day.

PRO TIP · Almond oil is, yes, the oil pressed from almonds. It has a mildly sweet flavor. Don't use toasted almond oil; its flavor is too pronounced. Once opened, store almond oil, covered, in the refrigerator for a couple of months. If you detect an acrid aroma, throw it out and buy a new bottle.

BANANA-NOUGATINE ICE CREAM

· YIELD: 1 FULL QUART ·

—— ◈ ——

Nougatine is almond brittle, a thin sheet of caramelized sugar holding the nuts. It's sometimes ground up and folded into pastry cream to create the almond filling for French pastries like the incomparable Paris-Brest. In ice cream, it gives a slightly bitter, sophisticated finish to the bananas, a real treat with this sweet pie. Pulverize the nougatine into fine sand so there are no shards.

FOR THE NOUGATINE

½ cup sliced almonds

½ cup confectioners' sugar

FOR THE ICE CREAM

2 cups heavy cream

⅔ cup granulated white sugar

⅓ cup whole milk

3 very ripe medium bananas, peeled

2 tablespoons crème de banane liqueur

TO MAKE THE NOUGATINE

1 · Cover a large baking sheet with a silicone mat. Combine the sliced almonds and confectioners' sugar in a large skillet set over medium heat. Cook, stirring occasionally at first and then less and less, until the sugar melts and turns dark amber. Pour into a thin layer on the prepared baking sheet. Cool to room temperature, about 2 hours.

2 · Break the nougatine into chunks, then pulverize these in a food processor fitted with the chopping blade or seal them in a large baggie and strike the bits gently but repeatedly with a rolling pin until they are the consistency of fine sand. Set aside in the sealed bag for up to 1 day.

TO START THE ICE CREAM

3 · Stir the cream, granulated white sugar, and milk in a large saucepan set over medium heat until the sugar dissolves. Break the bananas into pieces and drop them into the mixture. Bring to a simmer, stirring occasionally. Cover, reduce the heat to low, and simmer slowly for 10 minutes. Cover and set aside off the heat for 10 minutes.

4 · Pour the contents of the saucepan into a large blender, add the liqueur, and cover, removing the center knob in the lid. Cover the lid with a clean kitchen towel and blend until smooth, scraping down the inside of the canister at least once. Reinsert the knob in the lid and chill the canister in the refrigerator for at least 4 hours or up to 12 hours.

TO FREEZE IT

5 · Prepare an ice-cream machine. Blend the cold banana mixture one more time, then freeze it in the machine according to the manufacturer's instructions, until the ice cream can mound on a spoon.

6 · During the last few moments of churning, pour in the crushed nougatine and let the machine's dasher fold it in with the final few turns. Scoop into a container, seal, and store in the freezer for up to 1 week.

À LA MODE IT · Serve this messy pairing in shallow bowls.

PRO TIP · It's tricky to get the nougatine the right color. In essence, the darker it is, the more intense its flavor. But there's a very fine line between darkly flavorful and burned.

RHUBARB PIE

— ◆ —

STRAWBERRY JAM ICE CREAM

Consider this our playful deconstruction of strawberry-rhubarb pie. Unfortunately, we find rhubarb on its own a tad overwhelming: too vegetal, too sour, a sledgehammer. For balance, we add vanilla and orange zest. The former gives it a mellow, wintry finish, better in keeping with the changing time of year that is rhubarb season. The orange zest mutes the inherent sourness with subtle, vanilla accents, twisting the rhubarb away from its savory roots and into solid dessert fare. All that's left after that is to make the strawberry ice cream—which is very soft, even when frozen solid. Dig in without delay.

RHUBARB PIE

· YIELD: ONE 9-INCH PIE ·

— · ◆ · —

Slice the rhubarb into thin bits, not more than ¼ inch. They'll begin to melt into a filling, offering a little texture without the decided chew of, say, apple pie. If you get exuberant and slice the rhubarb into very thin bits, the pie may cook more quickly. In any event, start checking at about the 50-minute mark to see when the filling is truly bubbling through the cracks and the crust is set.

FOR THE FILLING

2 pounds fresh rhubarb, thinly sliced

1½ cups granulated white sugar

3 tablespoons instant tapioca

2 tablespoons all-purpose flour

I teaspoon pure vanilla extract

½ teaspoon finely grated orange zest

¼ teaspoon salt

FOR THE CRUST

2 cups all-purpose flour, plus additional for dusting

I teaspoon salt

²/₃ cup solid vegetable shortening

2 tablespoons cold unsalted butter, cut into small bits

At least ¼ cup very cold water

I teaspoon distilled white vinegar

OVEN RACK · center | **OVEN TEMPERATURE** · 350°F

TO MAKE THE FILLING

1 · Mix the rhubarb, sugar, tapioca, flour, vanilla extract, zest, and salt in a clean, large bowl. Set aside while you make the crust.

TO MAKE THE CRUST

2 · Mix the flour and salt in a large bowl. Add the shortening and butter; cut them into the flour mixture with a pastry cutter or a fork until the mix resembles white, coarse sand.

3 · Stir ¼ cup of cold water and the vinegar in a small cup or bowl. Add it to the flour mixture and stir until you have a soft, pliable, but not sticky dough, adding more cold water in ½-tablespoon increments as necessary. Gather the dough into a ball and divide it into two sections, one slightly larger than the other (about a 60/40 split). Dust the larger one with flour and roll it into an 11-inch circle, following the instructions that begin on page 22. Center and set the crust into a 9-inch pie plate. Cover both the pie crust in the plate and the second ball of dough with clean kitchen towels.

TO PUT IT TOGETHER

4 · Roll the remaining dough ball into a 10-inch circle, using the same technique as for the first one. Set it on the pie, then seal the edges, trimming any excess and crimping the two crusts

together so no filling can leak out. If desired, flute or decorate the edge. Using a sharp paring knife, cut several slits in the top crust in a decorative pattern to release steam.

5 · Bake the pie until the crust is lightly browned and flaky, until the filling is bubbling through the slits, about 1 hour 10 minutes. If the crust is browning too deeply, drape a sheet of aluminum foil over the pie as it continues to bake. Cool the pie on a wire rack for at least 1 hour or to room temperature before slicing into wedges to serve. Store tightly covered with plastic wrap in the refrigerator for up to 2 days.

PRO TIP · Rhubarb stalks can be stringy, like celery on steroids. If possible, choose thinner stalks for fewer strings. You can also peel off some of the stringiness by using a paring knife to nick up the strands at the fatter end and zip them down the stalk. However, you'll also lose some of the characteristic red color.

STRAWBERRY JAM ICE CREAM
· YIELD: ABOUT 1 QUART ·

Here's a true ice cream: no eggs. But we do thicken it. These days, most of us like the consistency of creamier ice cream; even store-bought premium ice creams usually include thickeners. There's also a double hit of berries here: both the sliced strawberries and the jam. For the best flavor, use a high-quality strawberry jam. Do not substitute strawberry jelly or preserves. And do not substitute an all-fruit spread. The ice cream needs the extra sugar for texture. Because of the jam, the ice cream will never freeze rock hard, even if set in a container on the floor of your freezer for weeks.

1½ cups heavy cream
1 cup whole milk
2 tablespoons cornstarch
1 cup hulled, thinly sliced strawberries
½ cup strawberry jam
½ cup granulated white sugar
½ teaspoon pure vanilla extract

TO START THE ICE CREAM
1 · Whisk the cream, milk, and cornstarch in a medium saucepan set over medium heat. Continue whisking until the mixture thickens and just begins to bubble, almost like pudding does at this stage, about 3 minutes.

2 · Pour the contents of the saucepan into a large blender. Add the strawberries, jam, sugar, and vanilla extract. Cover the canister but remove the center knob in the lid. Cover the lid with a clean kitchen towel. Blend the mixture until smooth, scraping down the inside of the canister at least once. Set the knob back in the lid and refrigerate for at least 4 hours or up to 2 days.

TO FREEZE IT
3 · Prepare an ice-cream machine. Blend the cold strawberry mixture one more time, then freeze it in the machine according to the manufacturer's instructions, until you can scoop up a small mound with edges that do not immediately begin to melt. Store in a sealed container in the freezer for up to 1 month.

À LA MODE IT · Because the ice cream is naturally soft, make sure that the serving plates are at room temperature, even a little chilled (perhaps refrigerated for 10 minutes).

PRO TIP · In truth, you could turn this ice cream into any flavor, using a fruit/jam combination of your choice.

BACON–MAPLE WALNUT PIE

MALT FROZEN CUSTARD

Think of this as breakfast morphed into dessert: maple syrup, bacon, waffles—if they were served with a vanilla malt! This is a stellar pairing of flavors, nothing held back. Don't even think of using a fine-grade maple syrup like light or even medium amber. Go for the robust, dark stuff to stand up to the excesses.

BACON–MAPLE WALNUT PIE

· YIELD: ONE 9-INCH PIE ·

Even if you like your morning bacon limp, fry it crisp enough that you can shard it into pieces. These will soften in the pie, providing a distinctly porky flavor to go with the walnuts and maple syrup. You don't want to burn the bacon—doing so can add unpleasantly bitter notes. But get it crisp enough to stand up to the long baking time and still release lots of sophisticated, caramelized flavor without ending up as chewy, rubbery bits.

FOR THE CRUST

4 ounces thin-cut bacon slices

Up to 5 tablespoons solid vegetable shortening

I cup all-purpose flour, plus additional for dusting

At least 2 tablespoons very cold water

1/2 teaspoon apple cider vinegar

FOR THE FILLING

3 large eggs, at room temperature

I cup maple syrup, preferably grade B or 2

1/2 cup granulated white sugar

1/2 cup packed dark brown sugar

I tablespoon pure vanilla extract

2 cups chopped walnuts

OVEN RACK · center | OVEN TEMPERATURE · 350°F

TO MAKE THE CRUST

1 · Fry the bacon, turning occasionally with a fork, in a large skillet set over medium heat, until crisp, 3 to 4 minutes. Transfer the bacon to a paper towel–lined plate and set aside.

2 · Reserve 2 tablespoons of the rendered bacon fat from the skillet, then measure the remainder of the fat in the skillet into a heat-safe liquid measuring cup. Cool for 10 minutes at room temperature. Add enough solid shortening so that the total volume in the cup measures 6 tablespoons (1/4 cup plus 2 tablespoons).

3 · Pour the flour into a large bowl and add the combined fat in the measuring cup. Using a pastry cutter or a fork, work the fat through the flour until the mixture resembles coarse cornmeal.

4 · Stir 2 tablespoons of cold water and the vinegar in a small cup or bowl. Add to the flour mixture and stir until a soft, pliable, but not sticky dough forms, adding more cold water in 1-teaspoon increments as necessary. Gather the dough into a ball, dust it with flour, and roll it into an 11-inch crust, using the techniques on page 22. Center and set the crust into a 9-inch pie plate. Trim the edges and flute them as desired.

TO MAKE THE FILLING

5 · Beat the eggs, maple syrup, the white and brown sugars, and the vanilla extract in a large bowl with an electric mixer at medium speed until smooth and uniform, even a little foamy at the top. Beat in the reserved 2 tablespoons bacon fat.

6 · Working by hand, crumble the bacon into tiny bits in the bowl. Stir in the walnuts until well combined and pour into the prepared pie crust.

TO FINISH UP

7 · Bake the pie until puffed and brown, until there is only a slight jiggle in the filling at the center of the pie when the rim of the plate is tapped, about 55 minutes. Cool the pie on a wire rack for at least 1½ hours or to room temperature before slicing into wedges to serve. Store tightly sealed with plastic wrap in the refrigerator for up to 2 days.

PRO TIP · A nut pie is underdone (and gooey) if its center moves in waves when the side is tapped. However, it's overdone (and dried out) when the middle is firm while the pie is still in the oven. Remove it from the oven when there's a slight jiggle at the center.

MALT FROZEN CUSTARD
· YIELD: ABOUT 1 QUART ·

We're not fooling around! We want an intense malt taste to stand up to the bacon. That said, the malted milk powder may never fully melt into the cream and milk over the heat. But you're going to beat it into the egg yolks and then strain it, so there's little chance of a grainy frozen dessert. And if it's all not enough for you (wow!), add up to 1⅓ cups chopped malted milk balls to the mix during the final 2 minutes or so in the ice-cream machine.

1¾ cups heavy cream

1¼ cups whole milk

⅔ cup malted milk powder

½ teaspoon pure vanilla extract

4 large egg yolks, at room temperature

½ cup white granulated sugar

¼ teaspoon salt, optional

TO MAKE THE CUSTARD

1 · Stir the cream, milk, malt, and vanilla extract in a large saucepan set over medium heat until the powder has mostly dissolved and small bubbles form around the inside perimeter of the pan. Meanwhile, using an electric mixer, beat the egg yolks, sugar, and salt (if using) in a large bowl until thick and pale yellow, until wide ribbons slide off the turned-off beaters, about 4 minutes.

2 · Beat about half the hot cream mixture into the egg mixture in a slow, steady stream until smooth, then beat this combined mixture into the remaining cream mixture in the pan. Set the pan over low heat and cook, stirring constantly, until the mixture thickly coats the back of a wooden spoon and the temperature registers 170°F, 4 to 7 minutes.

3 · Strain the mixture through a fine-mesh sieve into a bowl and refrigerate for at least 4 hours or up to 2 days, covering once the mixture is cold.

TO FREEZE IT

4 · Prepare an ice-cream maker. Stir the cold custard and freeze it in the machine according to the manufacturer's instructions, until you can scoop up a small mound with edges that do not immediately start melting. Store in a sealed container in the freezer for up to 1 month.

À LA MODE IT · Yes, serve slices with scoops, as usual. But to take the pair over the top, fry up a couple of extra bacon slices and crumble them over the scoops.

PRO TIP · Malted milk powder is a combination of barley, malt, wheat, milk solids, and sometimes salt. Check the label—although we like a little salt in this frozen custard, you may already be adding some with the malted milk powder and therefore don't need more. Do not confuse malted milk powder with diastatic malt powder, a bread-baking additive with enzymes that break starches into sugars.

CHOCOLATE PECAN PIE

---◆---

DRAM GELATO

Bring on winter for this full-flavored combo! Okay, who are we kidding? You wouldn't wish winter on yourself even for a good à la mode pairing if you lived where we do in rural New England. But even on a summer night, this cold-weather duo would make a treat: lots of chocolate, lots of pecans, and the pleasant surprise of allspice, the dominant note in a rich gelato, some holiday spirit even if you serve it on a July night. Put on some Christmas carols. The neighbors won't mind.

CHOCOLATE PECAN PIE

· YIELD: ONE 9-INCH PIE ·

---◆---

We always mix maple syrup into the classic, candylike filling of a pecan pie because we like the woodsy aromatics with the slightly tannic nuts. However, we don't use *only* maple syrup because its flavor begins to overwhelm the subtle pecans. Plus, the filling becomes looser with the added moisture of maple syrup (from the little water content left after sugaring the sap). So a mix of maple syrup and dark corn syrup will bring the right flavor and texture.

FOR THE CRUST

I cup all-purpose flour, plus additional for dusting

1/2 teaspoon salt

1/3 cup solid vegetable shortening

I tablespoon cold unsalted butter

At least 3 tablespoons very cold water

1/2 teaspoon distilled white vinegar

FOR THE FILLING

3 large eggs, at room temperature

3/4 cup dark corn syrup

6 tablespoons (3/4 stick) unsalted butter, melted and cooled

1/4 cup maple syrup, preferably grade B or 2

2 teaspoons pure vanilla extract

3 ounces unsweetened chocolate, chopped, melted, and cooled to room temperature

1/3 cup granulated white sugar

1/3 cup packed dark brown sugar

1/2 teaspoon salt

I1/2 cups chopped pecans

OVEN RACK · center | OVEN TEMPERATURE · 375°F

TO MAKE THE CRUST

1 · Mix the flour and salt in a large bowl. Add the shortening and butter; cut into the mixture with a pastry cutter or a fork until the whole thing resembles a floury version of very coarse salt.

2 · Stir 3 tablespoons of cold water and the vinegar in a small bowl or cup. Add it to the flour mixture and stir with a fork until you have a soft, pliant, smooth dough, adding more cold water in 1/2-tablespoon increments as necessary. Gather the dough into a ball, dust it with flour, and roll it into an 11-inch circle, following the instructions that begin on page 22. Center and set the crust into a 9-inch pie plate. Trim the edges; flute them if desired.

TO MAKE THE FILLING

3 · Whisk the eggs, corn syrup, melted butter, maple syrup, and vanilla extract in a large bowl until smooth. Whisk in the melted chocolate. Then whisk in the white and brown sugars and the salt until all have dissolved and the mixture is again smooth. Stir in the pecans and pour the filling into the prepared pie crust.

TO FINISH UP

4 · Bake the pie until slightly puffed with only a bit of jiggle at the center when the rim of the pie plate is tapped, 40 to 50 minutes. Cool the pie on a wire rack for at least 1 hour or to room temperature before slicing into wedges to serve. Store tightly sealed in plastic wrap in the refrigerator for up to 2 days.

PRO TIP · To melt chocolate, set up a double boiler and stir the chocolate in the top half over barely simmering water below until half melted—then remove the top half of the double boiler from the heat and continue stirring the chocolate until smooth. Or try the microwave. Melt the chocolate in a bowl on high in 10-second increments, stirring well with a rubber spatula after each heating. Once about three-quarters has melted (and you should begin to cut down the length of the increments as the chocolate melts), remove the bowl and stir at room temperature until smooth. Cool for 10 to 15 minutes at room temperature unless directed otherwise by the recipe.

DRAM GELATO
· YIELD: ABOUT 1 QUART ·

———— · ◈ · ————

Dram liqueur, sometimes called *pimento dram*, is an allspice-flavored distilled spirit, a favorite in the Caribbean. It's sweet, a bit herbal, and very aromatic—a punch of flavor. We've used plenty of egg yolks here to tone it down and turn the flavor into that characteristic nutmeg-cinnamon-clove hybrid of the allspice berry that better fits the pie. We've also added cornstarch to the gelato because the extra liquid from the liqueur can make it icy.

2½ cups whole milk

¼ cup heavy cream

7 large egg yolks, at room temperature

⅔ cup granulated white sugar

¼ cup dram liqueur, such as St. Elizabeth's Allspice Dram

1½ tablespoons cornstarch

TO MAKE THE CUSTARD

1 · Mix the milk and cream in a large saucepan and set over medium heat until little bubbles fizz around the inside perimeter of the pan. Meanwhile, using an electric mixer at medium speed, beat the eggs and sugar in a large bowl until thick ribbons slide off the turned-off beaters, about 6 minutes. Add the dram liqueur and cornstarch; beat until smooth.

2 · Beat about half the hot milk mixture into the egg yolk mixture in a small, steady stream until smooth, then beat this combined mixture into the remaining milk mixture in the pan. Set the pan over low heat and cook, stirring constantly, until the mixture thickly coats the back of a wooden spoon and the temperature registers 170°F, 5 to 7 minutes.

3 · Pour the mixture through a fine-mesh sieve into a medium bowl or container. Refrigerate for at least 4 hours or up to 1 day, covering once the mixture is cold.

TO FREEZE IT

4 · Prepare an ice-cream maker. Stir the cold custard and freeze it in the machine according to the manufacturer's instructions, until glossy and smooth, until you can mound it on a spoon. Store in a covered container in the freezer for up to 1 month.

PRO TIP · To make your own dram liqueur, mix ¼ cup crushed allspice berries with 1 cup overproof bourbon, such as Booker's, in a large glass jar. Cover and set aside for 4 days at room temperature. Stir 1 cup packed dark brown sugar and 1 cup water together in a small saucepan; set over medium heat until the brown sugar dissolves and bubbles fizz inside the perimeter of the pan. Set off the heat and cool to room temperature, about 2 hours. Strain the bourbon mixture through a fine-mesh sieve and into the glass container. Squeeze gently to get the last drops from the allspice berries. Stir well, cover, and store in the fridge for up to 2 months.

CHOCOLATE SUGAR PIE

—◆—

PEANUT BUTTER–CHOCOLATE RIPPLE FROZEN CUSTARD

Sometimes you try to balance the natural sweetness of a dessert with savory, herbal, or bitter notes. And sometimes you just chuck it all and indulge your sweet tooth. This combo is undoubtedly sugary: the peanut butter in the frozen dessert is the only help! If you're offering this as the dessert after dinner, make sure the main course has no extra sweetness: no honey in the sauce, no dried fruit in the braise, no white pasta. You want this pie and ice cream to wake up the palate, not exhaust it.

CHOCOLATE SUGAR PIE
· YIELD: ONE 9-INCH PIE ·

—◆—

This one's a Midwestern tradition: supersweet, as you'd expect from its name, a bit of sugary crunch in every bite. We've added chocolate because, well, duh. (Also, for a silkier finish.) Most sugar pie recipes don't include flour as ours does. The pie is supposed to quiver when cut. But we added flour to change the texture from something like the center of a pecan pie to something like a fudgy brownie—and thus better with ice cream.

FOR THE CRUST

I cup all-purpose flour, plus additional for dusting

¼ teaspoon salt

5 tablespoons cold unsalted butter, cut into small bits

1½ tablespoons solid vegetable shortening

At least 3 tablespoons very cold water

½ teaspoon distilled white vinegar

FOR THE FILLING

4 tablespoons (½ stick) unsalted butter

I ounce unsweetened chocolate, chopped

I cup packed dark brown sugar

¼ cup unsweetened cocoa powder, preferably natural style

¾ cup regular or low-fat evaporated milk

2 large eggs, plus I large egg yolk, at room temperature

2 teaspoons pure vanilla extract

¼ cup all-purpose flour

OVEN RACK · center | **OVEN TEMPERATURE** · 375°F

TO MAKE THE CRUST

1 · Mix the flour and salt in a large bowl. Cut in the butter and shortening with a pastry cutter or a fork until the mixture resembles coarse cornmeal.

2 · Stir 3 tablespoons of cold water and the vinegar in a small bowl; add to the flour mixture and stir until you have a supple, soft, but not sticky dough, adding more cold water in 1-teaspoon increments as necessary. Gather the dough into a ball, dust it with flour, and roll it into an 11-inch circle, following the techniques on page 22. Center and set the crust into a 9-inch pie plate; trim the edges and flute them as desired.

TO MAKE THE FILLING

3 · Melt the butter and chocolate in a small saucepan set over low heat, stirring more and more often as it melts, until smooth. Cool for 5 minutes. Meanwhile, whisk the brown sugar and cocoa powder in a small bowl to break up the grains. Set aside.

4 · Whisk the evaporated milk, eggs, egg yolks, and vanilla extract in a large bowl until smooth. Whisk in the brown sugar mixture until dissolved. Then whisk in the chocolate mixture along with the flour until smooth. Pour the filling into the prepared crust.

TO FINISH UP

5 · Bake the pie until the filling is set with no jiggle at the center when the rim of the pie plate is tapped and a crusted, crackled top has formed, about 45 minutes. Cool the pie on a wire rack for at least 1½ hours or to room temperature before slicing into wedges. Store tightly covered in plastic wrap at room temperature for 1 day.

PRO TIP · Natural-style cocoa powder has a more pronounced flavor, despite being lighter in color than Dutch-processed cocoa powder. The latter also has an alkali added to help it dissolve more quickly. Yes, either will work, but despite its darker color, the natural-style powder will offer a deeper, more intense flavor.

PEANUT BUTTER–CHOCOLATE RIPPLE FROZEN CUSTARD
· YIELD: A LITTLE MORE THAN 1 QUART ·

You can't top a classic. But you can better a technique. Rather than letting the ice-cream machine churn the chocolate sauce into the custard for the last few turns, we layer the peanut butter concoction and sauce in a loaf pan. When you scoop it up, don't dig down—rather, run your ice cream scoop along the surface, creating ribbons of chocolate in each ball.

2 cups heavy cream

1 cup whole milk

3/4 cup granulated white sugar

1/2 cup smooth natural-style peanut butter

6 large egg yolks, at room temperature

2 teaspoons pure vanilla extract

1/4 cup crunchy natural-style peanut butter

1/4 cup jarred chocolate syrup (see Pro Tip)

TO MAKE THE CUSTARD

1 · Heat the cream and milk in a large saucepan over medium-low heat until small bubbles appear around the inner perimeter of the pan.

2 · Put the sugar, smooth peanut butter, egg yolks, and vanilla extract in a large blender. Cover and remove the top knob in the lid. Blend while pouring the hot cream mixture through the hole in the lid in a slow, steady stream. Scrape down the inside of the canister and blend until smooth.

3 · Put the knob back in the lid and refrigerate the canister for at least 4 hours or up to 2 days.

TO FREEZE IT

4 · Prepare an ice-cream machine. Stir the cold custard and freeze it in the machine according to the manufacturer's instructions, until you can scoop up a mound of the ice cream with edges that do not instantly start melting.

5 · Meanwhile, mix the crunchy peanut butter and chocolate syrup in a small bowl until smooth. When the ice cream is ready, spoon about one-quarter into a large loaf pan. Add about one-third of the chocolate mixture, spreading it as much as you can with a rubber spatula—and then repeat this two more times before ending with a layer of ice cream. Store in a covered container in the freezer for up to 2 weeks.

À LA MODE IT · Warm shallow soup bowls in a 200°F oven for 10 minutes or so, then serve the pie in them with a scoop of the frozen custard right on top, but not touching the bowl.

PRO TIP · For the best texture, look for high-end chocolate sauces, thick and rich even at room temperature, such as Torani Dark Chocolate Sauce or Ghirardelli's Black Label Chocolate Sauce.

FENNEL-RAISIN PIE

◆

PINE NUT FROZEN CUSTARD

Stick with us. Raisins and fennel are a time-tested duo in Italian cooking; raisins and fennel seeds, pretty common in Italian desserts—a sweet/caramel flavor with the anise. So we honored that tradition by using fresh fennel, not just fennel seeds, in this dessert. Vegetables in a pie? Sure. You use rhubarb, don't you? The pleasing licorice flavor of the fennel calms down and becomes a rich, almost savory filling against the fragrant, olive oil crust—and sets you up for a silky, frozen pine nut concoction with an earthy sweetness (and also another Italian delight, those *pinoli*, in the mix).

FENNEL-RAISIN PIE

· YIELD: ONE 9-INCH PIE ·

· ◆ ·

This pie's texture is something like old-school chess pie with fruit in it—if that were even possible. When you get the cooked fennel into the food processor, take care not to liquefy it. Pulse, don't process. You want many bits of fennel—no big chunks, of course, but a little chew to turn this rich filling into something extraordinary. Note that the crust is rolled out to a larger diameter circle than usual to create a thick lip to contain the very wet filling.

FOR THE CRUST

1¼ cups all-purpose flour, plus additional for dusting

½ teaspoon salt

4 tablespoons (½ stick) cold unsalted butter, cut into small pieces

¼ cup olive oil

At least ¼ cup very cold water

½ teaspoon apple cider vinegar

FOR THE FILLING

3 tablespoons unsalted butter

One 1½-pound fennel bulb, trimmed and chopped

⅔ cup granulated white sugar

1 large egg, plus 2 large egg yolks, at room temperature

2 tablespoons all-purpose flour

1 teaspoon finely grated lemon zest

¼ teaspoon freshly grated nutmeg

¼ teaspoon salt

2 cups golden raisins

OVEN RACK · center | OVEN TEMPERATURE · 350°F

TO MAKE THE CRUST

1 · Mix the flour and salt in a large bowl. Add the butter and olive oil; cut the fat into the flour mixture with a pastry cutter until it all resembles coarse (but white) cornmeal.

2 · Stir ¼ cup of cold water and the vinegar in a small cup or bowl, then add it to the flour mixture. Stir until you have a soft, pliable, but not sticky dough, adding more cold water in 1-teaspoon increments as necessary. Gather the dough into a ball, dust it with flour, and roll it into a 12-inch circle, following the techniques on page 22. Set and center in a 9-inch pie plate. Fold the excess dough under itself to make a thick lip that stands up on the rim of the pie plate. Flute or ornament the edge at will. Lay a clean kitchen towel over the crust.

TO MAKE THE FILLING

3 · Melt the butter in a large skillet set over medium heat. Add the fennel and cook, stirring often, until softened and sweet, about 10 minutes. Set aside off the heat to cool for 10 minutes.

4 · Put the sugar, egg, egg yolks, flour, lemon zest, nutmeg, and salt in a food processor; cover and process until smooth. Add the raisins and pulse to chop. Scrape the contents of the skillet into the food processor, cover, and pulse two or three times, just until the fennel has been chopped into fairly fine bits. Pour and scrape this mixture evenly into the prepared pie crust.

TO FINISH UP

5 · Bake the pie until set at the center and lightly browned, about 45 minutes. Cool the pie on a wire rack for at least 1½ hours or to room temperature before slicing into wedges. Store tightly covered with plastic wrap in the refrigerator for up to 2 days.

PRO TIP · To trim a fennel bulb, remove all the stalks and feathery fronds from the top of the bulb. Turn the bulb over and cut about ¼ inch off the bottom. Slice off any browned bits on the outer layer as well. Slice the bulb in half vertically, then remove any feathery fronds from inside. Cut the fennel into ½-inch-thick slices, then chop these into ½- to I-inch bits.

PINE NUT FROZEN CUSTARD
· YIELD: ABOUT I QUART ·

— · ✧ · —

This frozen custard will only be as good as its pine nuts—and they go rancid quickly! Check before using. They should smell "fir-tree-ish" and sweet, rather than musty or metallic. Toasting them will intensify their flavors.

⅔ cup pine nuts

½ cup granulated white sugar

6 large egg yolks, at room temperature

⅓ cup honey

¼ teaspoon salt

2 cups heavy cream

I cup whole milk

TO MAKE THE CUSTARD

1 · Toast the pine nuts in a large, dry skillet set over medium-low heat, stirring often, until fragrant and lightly browned, about 4 minutes. Pour into a bowl and cool to room temperature, about 20 minutes.

2 · Put the pine nuts, sugar, egg yolks, honey, and salt in a food processor; cover and process to a smooth paste, scraping down the inside of the canister at least once.

3 · Heat the cream and milk in a large saucepan set over medium heat until whiffs of steam come off the top. With the machine running, pour in half the hot cream mixture in a slow, steady stream through the feed tube, processing until smooth.

4 · Stir this combined mixture into the remaining cream mixture in the saucepan. Set over low heat and cook, stirring constantly, until the custard thickly coats the back of a wooden spoon, until the temperature registers 170°F, 4 to 7 minutes.

5 · Strain the mixture through a fine-mesh sieve into a medium bowl and refrigerate for at least 4 hours or up to 2 days, covering the bowl once the mixture is cold.

TO FREEZE IT

6 · Prepare an ice-cream maker. Stir the cold custard and freeze it in the machine according to the manufacturer's instructions, until you can scoop up a small mound with edges that do not instantly melt. Store in a sealed container in the freezer for up to 1 month.

À LA MODE IT · Set the frozen custard scoops beside (not on) pieces of the pie.

PRO TIP · Bringing any custard to the right thickness is not a matter of timing. Instead, it depends on how hot the ingredients were before the pan went back over the heat, how much residual moisture is in them, and the exact volume of the eggs. You can increase the heat a tad, but keep stirring at all times. Don't be impatient.

SQUASH AND HONEY PIE

—◆—

INDIAN PUDDING ICE CREAM

Here's the pie for your next Thanksgiving, a celebration of the New England settlers no matter where you live. This one's less sweet than the standard pumpkin pie—and more aromatic, with a luxuriously silky feel that doesn't veer toward that plastic chew. With the ice cream, it's a harvest festival. Or skip all that and serve this after steaks on the grill some summer night. It's particularly appealing in those last days of August when the light starts its slow salaam to autumn.

SQUASH AND HONEY PIE

· YIELD: ONE 9-INCH PIE ·

— ·◆· —

Because we use winter squash, not pumpkin, we end up with a heartier, somewhat more savory pie. You can, indeed, use frozen winter squash puree, available in almost all supermarkets, but it's wet once thawed. So pour the liquid out of the box—or line a colander with paper towels, put the puree inside, and let it drain for 10 or 15 minutes. If you want to go all out, make your own puree. Slice 2 medium acorn squash in half through the stems, then scoop out the seeds and membranes with a serrated grapefruit spoon. Roast them cut side down on a rimmed baking sheet in a 350°F oven until soft and beyond tender, about 1 hour. Cool on the baking sheet for 20 minutes, then turn them over and scrape out the flesh. You can peel off any too-brown bits if they bother you, but they add a sophisticated, vaguely bitter pop to the filling.

FOR THE CRUST

1 cup all-purpose flour, plus additional for dusting

1 teaspoon granulated white sugar

1/4 teaspoon salt

4 tablespoons (1/2 stick) cold unsalted butter, cut into small bits

2 tablespoons solid vegetable shortening

At least 2 tablespoons very cold water

1/4 teaspoon fresh lemon juice

FOR THE FILLING

1 large egg, plus 2 large egg yolks, at room temperature

6 tablespoons granulated white sugar

1/4 cup honey

2 cups frozen winter squash puree, thawed and drained of excess liquid

1 cup whole or low-fat milk

1/2 cup heavy cream

1/4 teaspoon freshly grated nutmeg

1/4 teaspoon salt

OVEN RACK · center | OVEN TEMPERATURE · 350°F

TO MAKE THE CRUST

1 · Mix the flour, sugar, and salt in a large bowl. Add the butter and shortening. Cut them in with a pastry cutter or a fork until the mixture resembles coarse, dry, white sand.

2 · Stir 2 tablespoons of cold water and the lemon juice in a small bowl or cup. Add to the flour mixture and stir with a fork until you have a soft, supple, but not sticky dough, adding more cold water in 1/2-tablespoon increments as necessary. Gather the dough into a ball, dust it with flour, and roll it into an 11-inch circle, using the techniques that begin on page 22. Center and set the

crust into a 9-inch pie plate. Trim the edge and flute it at will.

TO MAKE THE FILLING

3 · Beat the egg, egg yolks, sugar, and honey in a large clean bowl with an electric mixer at medium speed until smooth, a little foamy, but still thick, about 2 minutes. Beat in the squash puree, milk, cream, nutmeg, and salt until smooth. Pour the filling into the prepared crust.

TO FINISH UP

4 · Bake the pie until the crust is lightly browned and the filling set with the slightest jiggle at the center of the pie when the rim of the plate is tapped, about 1 hour 10 minutes. Cool the pie on a wire rack for at least 1½ hours before slicing into wedges. Store tightly sealed in plastic wrap in the refrigerator for up to 2 days.

PRO TIP · This pie bakes a long time. If the edge has been fluted, the crust may begin to burn. Watch carefully and lay strips of aluminum foil around the rim if you notice the crust getting too dark. Do not cover the middle of the pie.

INDIAN PUDDING ICE CREAM
· YIELD: ABOUT 1 QUART ·

Indian pudding is the New England version of British hasty pudding, made with cornmeal on this side of the pond since wheat supplies were scarce in the early days. It's also made with molasses, rather than maple syrup. Because New England lay at the crossroads of the Caribbean-European trading route (up the North American coast for fewer days in the open water), settlers often found themselves with a copious supply of molasses on their docks. These are bold, assertive flavors in a somewhat grainy ice cream. If you want a milder flavor, substitute maple syrup for the molasses.

1¾ cups heavy cream

1 cup whole milk

¼ cup finely ground yellow cornmeal

½ cup packed dark brown sugar

¼ cup molasses

1 large egg, plus 1 large egg yolk, at room temperature

½ teaspoon pure vanilla extract

½ teaspoon ground dried ginger

½ teaspoon ground cinnamon

⅛ teaspoon salt

TO START THE ICE CREAM

1 · Combine the cream, milk, and cornmeal in a large saucepan set over medium heat. Cook, whisking almost constantly, until bubbling. Reduce the heat to low and simmer slowly, whisking constantly, until thick and rich like cream of wheat cereal, about 10 minutes.

2 · Put the brown sugar, molasses, egg, egg yolk, vanilla extract, ginger, cinnamon, and salt in a large blender canister. Cover but remove the lid's center knob. With the blender running, pour the hot cream mixture through the hole in the lid in a slow, steady stream. Scrape down the inside of the canister and blend until smooth. Put the center knob back in the blender's lid and refrigerate for at least 4 hours or up to 8 hours.

TO FREEZE IT

3 · Prepare an ice-cream machine. Blend the cold custard one more time, then freeze it in the machine according to the manufacturer's instructions, until you can spoon up a mound with edges that do not instantly begin to melt. Store in a sealed container in the freezer for up to 1 week.

À LA MODE IT · Since the pie has a soft, delicate texture, set the scoops to the side of the slices.

PRO TIP · Most yellow cornmeal sold in the baking section of North American supermarkets is finely ground. However, if you buy organic cornmeal or cornmeal from a high-end supermarket, it may well be coarser. If it's not the texture of very fine sand, whir it several times in a food processor to grind it more finely.

DRIED FRUIT PIE

❖

PISTACHIO ICE CREAM

If it's winter in your neck of the woods—as it is in our New England ones, oh, eleven and a half months out of the year—decent, fresh fruit may be in short supply. Yeah, they truck in those hockey pucks masquerading as peaches and plums from South America; they're hardly worth the money. But we can't let our pie cravings go unfulfilled. Dried fruit makes a wonderful alternative filling, sort of like old-fashioned mincemeat (but without the suet). We find that this pale green, nutty gelato sets off the delicate flavor notes in the dried fruit.

DRIED FRUIT PIE

· YIELD: ONE 9-INCH PIE ·

❖

The only thing that can muck up this pie is inferior dried fruit. Here are the rules. Dried fruit should be pliable and moist, without desiccated or hardened bits. It should also smell like its fresh kin. If you're buying it in packages, check the expiration dates; make sure there are no dusty fragments in the package or squishy bits on the fruit. Dried pears can be hard to track down. Substitute dried nectarines for a slightly sweeter finish.

FOR THE FILLING

2 cups pitted prunes

1¼ cups packed dried apricots, preferably California dried apricots (see Pro Tip on page 56)

I cup dried cranberries

I cup chopped dried pears

I large egg, plus I large egg yolk, at room temperature

¾ cup packed light brown sugar

4 tablespoons (½ stick) unsalted butter, melted and cooled

2 teaspoons pure vanilla extract

½ teaspoon ground cinnamon

½ teaspoon salt

FOR THE CRUST

2½ cups all-purpose flour, plus additional for dusting

I teaspoon salt

12 tablespoons (¾ cup) solid vegetable shortening

3 tablespoons cold unsalted butter, cut into small bits

At least 6 tablespoons very cold water

I teaspoon apple cider vinegar

TO MAKE THE FILLING

1 · Put the dried fruit in a large saucepan and add enough water so that it's submerged by 2 inches. Bring to a boil over high heat. Reduce the heat and simmer for 5 minutes.

2 · Drain in a colander set in the sink and cool for 15 minutes. Pour the cooked fruit onto a large cutting board and rock a large chef's knife through the pieces to chop them into ½-inch bits, gathering them back together occasionally. Scrape the chopped fruit into a large, clean bowl. Stir in the egg, egg yolks, brown sugar, melted butter, vanilla extract, cinnamon, and salt until uniform.

OVEN RACK · center | OVEN TEMPERATURE · 400°F

TO MAKE THE CRUST

3 · Mix the flour and salt in a large bowl. Cut in the shortening and butter with a pastry cutter or a fork until the mixture resembles coarse, dry sand.

4 · Stir 6 tablespoons of the cold water and the vinegar in a small bowl or cup. Add to the flour mixture and stir with a fork until a soft, not-sticky dough forms, stirring in more water in

½-tablespoon increments as necessary. Divide the dough into two balls, one slightly larger than the other (about a 60/40 split). Dust the larger one with flour and roll it into an 11-inch circle, following the directions that begin on page 22. Center and set the crust into a 9-inch pie plate, letting the excess hang over the rim.

5 · Pour the prepared filling into the crust. Roll out the remaining dough into a 10-inch circle, following the same technique as for the first one. Center and set the crust on top of the pie. Trim and crimp the edges together to form a tight seal. Flute as you like. Make four 4-inch slits in the top crust—or a combination of smaller slits to create a decorative pattern.

TO FINISH UP

6 · Bake the pie for 20 minutes. Reduce the oven temperature to 350°F and continue baking until the crust is lightly browned and the filling bubbles through the slits, about 35 minutes more. Cool the pie on a wire rack for at least 1 hour or to room temperature before cutting into wedges. Store tightly covered in plastic wrap in the refrigerator for up to 2 days.

PRO TIP · Make sure the dried fruit has cooled before you add the eggs—then stir vigorously and well.

PISTACHIO ICE CREAM
· YIELD: ABOUT 1 QUART ·

If you can only find salted, shelled pistachios, rinse them in a colander set in the sink four or five times to get rid of some of the salt, then drain well and blot dry on paper towels. Omit the salt from the recipe, too. By the way, you needn't be too fussy about adding whole pistachios (or any nuts) to an ice cream in the machine. The point is to get them evenly distributed.

2 cups whole milk

½ cup heavy cream

1¼ cups unsalted and shelled pistachios

½ cup granulated white sugar

¼ teaspoon salt

2 tablespoons cornstarch

1 or 2 drops green food coloring, optional

TO START THE ICE CREAM

1 · Warm 1½ cups milk and cream in a large saucepan set over medium heat until puffs of steam rise off the surface. Meanwhile, put ¾ cup of the pistachios, the sugar, and salt in a food processor. Cover and process to a thick paste.

2 · With the machine running, pour the hot milk mixture through the feed tube into the canister. Scrape down the inside of the canister, pulse a couple of times, and set aside to steep at room temperature for 30 minutes.

3 · Pour and scrape the mixture from the canister into the large saucepan. Whisk the cornstarch into the remaining ¼ cup milk in a small bowl until smooth; whisk this mixture into the cream mixture in the saucepan. Set over low heat and cook, whisking almost constantly, until the mixture thickly coats a wooden spoon's back and the temperature registers 170°F, 4 to 7 minutes.

4 · Pour the mixture through a fine-mesh sieve into a clean bowl; using a rubber spatula, press against any pistachio solids in the strainer to extract every drop of liquid. Refrigerate for at least 4 hours or up to 1 day, covering once the mixture has cooled.

TO FREEZE IT

5 · Prepare an ice cream machine. If using, add the food coloring to the base. In any case, stir well. Freeze it in the machine according to the manufacturer's instructions. As the ice cream becomes moundable, add the remaining ½ cup pistachios and let the dasher stir and mix them into the ice cream. Store in a sealed container in the freezer for up to 1 month.

À LA MODE IT · Because there's so much dried fruit in each slice, as well as a very thick ice cream, make sure you offer both forks and spoons when serving.

APRICOT BRANDY SLAB PIE

◆

CHAI FROZEN CUSTARD
WITH A LEMON CURD SWIRL

Imagine a giant newton cookie. Now imagine it flattened like a Pop-Tart. And with apricots. Voilà: this big dessert for eight people. Although it's all-American, down-home fare, we've gussied it up with an aromatic, lemony frozen custard. Sure, you could make a slab pie and buy vanilla ice cream. But you'd miss what's unbelievable: the rustic/uptown intersection, the sour of the apricots matched by the lemon curd, given an warming tweak with the chai spices.

APRICOT BRANDY SLAB PIE
· YIELD: ONE 10-INCH-LONG SLAB PIE ·

◆

Slab pies are a Midwestern and Southern tradition. Some are made to fill an 11 x 17-inch baking sheet; others are a long slat like this one, like a big hand pie, baked rather than fried. They're made to serve crowds, but we've cut this one down a bit while still giving you a fairly large chunk of cookie dough/apricot goodness. Bake it on parchment paper, not a silicone baking mat, which would insulate the pie and prevent the cookie dough crust from firming up.

FOR THE FILLING
3/4 pound dried apricots, preferably California apricots

1/2 cup golden raisins

1/2 cup packed light brown sugar

1/4 cup water

3 tablespoons apricot brandy

3 tablespoons fresh lemon juice

1/4 teaspoon ground cinnamon

1/8 teaspoon salt

FOR THE CRUST
2 cups all-purpose flour, plus additional as needed

1/2 teaspoon baking powder

1/2 teaspoon baking soda

1/4 teaspoon salt

1/2 cup granulated white sugar

6 tablespoons packed light brown sugar

6 tablespoons (3/4 stick) cold unsalted butter, cut into little bits

2 large eggs, at room temperature

FOR THE DRIZZLE
At least 3/4 cup confectioners' sugar

1 teaspoon whole milk

1 teaspoon unsalted butter, melted and cooled

1/4 teaspoon pure vanilla extract

1/8 teaspoon salt

TO MAKE THE FILLING
1 · Put the dried apricots and golden raisins in a food processor, cover, and process until finely chopped, really almost a paste. Scrape into a large saucepan and mix in the brown sugar, water, brandy, lemon juice, cinnamon, and salt. Cook over medium heat, stirring often, until thick, pastelike, and bubbling, about 10 minutes. Scrape every last bit into a medium bowl and set aside to cool for 30 minutes or up to 2 hours.

OVEN RACK · center | OVEN TEMPERATURE · 400°F

TO MAKE THE CRUST
2 · Mix the flour, baking powder, baking soda, and salt in a large bowl. Set aside. Beat the granulated white, brown sugar, and butter in a second large bowl with an electric mixer at medium speed until light and quite fluffy, about

5 minutes. Scrape down the inside of the bowl, then beat in the eggs one at a time, making sure the first is thoroughly incorporated before adding the second.

3 · Stop the beaters, add the flour mixture, and beat at very low speed to form a soft dough. Depending on the day's humidity and the flour's moisture content, you may need to add a little more flour to turn this into a not-sticky, firm, but moist dough.

4 · Cut a piece of parchment paper to fit inside a large, rimmed baking sheet such as an 11 x 17-inch sheet pan. Set the paper on your work surface and dust it with flour. Gather the dough into a ball, divide it into two equal pieces, and set one on the parchment paper. Using your clean, dry hands, shape it into a small, squat rectangle. Dust it with flour. (Set the other dough ball under a clean kitchen towel.) Using a rolling pin, roll out the piece of dough on the parchment paper into a 8 x 10-inch rectangle. Transfer to the baking sheet.

TO FINISH UP

5 · Spoon the cooled apricot filling evenly down the long axis of the rectangle. Spread it to cover the piece, leaving a ¼-inch border.

6 · Lay a sheet of parchment paper on your work surface. The size of this piece is not as crucial, so long as it's big enough to roll out the second half of the dough. Dust the paper with flour, add the second ball of dough, and roll it exactly as you did the first one. Invert and lay the second piece on top of the first, peeling off the parchment paper. Crimp and seal closed on all edges.

7 · Bake the slab pie until lightly browned and slightly puffed, about 18 minutes. Transfer to a wire rack and cool on the baking sheet for at least 1 hour. Transfer the slab to a large serving platter and cool to room temperature, about 1 hour.

TO MAKE THE DRIZZLE

8 · Mix ¾ cup of confectioners' sugar, the milk, melted butter, vanilla extract, and salt in a bowl until smooth, adding a little more confectioner's sugar if the mixture won't run in a thin stream off the end of the mixing spoon. Using a fork, drizzle the mixture over the pie. Slice it into squares and rectangles to serve. The pie can be stored, before the drizzle, tightly covered in plastic wrap at room temperature for up to 2 days.

PRO TIP · Dried California apricots are bright orange and tart/sweet; dried Turkish apricots are brown and much sweeter. In truth, both are grown in a variety of places (Arizona, Armenia) but the names have stuck to divide the dried apricot world. Either will work here, although we decidedly prefer the brightly colored ones with the sour pop.

CHAI FROZEN CUSTARD WITH A LEMON CURD SWIRL
· YIELD: A LITTLE MORE THAN 1 QUART ·

In a frozen custard, warm spices like those in chai are exceptionally mellow and sweet. With lemon curd, they're unbelievable. If you want to go all out, make your own chai blend. Warm and steep the following in the milk: 1 heaping tablespoon black tea leaves, one 2-inch cinnamon stick, ½ teaspoon whole black peppercorns, 2 crushed green cardamom pods, and 4 whole cloves. Strain through a fine-mesh sieve, discarding the tea and spices before continuing.

2 cups whole milk, plus more if needed

3 small chai tea bags

1¼ cups heavy cream

4 large egg yolks, at room temperature

⅔ cup granulated white sugar

½ cup purchased lemon curd

TO MAKE THE CUSTARD

1 · Heat the milk in a medium saucepan set over medium-low heat until puffs of steam rise off its surface. Remove from the heat, add the tea bags, stir gently, cover, and steep for 30 minutes.

2 · Strain into a medium bowl. Measure what remains: add a little more milk if necessary to make sure you have at least 1¾ cups. Stir the steeped milk with the cream in a large saucepan. Set over medium-low heat and warm until you see those puffs of steam again.

3 · Meanwhile, beat the egg yolks and sugar in a large bowl with an electric mixer at medium speed until thick and pale yellow, until wide ribbons slide off the turned-off beaters, about 4 minutes.

4 · Beat in about half of the milk mixture in a slow, steady stream until smooth, then beat this combined mixture into the remaining milk mixture in the saucepan. Set over low heat and cook, stirring constantly, until it thickly coats the back of a wooden spoon and the temperature registers 170°F, 4 to 7 minutes.

5 · Strain the mixture through a fine-mesh sieve into a clean bowl, then refrigerate for at least 4 hours or up to 1 day, covering once the custard has cooled.

TO FREEZE IT

6 · Prepare an ice-cream machine. Stir the cold custard and freeze it in the machine according to the manufacturer's instructions, until you can spoon up a small mound with edges that do not immediately begin to melt.

7 · Pack about one-quarter of the frozen custard in a loaf pan or a 1-quart, squat container. Spread about one-third of the lemon curd over the frozen custard with your cleaned fingers or a rubber spatula. Make two more similar layers and end with a layer of frozen custard. When you scoop up the custard, you'll make ribbons in the balls. Store in a sealed container in the freezer for up to 2 weeks.

À LA MODE IT · Although we suggest squares and rectangles as slices, you can cut the slab across from short side to short side, making long, 1½-inch-thick slices with more crust per serving. If so, serve these with scoops of the frozen custard on dinner plates, rather than dessert plates.

PRO TIP · To make lemon curd, whisk 4 large, room-temperature egg yolks, ½ cup fresh lemon juice, and ½ cup granulated white sugar in the top half of a double boiler until combined (the sugar won't dissolve). Add 4 tablespoons (½ stick) room-temperature unsalted butter and set over 1 inch of simmering water in the bottom half of the double boiler. Reduce the heat so the water barely bubbles and whisk until smooth, glossy, and thick, 7 to 8 minutes. Scrape into a bowl and cool for at least 4 hours or up to 4 days in the refrigerator, covering tightly once chilled.

APPLE-DATE GALETTE

— ◆ —

CINNAMON—BROWN SUGAR FROZEN CUSTARD

If an old-school Parisian bistro pulled up stakes and plunked down in Madison, Wisconsin, the frozen custard capitol of the United States, it would serve this pairing. A galette is a round, free-form tart with the crust pulled a little more than halfway up and over the filling. Since it is grandmotherly fare with little fandango, we kept its frozen concoction pretty straightforward: autumnal notes to match those apples and dates.

APPLE-DATE GALETTE

· YIELD: ONE 12-INCH GALETTE ·

— · ◆ · —

We crafted a somewhat crunchier crust for this tart—not crackerlike, but a cross between a traditional crust and shortbread. That texture better matches the soft apples, rather like a shortbread cookie spread with preserves. The dates bring a sticky, sweet earthiness to the game, grounding the other flavors. To chop them more easily, spray your knife with nonstick cooking spray. As the galette bakes, some of the filling will undoubtedly run over the crust, but the lined baking sheet should make cleanup a snap. Don't use a silicone baking mat—it will insulate the dough and prevent it from crisping.

FOR THE CRUST

1½ cups all-purpose flour, plus additional for dusting

1½ tablespoons granulated white sugar

½ teaspoon salt

10 tablespoons (1 stick plus 2 tablespoons) cold unsalted butter, cut into small bits

Up to ⅓ cup very cold water

FOR THE FILLING

¾ cup chopped pitted Medjool dates (about 10 large Medjools)

1½ tablespoons packed dark brown sugar

3 large tart, green apples, such as Granny Smith apples, peeled, cored, and chopped

2 tablespoons granulated white sugar

2 tablespoons all-purpose flour

¼ teaspoon freshly grated nutmeg

¼ teaspoon ground dried ginger

2 tablespoons honey

OVEN RACK · center | OVEN TEMPERATURE · 375°F
PREP · Line a large, rimmed baking sheet with parchment paper.

TO MAKE THE CRUST

1 · Mix the flour, white sugar, and salt in a large bowl. Add the butter and cut it in with a pastry cutter or a fork until broken into hundreds of tiny bits coated in flour, each no bigger than the head of a pin.

2 · Stir in 3 tablespoons of the cold water with a fork, then more water in 1-teaspoon increments just until you create a soft, pliable, not-sticky dough. Gather the dough into a ball, dust it with flour, and roll it into a 12-inch circle, using the technique that begins on page 22. Lay the crust in the center of the parchment paper on the prepared baking sheet.

TO MAKE THE FILLING

3 · Toss the dates and brown sugar in a large bowl until well coated. Stir in the apples, white sugar, flour, nutmeg, and ginger until the fruit is evenly coated. Spread the filling onto the crust, leaving

a 1½-inch border all around the dough. Fold this edge up and over the filling, leaving a hole in the center of the galette. Drizzle the exposed fruit with the honey.

TO FINISH UP

4 · Bake the galette until lightly browned and a bit crunchy, with a bubbling filling, about 45 minutes. Cool the galette on the baking sheet set on a wire rack for at least 30 minutes or to room temperature before slicing into 6 or 8 wedges. Store tightly sealed in plastic wrap on the countertop for up to 2 days.

PRO TIP · No pro makes a perfect galette. It should have a rustic, homemade feel, definitely not made in a tart ring. If you want to get fancy, trim the edges with a fluted pastry wheel for a scalloped look. Fold the dough over the filling in sections, pushing them together a bit to seal closed, so you end up with minor bumps and waves in the top crust.

CINNAMON–BROWN SUGAR FROZEN CUSTARD

· YIELD: ABOUT 1 QUART ·

———— ◈ ————

This frozen dessert gets much of its flavor from the residual molasses in the brown sugar, a slightly bitter contrast in the cinnamon-rich custard. If you want to up the game, substitute demerara sugar, a "raw" sugar that retains quite a bit of the molasses from its caramelization process. You'll need to beat demerara sugar a bit longer to get it to dissolve into the egg yolks.

1 2/3 cups heavy cream

1 cup whole milk

1 tablespoon unsalted butter

5 large egg yolks, at room temperature

1/2 cup packed dark brown sugar

1/2 teaspoon ground cinnamon

1/4 teaspoon salt

TO MAKE THE CUSTARD

1 · Mix the cream, milk, and butter in a large saucepan set over medium heat. Stir until the butter has melted, then heat until whiffs of steam come off the surface, 3 to 4 minutes. Meanwhile, beat the egg yolks, brown sugar, cinnamon, and salt in a large bowl with an electric mixer at medium speed until thick and pastelike, about 4 minutes.

2 · Beat about half the cream mixture into the egg mixture until smooth, then beat this combined mixture into the remaining cream mixture until smooth. Set the pan over low heat and cook, stirring constantly, until the mixture thickly coats the back of a wooden spoon and the temperature registers 170°F, 4 to 7 minutes.

3 · Pour the mixture through a fine-mesh sieve into a clean bowl; refrigerate for at least 4 hours or up to 2 days, covering once chilled.

TO FREEZE IT

4 · Prepare an ice-cream machine. Stir the cold custard and freeze it in the machine according to the manufacturer's instructions, until you can scoop up a small mound with edges that do not immediately melt. Store in a sealed container in the freezer for up to 1 month.

À LA MODE IT · Since the crust is rather firm, make sure you've got knives, forks, and spoons at the table.

PRO TIP · If you want to serve this frozen custard on its own, spoon and spread some of it into a loaf pan or other long, shallow container. Spread a bit of apple butter over the top—and continue on, making layers of each until you finish up with a layer of frozen custard.

LINZER COOKIE TART

—◆—

DOUBLE DARK CHOCOLATE FROZEN CUSTARD

What is it about raspberries and nuts? You'd think that they wouldn't match up, that the sour berries would run right over the subtly sweet, slightly bitter notes in almonds and pecans. Miraculously, they don't; so we've kept them together in this jam-filled tart, modeled on Linzer cookies. And we probably don't need to sell you on the combo of raspberries and chocolate, right? In the end, it's going to hang together on the quality of the jam. Don't cheap out. Go for the good stuff.

LINZER COOKIE TART
· YIELD: ONE 10-INCH TART ·

—◆—

The dough is actually made of two sorts of nuts, almonds (yes, traditional) and pecans, something of an American original. Together, they offer a bit more earthy flavor to the crust so it can stand up to the dark, rich ice cream. This crust also has a cookie quality, rather than the short, crisp texture of many tarts. If you want to take the flavors over the top, warm the jam with 1 tablespoon raspberry liqueur such as Chambord in a bowl for 15 seconds in the microwave on high, stir well, and then spread it on the crust.

I cup sliced almonds

1/2 cup pecan pieces

I1/2 cups all-purpose flour, plus additional for dusting

2/3 cup granulated white sugar

I teaspoon ground cinnamon

1/2 teaspoon baking powder

1/4 teaspoon salt

I4 tablespoons (I stick plus 6 tablespoons) cold, unsalted butter, cut into small bits

2 large eggs, at room temperature

1/2 teaspoon pure vanilla extract

I1/2 cups raspberry jam

Confectioners' sugar, for garnishing

TO MAKE THE CRUST

1 · Put the almonds and pecans in a food processor, cover, and process until finely ground. Add the flour, granulated white sugar, cinnamon, baking powder, and salt; cover; and process until well blended.

2 · Add the butter, cover, and process until the consistency of coarse cornmeal. Add the eggs and vanilla extract. Cover and pulse until a dough forms. Gather the dough into a ball, divide it in half, form each into equal balls, and wrap separately in plastic wrap. Refrigerate for at least 2 hours or up to 1 day.

OVEN RACK · center | OVEN TEMPERATURE · 350°F

3 · Dust one of the balls with flour and roll it into an 11-inch circle, using the technique that begins on page 22. Center and set the crust into a 10-inch tart pan with a removable bottom; gently press the dough to fit the pan, making sure the edge conforms to the fluted edge and trimming off any excess.

TO FINISH UP

4 · Spread the jam evenly over the bottom of the crust. Dust the remaining dough with flour and roll it into an 11-inch circle as before. Using a pastry wheel or a sharp knife, cut the dough into 1/2-inch-wide strips. Peel these up one by one and lay them over the crust in a lattice pattern, the first one at the center in one direction, then another center one in the center at 90 degrees to

the first, and then working out to all edges, overlapping the strips. Trim the strips and seal them to the sides of the crust.

5 · Bake the tart until the crust is lightly browned and the jam is bubbling, about 30 minutes. Cool the tart in the pan on a wire rack for 10 minutes, then slip the tart out of its pan, still attached to its metal bottom. Continue cooling on a wire rack for at least 30 minutes or to room temperature. Slice into wedges and dust with confectioners' sugar to serve. Store tightly sealed in plastic wrap in the refrigerator for up to 2 days.

PRO TIP · You can remove the tart from its metal bottom, too. After you remove the sides of the pan, cool for another 15 minutes on a wire rack, then run a long, thin knife under the tart, separating it from the bottom. Slide it off onto a serving plate.

DOUBLE DARK CHOCOLATE FROZEN CUSTARD
· YIELD: ABOUT 1 QUART ·

Melted dark chocolate plus cocoa powder adds up to a glorious frozen custard. In fact, we used enough of both to take the custard right up the edge of being grainy. Don't worry: it's smooth and rich. And don't be tempted to use chocolate chips. They rarely give you a cocoa solid content above 40 or 50 percent. Instead use high-quality dark chocolate, even a bar you might enjoy eating on its own.

1 1/4 cups heavy cream

1 cup whole milk

6 ounces dark chocolate, preferably 70% to 80%, chopped

1/3 cup unsweetened cocoa powder, preferably natural-style cocoa powder

3 large egg yolks, at room temperature

2/3 cup granulated white sugar

1 teaspoon pure vanilla extract

1/4 teaspoon salt

TO MAKE THE CUSTARD
1 · Whisk the cream, milk, chocolate, and cocoa powder in a large saucepan set over medium heat until the chocolate has melted and the mixture is smooth and hot. Meanwhile, beat the egg yolks and sugar in a large bowl with an electric mixer at medium speed until pale and thick, until ribbons slide off the turned-off beaters, about 3 minutes. Beat in the vanilla extract and salt.

2 · Beat about half of the cream mixture in a slow, steady stream into the egg mixture until smooth, then beat this combined mixture into the remaining cream mixture in the saucepan. Set it over low heat and cook, stirring constantly, until it thickly coats the back of a wooden spoon and the temperature registers 170°F, 4 to 7 minutes.

3 · Strain the mixture through a fine-mesh sieve into a clean bowl. Refrigerate for at least 4 hours or up to 1 day, covering once the custard has cooled.

TO FREEZE IT
4 · Prepare an ice-cream machine. Stir the cold custard and freeze it in the machine according to the manufacturer's instructions, until the ice cream can hold its shape on a spoon without immediately melting at the edges. Store in a covered container in the freezer for up to 1 month.

À LA MODE IT · Since the tart has that jewel-like, raspberry filling, serve the scoops of frozen custard to the side of each piece, rather than on it.

PRO TIP · As the dark chocolate melts with the cream and milk, it will have a tendency to fall to the bottom of the saucepan and get trapped in the corners—where it will singe, creating a bitter accent. Make sure to whisk well so every last bit gets incorporated into the milk.

SALTY KEY LIME TART

TRIPLE COCONUT FROZEN CUSTARD

We have long been fans of salt in desserts: a little in ice cream, a little in chocolate cake. It highlights accents in a sweet palette that may get lost—helping bring to the foreground, say, the lime and coconut in this combo. But there's no doubt that this tart takes our love of salt over the top. If you're unsure, omit the flaked salt on top—there'll be enough salt in the crust to carry that mineral flavor forward in each bite.

SALTY LIME TART
· YIELD: ONE 9-INCH TART ·

This one's a salty shortbread crust topped with a sour lime curd. We used cake flour to create a shorter, crisper crust. And we added confectioners' sugar (with its attendant cornstarch) as well as extra cornstarch to pull out the moisture. There's no chance of this tart going boggy! Key lime juice is, of course, squeezed from key limes, smaller, more acidic, and more heavily perfumed limes than the standard, Persian limes. Key limes are actually grown in many places besides the Florida Keys—and were not even indigenous to those islands. You can use standard lime juice in this tart but the more moderated flavor will not stand up as well to a salt garnish.

FOR THE CRUST

1½ cups cake flour

9 tablespoons confectioners' sugar

5 teaspoons cornstarch

2 teaspoons kosher or coarse-ground sea salt

10½ tablespoons (1 stick plus 2½ tablespoons) cold unsalted butter, cut into small bits, plus additional for greasing

Up to ¼ cup heavy cream, as needed

FOR THE FILLING

One 14-ounce can sweetened condensed milk (do not use low-fat or fat-free)

¾ cup key lime juice

2 ounces regular cream cheese, at room temperature

1 large egg, plus 2 large egg yolks, at room temperature

1 tablespoon all-purpose flour

2 teaspoons finely grated lime zest

1 teaspoon flaked sea salt, such as Maldon

OVEN RACK · center | OVEN TEMPERATURE · 325°F
PREP · Lightly butter the inside of a 9-inch springform baking pan.

TO MAKE THE CRUST

1 · Put the cake flour, confectioners' sugar, cornstarch, and kosher salt in a food processor. Cover and pulse until well combined. Add the butter, cover, and pulse until the mixture resembles dry, coarse sand. With the machine running, pour in the cream in 1-tablespoon increments just until a slightly sticky dough forms when you press bits together between your fingers.

2 · Pour the crumbles into the prepared springform pan and press into a crust, evenly coating the bottom of the pan and pressing the crust 1 inch up the sides. Lay a sheet of aluminum foil in the pan to cover the crust. Bake to set for 17 minutes. Transfer to a wire rack; remove the foil. Maintain the oven temperature.

TO MAKE THE FILLING AND FINISH UP

3 · Clean and dry the food processor. Add the condensed milk, lime juice, cream cheese, egg, egg yolks, flour, and zest. Cover and process until smooth, scraping down the inside of the canister at least once. Pour the filling into the warm crust.

4 · Bake until puffed and set, about 17 minutes more. Transfer to a wire rack and cool for 1 hour. Remove the sides of the springform pan. Refrigerate the tart for at least 2 hours before serving, tenting loosely with plastic wrap when cold. Sprinkle with the flaked sea salt after slicing into wedges to serve. Store loosely covered in plastic wrap in the refrigerator for up to 2 days.

PRO TIP · The crust amalgam won't look like a dough when you've added the right amount of cream. In fact, if it comes together into a ball in the canister, you've added too much and need to start over. Instead, you should be able to press bits and crumbles together to form a dough—not that they've already gotten to that stage in the processor.

TRIPLE COCONUT FROZEN CUSTARD
· YIELD: ABOUT I QUART ·

Good grief, this one's rich! We didn't solely rely on the coconut fat in coconut milk to make an ice cream. We tried that—the texture was still too icy. So we added eggs. Then we added cream. Now it was worthy of that salty lime tart. But for an even more sophisticated flavor, toast the coconut on a baking sheet in a 325°F oven until aromatic, stirring occasionally, about 5 minutes. The coconut will brown a bit at the edges, so the ice cream will not be as white (and not as aesthetically pleasing), but the taste will be more reminiscent of coconut cream pie.

I¼ cups heavy cream

I cup canned cream of coconut

⅔ cup regular coconut milk (do not use "light" coconut milk)

½ cup packed sweetened shredded coconut

4 large egg yolks, at room temperature

I teaspoon pure vanilla extract

TO MAKE THE CUSTARD
1 · Mix the cream, cream of coconut, coconut milk, and shredded coconut in a large saucepan. Set over medium heat and warm until small bubbles begin to fizz around the pan's inner perimeter.

2 · Whisk the egg yolks and vanilla extract in a large bowl until smooth and creamy. Whisk in about half the hot cream mixture in a slow, steady stream until smooth, then whisk this combined mixture into the remaining cream mixture in the saucepan until smooth. Set over low heat and cook, stirring almost constantly, until the mixture thickly coats the back of a wooden spoon and the temperature registers 170°F, 4 to 7 minutes.

3 · Pour the mixture into a medium bowl and refrigerate for at least 4 hours or up to 1 day, covering once the mixture is cool.

TO FREEZE IT
4 · Prepare an ice-cream machine. Stir the cold custard and freeze it in the machine according to the manufacturer's instructions, until it can mound on a spoon without immediately melting at the edges. Store in a sealed container in the freezer for up to 1 month.

À LA MODE IT · If you serve the tart with flaked salt sprinkled on each serving, make sure you keep it on the lime curd, not on the nearby frozen custard. The frozen custard should be a salt-free break, as it were.

PRO TIP · Canned coconut milk will separate during storage. Stir it with a fork to redissolve the solids before measuring what you need. Store the remainder, covered, in the refrigerator for up to 2 weeks for another use.

PEANUT BRITTLE TART

POPCORN FROZEN CUSTARD

Here's our Cracker Jack fantasy! We started out by folding the boxed candy into vanilla gelato. Not bad, but the popcorn got mushy. So we went back to the drawing board and began pulling out individual flavor components until we got here: peanuts, caramel, and popcorn, separated in the preparation but together in every spoonful.

PEANUT BRITTLE TART
· YIELD: ONE 10-INCH TART ·

If you've got bridge work, turn the page. Imagine the flavors of peanut brittle, then imagine the texture of caramels. The filling is indeed a morphed technique from candy-making, poured into a buttery crust. Save it for a clear, bright day. Humidity and rain are its sworn enemies.

FOR THE CRUST

1½ cups all-purpose flour, plus additional for dusting

2 tablespoons granulated white sugar

8 tablespoons (1 stick) cold unsalted butter, cut into small pieces

At least 3 tablespoons very cold water, as needed

FOR THE FILLING

1¼ cups granulated white sugar

¼ cup water

⅔ cup heavy cream

2 tablespoons unsalted butter

1 tablespoon molasses

1 teaspoon pure vanilla extract

2 cups salted, shelled peanuts

OVEN RACK · center | OVEN TEMPERATURE · 375°F

TO MAKE THE CRUST

1 · Mix the flour and sugar in a large bowl. Add the butter and cut it into the mixture with a pastry cutter or a fork until it all resembles dry, coarse sand.

2 · Stir in 3 tablespoons of cold water with a fork, then more water, ½ tablespoon at a time, until a soft, not-sticky dough forms. Gather the dough into a ball, dust it with flour, and roll it into an 11-inch circle, following the instructions that begin on page 22. Center and set the crust into a 10-inch tart pan with a removable bottom. Press the dough to conform to the pan, even the fluting at the edges. Repeatedly prick the bottom of the crust and its sides with the tines of a fork, then line the pan with aluminum foil without pressing down onto the crust.

3 · Set the tart pan on a rimmed baking sheet and bake the crust for 15 minutes. Remove the foil and continue baking until lightly browned, about 5 minutes more. Transfer the tart pan to a wire baking rack.

TO MAKE THE FILLING

4 · Increase the oven temperature to 400°F.

5 · Stir the sugar and water in a large saucepan set over medium heat until the sugar has dissolved. Continue to cook without stirring until the mixture turns a dark amber color, 5 to 7 minutes. Meanwhile, warm the cream in a small saucepan set over medium-low heat until puffs of steam come up off its surface.

6 · Whisk the warmed cream into the amber syrup. Take care: it will roil up the sides of the pan. Whisk carefully but determinedly. Once smooth, whisk in the butter, molasses, and vanilla

extract. Remove from the heat and stir in the peanuts until well coated. Pour the filling into the still-warm crust.

TO FINISH UP

7 · Bake the tart until bubbling all over its surface, about 20 minutes. Transfer the tart to a wire rack and cool for at least 2 hours or to room temperature before slicing into wedges to serve. Store tightly sealed in plastic wrap on the countertop for up to 2 days.

PRO TIP · You'll have limited time to spread the peanuts evenly in the filling after it's been poured into the crust. Use an offset spatula sprayed with nonstick spray for the quickest, easiest job.

POPCORN FROZEN CUSTARD
· YIELD: ABOUT 1 QUART ·

Popcorn doesn't do right by ice cream. It collapses into an unappealing mush. But by soaking it in the cream and milk, we can infuse those flavors without the textural problems. If you buy already-popped popcorn in bags, make sure it includes no salt, sugar, or other flavors. Although kernel sizes vary, you'll need about 2½ tablespoons unpopped popcorn to give you 3 cups crushed, popped popcorn.

2 cups heavy cream

1 cup whole milk

3 cups crushed air-popped popcorn

6 large egg yolks, at room temperature

¾ cup granulated white sugar

½ teaspoon salt

TO MAKE THE CUSTARD

1 · Heat the cream and milk in a large saucepan over medium heat until puffs of steam rise off its surface. Stir in the popcorn, cover, and set aside

off the heat for 30 minutes. Strain the mixture through a fine-mesh sieve or a standard colander lined with cheesecloth. Using a rubber spatula, press gently against the popcorn to extract the last drips of liquid. Discard the solids.

2 · Pour the liquid into a clean, large saucepan. Set it over medium heat and again heat it until those puffs of steam appear. Meanwhile, using an electric mixer at medium speed, beat the egg yolks and sugar in a large bowl until thick and pale yellow, until thick ribbons slide off the turned-off beaters, about 4 minutes.

3 · Beat about half the cream mixture into the egg mixture until smooth, then beat this combined mixture into the remaining cream mixture in the pan until smooth. Set over low heat, add the salt, and cook, stirring constantly, until it thickly coats the back of a wooden spoon and the temperature registers 170°F, 4 to 7 minutes.

4 · Strain the mixture through a fine-mesh sieve into a medium bowl. Refrigerate for at least 4 hours or up to 1 day, covering the custard once it's chilled.

TO FREEZE IT

5 · Prepare an ice-cream machine. Stir the cold custard and freeze it in the machine according to the manufacturer's instructions, until the ice cream can mound on a spoon without immediately melting at its edges. Store in a sealed container in the freezer for up to 1 month.

À LA MODE IT · Since the tart is sticky, use a large, dampened chef's knife to cut it into wedges, wiping the blade after each slice. Serve with the frozen custard on the side—and with forks, rather than spoons.

PRO TIP · We actually didn't find that the more we soaked the popcorn, the better the frozen custard tasted. After more than 30 minutes, the cream mixture started picking up bitter notes, none too appealing.

CRISPS, COBBLERS, & FRUIT DESSERTS

IF YOU'RE TIRED OF ROLLING OUT CRUSTS, YOU'VE COME

to the right place. These are less formal fruit desserts to pair with frozen concoctions like Peach Ice Cream or Cherry-Vanilla Frozen Custard. (There's even a frozen riff on a classic French sauce in this mix of recipes; it's like a crème bavaroise morphed into a semifreddo.) We'll start with a collection of true-blue American classics: crisps and cobblers, yes, but also a pandowdy, a slump, and a brown betty. Ever heard of sonker or bird's nest pudding? You're about to. We'll round out the section with three vaguely Continental offerings: our version of apple strudel, a down-home take on the German tradition; an old-school dowager dessert that cries out for a rich frozen custard; and some poached pears worthy of a Left Bank bistro.

Although almost every recipe is less complicated than those pies and tarts were—we've even simplified the strudel to put it within weeknight reach—the flavor pairings are more ornate, thanks partly to the ways the baked desserts themselves often include more than one component. There's that crunchy topping over raspberries in the crisp or those wet biscuits over blueberries and ginger in the slump. To complement, we've also amped up the flavors in the ice creams and frozen custards, even tossing in a bright sherbet, all to work with, for, and even against the more complex flavor palates.

A WORD (OR SEVERAL) ABOUT FRUIT

The key to the overall success here is the fruit. We want it to be the cornerstone, despite a more ornate flavor palette all around. Thus, fruit is assumed fresh unless otherwise stated. Not only is the flavor better, but the baking times and sugar ratios were worked out for fresh fruit.

However, there are cases when frozen or even canned will work. We'll let you know. And we'll give you instructions on how to handle measuring frozen fruit (for example, measure it before thawing, then include any released juice). Otherwise, make no substitutions unless you're an experienced baker. A baking recipe is a call to the letter of the law—at least the first time you make it. Once you understand its intent, you can get more creative.

And one more thing, perhaps counterintuitive: if you can use frozen fruit and have a choice between inferior fresh fruit (bruised, hard, underripe, green, or fragrance-free) and the frozen variety, choose the frozen. Fruit meant for the supermarket's freezer section is picked riper than the fruit trucked to the produce section. Suppliers rely on the fresh stuff to continue to ripen in transit; the frozen fruit has no such chance and must be picked closer to perfection.

BASIC BAKING GUIDELINES

1 · BUY AN OVEN THERMOMETER. Like pianos, most ovens go out of whack over time. Many need an annual calibration. Some high-end ovens need it more often. If you hang an oven thermometer from the center rack, you'll know where your oven stands. You can also figure out how you have to adjust our required temperature or suggested timing to compensate. And you'll see if you need to call out a repair person.

2 · DON'T SWAP OUT PAN SIZES. We developed the recipes to work with a specific surface area and depth. Many baked desserts in this section are made in a 9-inch square, one in a 9 x 13-inch baking dish, and a few in other shaped vessels. We'll give you alternatives when they'll work.

3 · POSITION THE OVEN RACK AS STATED. Cakey toppings, biscuits on cobblers, and even oat-crunch crusts require a constant, even oven temperature. If yours doesn't have a middle slot for the rack, position it in the closest rung down from what would be center—and watch the baking more carefully to prevent scorching.

4 · USE A CONVECTION OVEN AT WILL. Drop the temperature by 25°F and reduce the baking time by 10, maybe 20 percent. But remember: not all convection ovens were created equal. You'll need to watch closely to discover how quickly your convection fan circulates air in the oven.

So let's move on to the down-home fruit desserts and their Continental kin. You may get reacquainted with some classics; you may find something brand-new. You'll certainly find plenty of vehicles for the rich ice creams and frozen custards, buttermilk to rum-nutmeg, lemon to walnut, even one with Grape-Nuts in the mix.

SOUR CHERRY COBBLER

— ✦ —

CANNOLI CREAM ICE CREAM

Late one night after a theater performance in New York City, we went to an Italian bakery for dessert and coffee. The woman behind the counter was definitely bleary-eyed. We asked for a couple of cannoli, as well as a slice of vanilla cake with a warm cherry sauce ladled on top. She poured the sauce over the cannoli. We never looked back. Because the cannoli shell got soft under the sauce, we morphed the duo into an American cobbler–Italian ice-cream fandango. Consider it sweetened ricotta and mascarpone with biscuits and a cherry sauce. Consider it ridiculous.

SOUR CHERRY COBBLER

· YIELD: ONE 9-INCH SQUARE COBBLER ·

— ✦ —

Cobblers have biscuit toppings—but not always true biscuits. This batter is more like a wet dough, like a super-thick waffle batter. We find that its wetter texture becomes cakier on top of the cobbler, a better fit to the fruit. And to that end, let's say that sour cherry season is very short, just a few weeks in midsummer. If you spot sour cherries at the market, snap them up, pit them, and freeze them in sealed plastic bags to make this combo later in the year. Or use purchased frozen pitted sour cherries. Thaw frozen sour cherries in a bowl in the refrigerator for a day or two, then measure the cherries with their liquid for this recipe. In a real dessert emergency, use canned pitted sour cherries although the flavor will be drastically muted, without the zing of the fresh fruit.

FOR THE FILLING

2¼ pounds sour cherries, pitted (about 6 cups)

⅔ cup granulated white sugar

1½ tablespoons instant tapioca

1 tablespoon all-purpose flour

¼ teaspoon salt

FOR THE TOPPING

¾ cup all-purpose flour

⅔ cup sliced almonds, finely ground

3 tablespoons granulated white sugar

1½ teaspoons baking soda

¼ teaspoon salt

½ cup buttermilk

2 tablespoons unsalted butter, melted and cooled, plus additional for greasing

¼ teaspoon almond extract

OVEN RACK · center | OVEN TEMPERATURE · 350°F
PREP · Lightly butter the inside of a 9-inch square baking pan.

TO MAKE THE FILLING

1 · Mix the sour cherries, sugar, tapioca, flour, and salt in a large bowl until the cherries are evenly coated. Pour into the prepared pan and set aside for 10 minutes.

TO MAKE THE TOPPING

2 · Wash and dry the bowl. Add the flour, ground almonds, sugar, baking soda, and salt; stir until uniform.

3 · In a second bowl, whisk the buttermilk, melted butter, and almond extract until smooth. Stir this mixture into the flour mixture just until you have a wet, soft batter that somewhat holds its shape but is still a bit runny. Dollop by

heaping tablespoonfuls across the sour cherry mixture. The more rustic, the better! They will spread out a lot as they bake, many fusing together.

TO FINISH UP

4 · Bake the cobbler until the biscuit topping is browned and the fruit filling is bubbling underneath, about 45 minutes. Cool the cobbler on a wire rack for 15 minutes or to room temperature before serving by the bowlful. Store tightly covered at room temperature for up to 1 day.

PRO TIP · To grind almonds, put them in a food processor, cover, and whir away until they're the consistency of fine, dry sand. Or look for ground almonds at high-end supermarkets and health-food stores.

CANNOLI CREAM ICE CREAM
· YIELD: ABOUT 1 QUART ·

This ice cream is like an easy, no-cook-but-frozen version of the filling in cannoli: a mix of sweetened ricotta, mascarpone, and even minced citron (that is, a candied citrus peel). While the flavor of the candied citron is muted in the frozen concoction, it'll add both eye appeal and an interesting, chewy texture, a good pairing with the soft cherry filling in the cobbler. Look for candied citron with the glacéed fruit at the supermarket.

1½ cups heavy cream

1 cup whole-milk ricotta

¾ cup granulated white sugar

½ cup (4 ounces) mascarpone

½ cup whole milk

1 tablespoon pure vanilla extract

½ cup finely chopped citron or candied citrus peel

TO START THE ICE CREAM

1 · Put the cream, ricotta, sugar, mascarpone, milk, and vanilla extract in a blender. Cover and blend until smooth, scraping down the inside of the canister at least once. Set the covered canister in the refrigerator and chill for at least 4 hours or up to 2 days.

TO FREEZE IT

2 · Prepare an ice cream machine. Stir the cold cream mixture and freeze in an ice-cream machine according to the manufacturer's instructions just until moundable.

3 · Sprinkle the chopped citron into the machine and let the dasher churn it into the ice cream during the last couple of minutes. Store in a sealed container in the freezer for up to 2 weeks.

À LA MODE IT · Serve the pair in bowls. The ice cream is pretty soft, even when stored in the freezer, so there's no need to set it out at room temperature before serving.

RASPBERRY CRISP
WITH A BUTTERY OAT-ALMOND TOPPING

PEACH ICE CREAM

A crisp is fruit baked under crunch. And here's our Peach Melba fantasy! It's got a topping like nutty oatmeal cookies over the berries, all to ground the natural sweetness of the peach ice cream. We tried reversing them (peach crisp/raspberry ice cream) but the raspberries ganged up and took over. As the pair now stands, they practically scream "summer," a tribute to those warm days when the light never stops.

RASPBERRY CRISP
WITH A BUTTERY
OAT-ALMOND TOPPING

· YIELD: ONE 9-INCH SQUARE CRISP ·

The fulcrum to balance the tart filling and the nutty topping is actually the lemon zest. That spark perks it all up, keeping the dessert from being too sweet, balancing the almonds and honey with the fruit. If you use frozen raspberries, don't thaw them. Toss them with the other filling ingredients and set aside for 15 minutes (rather than 10). Increase the baking time by 5 minutes or so, until bubbling.

FOR THE FILLING

6 cups fresh or frozen raspberries
    (about I pound IO ouces)

½ cup granulated white sugar

2 tablespoons instant tapioca

2 teaspoons finely grated lemon zest

¼ teaspoon salt

FOR THE TOPPING

½ cup all-purpose flour

½ cup rolled oats (do not use quick-cooking or
    steel-cut)

6 tablespoons packed dark brown sugar

6 tablespoons sliced almonds

4 tablespoons (½ stick) unsalted butter, melted and
    cooled, plus additional for greasing

2 tablespoons honey

½ teaspoon ground cinnamon

½ teaspoon almond extract

¼ teaspoon salt

OVEN RACK · center | **OVEN TEMPERATURE · 350°F**
PREP · Lightly butter the inside of a 9-inch square baking pan.

TO MAKE THE FILLING

1 · Mix the raspberries, white sugar, tapioca, lemon zest, and salt in a large bowl until the berries are well coated. Pour into the prepared pan and set aside for 10 minutes.

TO MAKE THE TOPPING

2 · Wash and dry the bowl. Mix the flour, oats, brown sugar, almonds, melted butter, honey, cinnamon, almond extract, and salt in the bowl. Crumble the topping evenly over the raspberry mixture.

TO FINISH IT UP

3 · Bake the crisp until the filling is bubbling and the topping has browned, about 45 minutes. Cool the crisp on a wire rack for at least 30 minutes or to room temperature before dishing up by the big spoonful into bowls. Store tightly covered in the refrigerator for up to 2 days.

PRO TIP · Getting the topping onto the fruit is easier said than done. Crumble the oat mixture between your fingers, creating a single, top layer with lots of bumps, ridges, and waves.

PEACH ICE CREAM
· YIELD: ABOUT 1 QUART ·

Surprisingly, there are no sliced peaches in our peach ice cream. We find they become icy chips, ruining the texture. If you lament the lack, add some. Prepare the recipe as indicated; then peel, pit, and dice a fresh peach to let the machine's dasher stir it into the custard for the final few turns. With a diced peach in the mix, eat the ice cream fresh out of the machine, rather than letting it harden up in the freezer.

1½ cups heavy cream

1 cup whole milk

½ cup granulated white sugar

1 tablespoon cornstarch

2 large sweet peaches, peeled, pitted, and thinly
   sliced

¼ cup peach nectar

¼ teaspoon pure vanilla extract

⅛ teaspoon salt

TO START THE ICE CREAM

1 · Whisk the cream, milk, sugar, and cornstarch in a large saucepan over medium heat until the mixture bubbles and thickens a bit, 3 to 4 minutes.

2 · Put the peaches, peach nectar, and vanilla extract in a blender. Add the hot cream mixture. Cover but remove the center knob from the lid. Cover the lid with a clean kitchen towel and blend until thick and smooth, scraping down the inside of the canister at least once. Put the knob in the lid and refrigerate the canister for at least 4 hours or up to 1 day.

TO FREEZE IT

3 · Prepare an ice cream machine. Give the cold ice cream base one more spin in the blender, then freeze it in the machine according to the manufacturer's instructions, until you can scoop up a spoonful with edges that do not immediately melt. Store in a sealed container in the freezer for up to 1 week.

À LA MODE IT · Best served in bowls, the crisp should be a bit warm. If you've made it the day before, nuke bowlfuls on high for 15 seconds to make sure there's no chill.

PRO TIP · Peach nectar is a sweetened fruit drink, made from peach puree and sometimes cut with unsweetened apple juice. It's not peach juice or pure peach puree, neither of which has enough sugar to make this a successful ice cream.

FIG CRISP WITH A WALNUT-MAPLE TOPPING

LEMON ICE CREAM

Fresh figs are almost too opulent to cook into a crisp. Almost. They melt into a sweet, jamlike filling, here topped with a sweet-nutty crunch. It's an old-fashioned dessert, fit for this tart-sweet lemon ice cream, our version of frozen lemon curd. Believe it or not, it's the butter in the crisp and the ice cream (ahem) that harmonizes them both, a common bass note among the lighter, brighter tones.

FRESH FIG CRISP WITH A WALNUT-MAPLE TOPPING

· YIELD: ONE 9-INCH SQUARE COBBLER ·

Although the flavor of fresh figs always benefits from a little acid, lemon juice easily overwhelms their delicate aroma. White balsamic vinegar to the rescue! It's a mild, vaguely sweet vinegar with a clean, bright finish, made into a syrup by boiling the pressings (or "must") from white Trebbiano grapes.

FOR THE FILLING

Unsalted butter, for greasing

3 pints large fresh figs (about 18 medium figs), stemmed and quartered

1/3 cup granulated white sugar

1 tablespoon instant tapioca

1 teaspoon white balsamic vinegar

1 teaspoon finely grated orange zest

1/2 teaspoon salt

FOR THE TOPPING

1/2 cup all-purpose flour

1/2 cup rolled oats (do not use quick-cooking or steel-cut)

6 tablespoons packed light brown sugar

1/3 cup finely chopped walnuts

4 tablespoons (1/2 stick) unsalted butter, melted and cooled

2 tablespoons maple syrup

1/2 teaspoon ground cinnamon

1/4 teaspoon salt

OVEN RACK · center | **OVEN TEMPERATURE · 375°F**
PREP · Lightly butter the inside of a 9-inch square baking pan.

TO MAKE THE FILLING

1 · Stir the figs, white sugar, tapioca, vinegar, zest, and salt together in a large bowl. Pour into the prepared pan and set aside for 10 minutes. Wash and dry the bowl.

TO MAKE THE TOPPING

2 · In the clean bowl, mix together the flour, oats, brown sugar, walnuts, butter, maple syrup, cinnamon, and salt until crumbly and moist. Sprinkle the topping over the fig mixture, coating it evenly and thoroughly.

TO FINISH UP

3 · Bake the crisp until the filling is bubbling and the topping is lightly browned, about 40 minutes. Cool the crisp on a wire rack for at least 30 minutes or to room temperature. Scoop up by the big spoonful into bowls to serve. Store tightly covered in the refrigerator for up to 1 day.

PRO TIP · Use almost any sort of fresh figs here: yellowish green Calimyrna figs will be tarter but lighter in flavor; Black Mission figs, sweeter and more assertive. Just don't use dried figs! The fresh figs should be quite ripe but not squishy; they should cut into discrete quarters.

LEMON ICE CREAM

· YIELD: A LITTLE LESS THAN 1 QUART ·

— · ◈ · —

Mixing cream into thickened lemon curd is a great idea and a French tradition. Freezing the results is a better idea. What's more, it's about the only way you can work with fresh lemon juice in an ice cream; otherwise, the juice curdles the dairy. This ice cream is best if you serve it right from the machine—or let the container stand at room temperature for 10 minutes.

2 whole eggs, at room temperature

1 cup granulated white sugar

1/2 cup fresh lemon juice

2 tablespoons unsalted butter

1 teaspoon lemon extract (not pure lemon oil)

1 2/3 cups heavy cream

1/3 cup whole milk

TO BEGIN THE ICE CREAM

1 · Whisk the eggs, sugar, lemon juice, butter, and lemon extract in the top half of a double boiler until foamy. Set it over about 1 inch of slowly simmering water in the bottom half. Or do this operation in a heat-safe medium bowl set over a medium saucepan with the same amount of simmering water. Whisk constantly until the mixture thickens, 7 to 8 minutes.

2 · Remove the top half of the double boiler or the bowl from the heat and set aside at room temperature for a couple of minutes. Whisk in the cream and milk. Cover and refrigerate until cold, about 6 hours, or even overnight.

TO FREEZE IT

3 · Prepare an ice-cream machine. Stir the custard base and freeze it in the machine according to the manufacturer's instructions, until moundable on a spoon. Store in a sealed container in the freezer for up to 1 month.

À LA MODE IT · Serve this duo with flatware tablespoons to hold the figs, topping, and ice cream in each bite.

PRO TIP · Look for a definite thickening in the curd: a change in its viscosity as well as a sheen on its surface. Don't cook it until it's firm on a spoon; rather, you should be able to drop a little back on the surface and it should hold its shape for a few seconds. It will continue to set as it cools.

BLACKBERRY PANDOWDY

—◆—

BUTTERMILK FROZEN CUSTARD

Back in the day—and we're talking even before we came along, not just in our disco '70s—blackberries and buttermilk were a summer-in-the-American-South treat (or at least it was so in one of our families). The blackberries would be mixed with sugar and set aside to macerate, then cool buttermilk would be poured on top. Here's a pairing to celebrate that old-school treat.

BLACKBERRY PANDOWDY

· YIELD: ONE 12-INCH OVAL PANDOWDY ·

—·◆·—

A pandowdy is made by putting a crust over fruit, then cracking the crust partway through baking so that the filling bubbles over its edge. Don't get all OCD when you break up the crust. It should be in chunks, nothing regular but nothing too small. If you don't have a 12-inch oval pan, use an 11 x 7-inch rectangular baking pan but reduce the cooking time by 5 or 10 minutes.

FOR THE FILLING

6 cups fresh blackberries

6 tablespoons granulated white sugar

2 tablespoons unsalted butter, melted and cooled, plus additional for greasing

I tablespoon fresh lemon juice

I tablespoon cornstarch

FOR THE CRUST

I¹⁄4 cups all-purpose flour, plus additional for dusting

¹⁄4 cup yellow cornmeal

I tablespoon granulated white sugar

¹⁄2 teaspoon salt

10 tablespoons (1 stick plus 2 tablespoons) cold unsalted butter, cut into small bits

At least ¹⁄4 cup very cold water

I large egg white, beaten in a small bowl until foamy

I tablespoon packed light brown sugar

OVEN RACK · center | OVEN TEMPERATURE · 375°F
PREP · Butter the inside of a 12-inch oval au gratin dish or an II x 7-inch baking dish.

TO MAKE THE FILLING

1 · Gently stir the blackberries, white sugar, melted butter, lemon juice, and cornstarch in a large bowl until the sugar evenly coats the berries. Pour into the prepared baking pan. Wash and thoroughly dry the bowl.

TO MAKE THE CRUST

2 · Add the flour, cornmeal, sugar, and salt to the clean bowl; stir well. Cut in the butter with a pastry cutter or a fork until the mixture resembles dry, coarse cornmeal. Stir in ¹⁄4 cup cold water, then more water in 1-teaspoon increments until the mixture becomes a soft but firm, supple, not-sticky dough.

3 · Gather the dough into a ball, dust it with flour, and roll it into a shape similar to the top of the au gratin dish (or the baking dish), following the instructions that begin on page 22. It can be rustic and a bit malformed; it shouldn't come up over the sides of the baking dish. Set it over the fruit. Brush it with the foamy egg whites and sprinkle evenly with the brown sugar.

TO FINISH UP

4 · Bake the pandowdy for 30 minutes. Using the handle of a flatware knife, break the crust into irregular chunks and shards, maybe 7 or 8 large pieces. Continue baking until the filling bubbles

up through the crust's cracks and coats its ragged edges, about 20 minutes more. Cool the pandowdy on a wire rack for at least 25 minutes or to room temperature before scooping into bowls to serve. Store tightly covered in the refrigerator for up to 2 days.

PRO TIP · The less you can work the crust, the more tender it will be. Gather the dough into a ball without making it too compact, dust it with flour as lightly as possible, and roll it in gentle but even strokes.

BUTTERMILK FROZEN CUSTARD
· YIELD: ABOUT 1 QUART ·

Most buttermilk these days isn't buttermilk at all—that is, it's not the leftover liquid from the butter-making process. It's a cultured product, similar to wet yogurt. (You'll see it so labeled on the carton.) We tested this recipe using "real" buttermilk, available at high-end or large supermarkets. It has more sour punch but a thinner texture. If you can only find cultured buttermilk, use 6 large egg yolks to keep the mixture from becoming too thick.

1¹/₃ cups heavy cream

1¹/₃ cups buttermilk

³/₄ cup granulated white sugar

8 large egg yolks, at room temperature

1 teaspoon pure vanilla extract

¹/₈ teaspoon salt

TO MAKE THE CUSTARD

1 · Mix the cream and buttermilk in a large saucepan, then set it over medium heat and warm until small bubbles fizz around the inside perimeter of the pan. Meanwhile, use an electric mixer at medium speed to beat the sugar and egg yolks in a large bowl until pale yellow but very thick, until wide ribbons slide off the turned-off beaters, about 5 minutes.

2 · Beat about half the hot cream mixture into the egg yolk mixture in a slow steady stream until smooth, then beat this combined mixture into the remaining cream mixture in the pan until smooth. Beat in the vanilla extract and salt. Set the pan over low heat and cook, stirring constantly, until the custard thickly coats the back of a wooden spoon and the temperature registers 170°F, 4 to 7 minutes.

3 · Strain the mixture through a fine-mesh sieve into a clean bowl. Refrigerate for at least 4 hours or up to 2 days, covering once the custard is cold.

TO FREEZE IT

4 · Prepare an ice-cream machine. Stir the cold custard and freeze it in the machine according to the manufacturer's instructions, until you can scoop up a mound with edges that do not immediately melt. Store in a sealed container in the freezer for up to 2 months.

À LA MODE IT · Set the frozen custard slightly to the side of any crust so that it melts into the blackberries but doesn't soften said crust.

PRO TIP · For a kick, add up to 1/8 teaspoon cayenne with the salt.

BLUEBERRY-GINGER SLUMP

FROZEN BAVARIAN CREAM

Ginger may be a miracle flavor in savory fare, but it can be something like napalm in desserts. With added sugar, it can TKO all else. We find that blueberries are one of its best matches. They offer a slightly herbaceous edge that keeps the ginger in balance. Still, that ginger needs to meet its match—and it will definitely do so with our take on Bavarian cream. Put away the ice cream maker: this is not an ice cream. It's a frozen sauce, pillowy soft. Add its uptown texture to the down-home slump and you'll know why we find this a most intriguing duo.

BLUEBERRY-GINGER SLUMP
· YIELD: 6 OR 8 BOWLFULS ·

A slump is another old-school dessert, sort of like a fruit cobbler—or maybe like a dessert version of pot pie. It's messier than either, the fruit mixture wet and thick, shellacking the biscuitlike topping as it bakes. In fact, the biscuits "slump" into the filling, thereby giving you a firm texture on top with soft, rich undersides. It's wonderfully sumptuous.

FOR THE FILLING

5 cups fresh blueberries

1/2 cup granulated white sugar

1/2 cup water

1 tablespoon fresh lemon juice

1 tablespoon minced peeled fresh ginger

1 tablespoon cornstarch

1/2 teaspoon ground cinnamon

1/2 teaspoon ground dried ginger

1/4 teaspoon salt

FOR THE TOPPING

1 1/2 cups self-rising flour, preferably self-rising white Southern biscuit flour

3 tablespoons cold unsalted butter, cut into small bits

1 tablespoon plus 2 teaspoons granulated white sugar

6 tablespoons whole milk

1/2 teaspoon ground cinnamon

TO MAKE THE FILLING

1 · Mix the blueberries, sugar, water, lemon juice, fresh ginger, cornstarch, cinnamon, dried ginger, and salt in a 4-quart oval French casserole or Dutch oven. Set over medium heat and bring to a boil, stirring often.

2 · Reduce the heat to low and simmer, uncovered but stirring occasionally, until thickened, like warm, melted jam out of the microwave, about 10 minutes.

TO MAKE THE TOPPING AND FINISH UP

3 · Put the self-rising flour, butter, and 1 tablespoon of sugar in a food processor. Cover and pulse until the butter has been finely ground into the flour. Add the milk, cover, and pulse a few times to form a somewhat wet dough. Drop by rounded spoonfuls onto the top of the blueberry mixture. Cover and simmer for 15 minutes.

4 · Mix the remaining 2 teaspoons sugar and the cinnamon in a small bowl. Sprinkle over the dumplings and continue simmering, covered, until the sugar has melted into a glaze, about 5 minutes more.

5 · Uncover and cool the slump off the heat for at least 30 minutes or to room temperature before serving in bowls. Store tightly covered in the refrigerator for up to 1 day (breakfast!).

PRO TIP · Soft white wheat flour, particularly the self-rising variety, has been a staple of Southern biscuit-making for years. It gives the biscuits a super-tender texture. Look for brands like White Lily or King Arthur, either in large supermarkets or from online suppliers.

FROZEN BAVARIAN CREAM
· YIELD: ONE 9 X 5-INCH FROZEN LOAF BAVARIAN CREAM ·

Bavarian cream (*crème bavaroise* in its chef-school nomenclature) is pastry cream thickened with gelatin rather than flour or cornstarch. It's often chilled until firm, then unmolded—except we decided to freeze it, not in an ice-cream maker, but in a loaf pan. To get the right texture, you must beat and beat the egg yolk mixture—if you think you're overbeating it, you'll get it about right. But don't beat the egg whites until they're stiff and don't beat the cream until it's buttery. These should be soft to give the frozen concoction a marshmallowy, luxurious texture.

1½ cups whole milk

One ¼-ounce package unflavored powdered gelatin

4 large egg yolks, at room temperature

12 tablespoons granulated white sugar

1 tablespoon pure vanilla extract

3 large egg whites, at room temperature

½ cup heavy cream

TO MAKE THE THICKENED CUSTARD
1 · Mix ¼ cup of the milk and the gelatin in a small bowl. Set aside for 5 minutes until the gelatin dissolves and stiffens the milk.

2 · Heat the remaining 1¼ cups milk in a large saucepan set over medium heat until puffs of steam come up off its surface.

3 · Meanwhile, beat the egg yolks and 6 tablespoons of sugar in a large bowl with an electric mixer at medium speed until thick and pale yellow, until wide ribbons slide off the turned-off beaters, about 4 minutes. Beat in the vanilla extract.

4 · Beat in about half the hot milk in a slow, steady stream until smooth, then beat this combined mixture into the remaining milk mixture in the pan. Set the pan over low heat and cook, stirring almost constantly, until the mixture thickly coats the back of a wooden spoon, 4 to 6 minutes.

5 · Stir in the gelatin mixture until smooth, then pour into a clean bowl and refrigerate until cooled and just starting to set up, about 2 hours.

TO MAKE THE REMAINING COMPONENTS
6 · Beat the egg whites in a large bowl with an electric mixer at low speed until foamy, then at medium speed and finally at high speed until they can form droopy points and peaks when the turned-off beaters are dipped into them. Beat in the remaining 6 tablespoons sugar in 2-tablespoon increments, beating at high speed until you can no longer feel any grainy sugar in the mixture when rubbed between your fingers. Set aside. Clean and dry the beaters.

7 · Beat the heavy cream in a second large bowl with the mixer, fitted with the clean beater, at high speed until it can hold its shape on a spoon, about 3 minutes.

TO PUT IT TOGETHER
8 · Using a rubber spatula, fold the egg white mixture into the chilled custard until smooth. Fold in the beaten cream until smooth.

9 · Line a 9 x 5-inch loaf pan with plastic wrap. Spoon and spread the chilled Bavarian cream into the pan. Cover with plastic wrap and freeze for at least 8 hours or up to 1 week. Store, tightly covered in the freezer for up to 1 month.

À LA MODE IT · Unmold the Frozen Bavarian Cream on a cutting board and unwrap it. Using a sharp, heavy knife, slice it the short way into 1-inch-thick pieces. Set these in bowls, then spoon the warm slump on top.

PRO TIP · Use a metal loaf pan. Plastic wrap sticks irredeemably to glass, making it impossible to get a smooth coating.

PLUM COBBLER

— ✦ —

ORANGE SHERBET

Here's an adventurous pairing. The flavors are bold: bright and fresh, more a collage than amalgam. The plums should be ripe and fragrant since their natural sugars will provide the major counterpunch to the creamy sherbet made from fresh orange juice. The biscuit topping also has warming spices like ginger and nutmeg to balance the tartness of the plums.

PLUM COBBLER

· YIELD: ONE 9-INCH SQUARE COBBLER ·

— ✦ —

This somewhat stiff biscuit dough is a better fit for the plums since they don't break down but retain some of their original texture. Although we suggest red plums here, you can use other varieties: Italian prune plums will create a thick, sweet filling; green plums will make for a rather lurid color but are mildly sweet with a bit more perfume. Just don't use canned plums.

FOR THE FILLING

2 1/2 pounds ripe red plums, pitted and sliced (about 6 cups)

1/3 cup granulated white sugar

2 tablespoons instant tapioca

1/4 teaspoon freshly grated nutmeg

1/4 teaspoon salt

FOR THE TOPPING

3 tablespoons heavy cream

3 tablespoons unsalted butter, melted and cooled, plus additional for greasing

1 large egg, plus 1 large egg yolk, at room temperature

1 teaspoon pure vanilla extract

1 cup all-purpose flour

3 tablespoons granulated white sugar

1/2 tablespoon baking powder

1/2 teaspoon salt

1/4 teaspoon ground dried ginger

1/4 teaspoon ground cloves

OVEN RACK · center | **OVEN TEMPERATURE · 350°F**
PREP · Lightly butter the inside of a 9-inch square baking pan.

TO MAKE THE FILLING

1 · Mix the plums, sugar, tapioca, nutmeg, and salt in a large bowl until the plums are evenly coated. Pour into the prepared pan and set aside for 10 minutes. Wash and dry the bowl.

TO MAKE THE TOPPING

2 · Whisk the cream, melted butter, egg, egg yolk, and vanilla extract in the clean bowl until smooth.

3 · Stir the flour, sugar, baking powder, salt, ginger, and cloves in a second large bowl. Add the cream mixture and stir with a wooden spoon until you have a soft dough that's just a bit wetter than a standard dough for biscuits. Drop by heaping tablespoonfuls onto the plum filling.

TO FINISH UP

4 · Bake the cobbler until the biscuit topping has browned and the filling is bubbling underneath, about 50 minutes. Cool the cobbler on a wire rack for at least 30 minutes or to room temperature. Spoon into bowls to serve. Store tightly covered in the refrigerator for up to 2 days.

PRO TIP · For a less rustic topping, use two, large, flatware tablespoons to form the biscuit mixture into oblong dumplings (like quenelles). Coat the spoons with nonstick spray, then scoop up some of the mixture in one spoon before passing it back and forth between the spoons to create an oblong shape. Set this on top of the filling and carry on making more.

ORANGE SHERBET
· YIELD: ABOUT I QUART ·
— · ◈ · —

As we've mentioned previously, sherbets originally involved mare's milk. Few of us live the sultan life but we have come to expect a creamier texture from sherbet. Rather than morphing the basic notion of a sherbet too far, we used half-and-half (more in keeping with the thickness of that exotic milk). We also added some gelatin to give the sherbet a creamy set while keeping the fruit juice at the fore of the flavors.

I teaspoon granulated gelatin

I tablespoon cold water

2¼ cups half-and-half

½ cup granulated white sugar

¼ cup light corn syrup

⅛ teaspoon salt

I cup fresh orange juice

2 tablespoons finely minced orange zest

TO START THE SHERBET

1 · Sprinkle the gelatin over the water in a small bowl. Set aside for 5 minutes until the water has become a soft gel.

2 · Mix the half-and-half, sugar, corn syrup, and salt in a large saucepan. Stir until the sugar has dissolved, then warm over medium heat until little puffs of steam come off the surface. Remove from the heat and stir in the gelatin mixture until dissolved.

3 · Pour and scrape the contents of the saucepan into a blender. Add the orange juice and zest. The mixture may begin to curdle from the added acid. Cover and remove the center knob from the lid. Cover the lid with a clean kitchen towel and blend until smooth, scraping down the inside of the canister at least once (and thus taking care of the curdling problem).

4 · Set the knob back in the lid. Place the covered canister in the refrigerator and chill the mixture for at least 4 hours or up to 8 hours.

TO FINISH UP

5 · Prepare an ice-cream machine. Blend the chilled mixture in the canister one more time, then pour its contents into the machine and freeze according to the manufacturer's instructions, until the sherbet will mound on a spoon. Store in a sealed container in the freezer for up to 1 month.

À LA MODE IT · Since the biscuits in the cobbler are a bit stiffer, serve the pair in bowls with a fork and spoon.

PRO TIP · If you buy orange juice at the store, make sure it is indeed fresh, not "from concentrate."

PEAR BROWN BETTY

◆

GRAPE-NUTS AND TURBINADO FROZEN CUSTARD

Autumnal and comforting, this pairing may well be the most all-American of the lot—or certainly the most New England. A brown betty is a dessert born out of that Puritan waste-not-want-not spirit, a way to use up yesterday's bread by turning it into buttery, bread-crumb "pudding" without using up the eggs. Don't worry: we make good use of them in the frozen custard, laced with that crunchy cereal and some crunchy sugar granules, too.

PEAR BROWN BETTY
· YIELD: SIX 1½- TO 2-CUP RAMEKINS ·
— · ◆ · —

There's no need for perfection when prepping the pears. They'll melt into those buttery bread crumbs—which should be fresh, not dried. (You don't want a sandy texture.) Look for fresh bread crumbs in the bakery section of most large supermarkets. Or buy a baguette, set it out on the countertop overnight, then cut it into small slices and whir these in a food processor until coarsely ground.

5 cups fresh bread crumbs

I cup finely ground walnuts or pecans

I cup packed dark brown sugar

½ teaspoon ground cinnamon

½ teaspoon freshly grated nutmeg

¼ teaspoon salt

12 tablespoons (1½ sticks) unsalted butter, melted and cooled

6 large ripe but firm Comice or Anjou pears

OVEN RACK · center | OVEN TEMPERATURE · 350°F
PREP · Set six 1½- to 2-cup oven-safe ramekins on a large rimmed baking sheet.

TO START THE BROWN BETTY
1 · Mix the bread crumbs, ground nuts, brown sugar, cinnamon, nutmeg, and salt in a large bowl until uniform. Pour in the melted butter and stir until moistened.

2 · Peel, stem, halve lengthwise, and core the pears. Slice each half into 10 to 12 very thin slices. Fit 10 to 12 pear slices in each ramekin (that is, about half a pear), then crumble ⅓ cup bread-crumb mixture on top. Repeat: same number of pear slices, same amount of the bread-crumb mixture.

TO FINISH UP
3 · Bake the brown betty until browned and bubbling, 35 to 40 minutes. Cool on a wire rack for at least 15 minutes or to room temperature before serving. Store tightly covered with plastic wrap in the refrigerator for up to 2 days.

PRO TIP · Use a melon baller to scoop the seeds from each pear half.

GRAPE-NUTS AND TURBINADO FROZEN CUSTARD
· YIELD: A LITTLE MORE THAN I QUART ·
— · ◆ · —

Since we use soft, fresh bread crumbs in the brown betty, we want the crunch here—and so we get it in two ways: with 1) a time-honored cereal that stays crisp and 2) coarse-grained turbinado sugar. The latter is made from cane juice, spun in a turbine (hence, the name) until coarse crystals form. It's always available in gourmet supermarkets and sold in most supermarkets under brand names like Sugar in the Raw. Both the cereal and the sugar have molasses notes,

giving the frozen custard an earthiness that's missing in the brown betty.

2 cups heavy cream

I cup whole milk

6 large egg yolks, at room temperature

1/2 cup granulated white sugar

2 teaspoons pure vanilla extract

I cup Grape-Nuts cereal

3 tablespoons coarse ground turbinado sugar

TO MAKE THE CUSTARD

1 · Heat the cream and milk in a large saucepan set over medium heat until whiffs of steam come up off the surface. Meanwhile, use an electric mixer at medium speed to beat the egg yolks and sugar in a large bowl until pale yellow and quite thick, until wide ribbons slide off the turned-off beaters, 3 to 4 minutes. Beat in the vanilla extract.

2 · Beat in about half the hot cream mixture in a slow, steady stream until smooth; then beat this combined mixture into the remaining hot cream mixture in the pan. Set the pan over low heat and cook, stirring almost constantly, until the mixture thickly coats the back of a wooden spoon and the temperature registers 170°F, 4 to 7 minutes.

3 · Strain the mixture through a fine-mesh sieve into a large bowl. Refrigerate for at least 4 hours or up to 1 day, covering the bowl once the custard has cooled.

TO FREEZE IT

4 · Prepare an ice-cream machine. Stir the cold custard and freeze it in the machine according to the manufacturer's instructions, until moundable.

5 · Add the cereal and let the machine's dasher fold it into the custard. Just as the ice cream is ready to serve, add the turbinado sugar and let the machine stir it in only for a few turns. Store in a sealed container in the freezer for a few days.

À LA MODE IT · If you've made the brown betty in advance, cover the ramekins with aluminum foil and warm them in a 300°F oven for 10 to 15 minutes. Set a scoop of the frozen custard in each ramekin.

PRO TIP · Let the machine stir in the turbinado sugar only during the last few churns so it's evenly distributed but not dissolved.

BING CHERRY SONKER

— ✦ —

CHERRY-VANILLA FROZEN CUSTARD

Sour cherries have all the creds. There are all sorts of newspaper articles and blog posts singing their praises. Then there are sturdy Bing cherries, around far longer but with little respect. We always have bowls of them in the house in the summer. We thought it high time they got their due in both halves of this pairing.

BING CHERRY SONKER

· YIELD: ONE 9-INCH SQUARE SONKER ·

— · ✦ · —

North Carolinians know what we're talking about. It's time the rest of you all caught up. A "sonker" is a take on cobbler: a dense, slightly gooey, buttermilk sponge cake baked over a melted butter and fruit concoction that gets absorbed into the cake. While fresh Bing cherries would be best, frozen or even canned will work here. If you're using frozen, pitted cherries, measure them before thawing, then use the fruit and juice in the bowl after thawing. If you're using canned, drain them.

FOR THE FILLING

5 cups stemmed and pitted Bing cherries (about 2 pounds)

2/3 cup granulated white sugar

2 tablespoons cornstarch

1/2 teaspoon ground cinnamon

1/4 teaspoon salt

4 tablespoons (1/2 stick) unsalted butter, melted and cooled, plus additional for greasing

FOR THE TOPPING

1 cup buttermilk

3/4 cup granulated white sugar

1 large egg, at room temperature

1 teaspoon pure vanilla extract

1 cup self-rising flour, preferably Southern white self-rising flour (see page 88)

OVEN RACK · center | OVEN TEMPERATURE · 350°F
PREP · Butter the inside of a 9-inch square baking dish.

TO MAKE THE FILLING

1 · Mix the cherries, sugar, cornstarch, cinnamon, and salt in a large bowl until the cherries are well coated and the cornstarch has dissolved. Pour into the prepared pan, smooth to an even depth, and pour the melted butter evenly on top. Clean and dry the bowl.

TO MAKE THE TOPPING

2 · Add the buttermilk, sugar, egg, and vanilla extract to the clean bowl; whisk until smooth and uniform. Whisk in the self-rising flour just until a loose, wet batter forms. Pour the batter evenly over the top of the cherry mixture.

TO FINISH UP

3 · Bake the sonker for 30 minutes. Reduce the oven temperature to 325°F and continue baking until puffed and brown, until the topping is set when the pan is tapped on the side, about 30 minutes more. Cool on a wire rack for at least 30 minutes or to room temperature. Serve by big spoonfuls in bowls. Store tightly covered with plastic wrap at room temperature for 1 day.

PRO TIP · The topping is a batter; you pour it over the cherries. Some of it's going to go down between them. These cherries will get baked into the topping. Make sure all the fruit is evenly covered.

CHERRY-VANILLA FROZEN CUSTARD

· YIELD: ABOUT 5 CUPS ·

Let's leave the maraschino cherries to cocktails. They've too long been a tasteless addition to this frozen custard. Although we prefer fresh fruit in most dessert recipes, don't be tempted to use fresh cherries. Canned Bing (or sweet) cherries in syrup are already softened, almost (well) "confited." They won't end up as icy chunks. Plus, their flavor will be delicate but straightforward, a sweet spike.

1³/₄ cups heavy cream

³/₄ cup whole milk

³/₄ cup granulated white sugar

4 large egg yolks, at room temperature

1 tablespoon pure vanilla extract

¹/₄ teaspoon salt

1 cup canned pitted sweet cherries in syrup (not water), drained but 2 tablespoons syrup reserved

TO MAKE THE CUSTARD

1 · Warm the cream and milk in a large saucepan over medium heat until little bubbles fizz around the inside perimeter of the pan. Meanwhile, whisk the sugar, egg yolks, vanilla extract, salt, and 2 tablespoons reserved cherry syrup in a large bowl until smooth and uniform.

2 · Whisk about half the cream mixture into the egg mixture in a slow, steady stream until smooth, then whisk this combined mixture into the remaining cream mixture in the pan. Set the pan over low heat and cook, stirring almost constantly, until the mixture thickly coats the back of a wooden spoon and the temperature registers 170°F, 4 to 7 minutes.

3 · Strain the mixture through a fine-mesh sieve into a bowl. Refrigerate for at least 4 hours or up to 1 day, covering once the custard is cold.

TO FREEZE IT

4 · Prepare an ice-cream machine. Stir the cold custard and freeze it in the machine according to the manufacturer's instructions, until the ice cream can mound on a spoon without immediately melting at its edges.

5 · During the last minute or so in the ice-cream machine, add the cherries and let the dasher stir them in. Store in a sealed container in the freezer for up to 2 weeks.

À LA MODE IT · Set a scoop of the frozen custard to the side of a big scoop of the sonker, rather than on top of it.

BIRD'S NEST PUDDING

— ◆ —

WALNUT GELATO

Frozen desserts don't pair well with custards. Who puts ice cream on pudding? Or on coconut cream pie? But this pairing is as close as we can get: the apples are baked in a dense, spongy cake, sort of like a clafouti except thicker. The apples are also positioned cut side up, so they look like little nests. We need a frozen dessert with lots of body to stand up to this unusual fare. We can't think of a much better one than this rich gelato, best in small scoops.

BIRD'S NEST PUDDING
· YIELD: A FULL 9 X 13-INCH PUDDING ·

— · ◆ · —

Cookbooks are a nineteenth-century concoction, part of the growing "home economy" movement. Most were small affairs and included recipes like this one, first appearing in an 1894 cookbook called *Recipes Tried and True*, published by the Ladies' Aid Society of the First Presbyterian Church of Marion, Ohio. The instructions are rudimentary ("bake in a quick oven") but we've adapted it as well as some of its ingredients to our more modern way of cooking so that you can experience one of the frontier's favorite desserts: stuffed apples baked in a light sponge cake.

FOR THE APPLES
4 large sweet apples, such as Honeycrisps
1/2 cup walnut pieces, finely ground
1/3 cup packed light brown sugar

FOR THE SPONGE CAKE
3 large eggs, separated
I cup all-purpose flour
1/2 teaspoon baking powder

1/4 teaspoon salt
I cup whole or low-fat milk
1/4 cup granulated white sugar
I teaspoon pure vanilla extract

OVEN RACK · center | **OVEN TEMPERATURE** · 350°F
PREP · Butter the inside of a 9 x 13-inch baking dish.

TO PREPARE THE APPLES
1 · Peel and halve the apples, then scoop out the cores and seeds with a small spoon, making a long indentation down the center of the apple that doesn't break through either end.

2 · Mix the ground nuts and brown sugar in a small bowl; pack this mixture into the hollows in the apple halves, mounding it up as necessary. (Use up all the brown sugar filling, even if it spills out onto the sides.) Set the apples cut side up in the prepared dish and bake for 30 minutes.

TO MAKE THE SPONGE CAKE
3 · Put the 3 egg whites in a bowl and beat them with an electric mixer at low speed until foamy, then at medium-high speed until they form soft, droopy points and peaks when the turned-off beaters are dipped into them. Set aside. Whisk the flour, baking powder, and salt in a medium bowl; set aside as well.

4 · Whisk the milk, white sugar, vanilla extract, and 3 egg yolks in a second large bowl until smooth and uniform. Add the flour mixture and whisk just until thoroughly moistened, no dry pockets anywhere. Use a rubber spatula to fold in the beaten egg whites, working in steady, gentle arcs to incorporate as much air as possible but until there are no visible streaks of egg white.

TO FINISH UP

5 · Pour this mixture over the hot apples and into the pan, taking care not to dislodge any of the stuffing. Continue baking until puffed and browned, about 30 minutes more. Cool on a wire rack for at least 25 minutes or to room temperature. To serve, scoop up apple halves and some of their surrounding sponge cake into individual bowls. Store tightly covered in plastic wrap in the refrigerator for up to 3 days.

PRO TIP · Folding in egg whites can be a challenge: you want uniformity with little deflation. Many bakers recommend folding in half of the beaten mixture more thoroughly, then the remainder more slowly. If you work methodically in large arcs with small amounts (as in this recipe), you can often get the whole batch into the bowl at once without losing too much air.

WALNUT GELATO
· YIELD: ABOUT 1 QUART ·

Rather than folding walnuts into vanilla gelato, we steep the milk with the nuts. So the more you toast the walnuts, the deeper this gelato's flavor. However, there is a limit to this process. There should be no blackened bits on the nuts or the custard may pick up a bitter edge, not a fine match to the sponge cake and apples.

2 cups walnut pieces (about 10 ounces)

2¾ cups whole milk

¼ cup heavy cream

4 large egg yolks, at room temperature

¾ cup packed light brown sugar

2 teaspoons pure vanilla extract

¼ teaspoon salt

TO MAKE THE CUSTARD

1 · Toast the nuts in a dry skillet over medium-low heat, stirring often, until lightly browned and aromatic, 4 to 6 minutes. Pour them into a large saucepan and add the milk. Set the pan over medium heat and bring to a bare simmer, stirring often. Cover and set aside off the heat for 30 minutes.

2 · Pour and scrape the contents of the pan into a blender. Cover but remove the center knob from the canister. Cover the lid with a clean kitchen towel, then blend until smooth, scraping down the inside of the canister at least once.

3 · Clean and dry the large saucepan. Pour the puree through a fine-mesh sieve into the pan. Gently press against the nut solids in the sieve to release as much liquid as you can. Stir in the cream, set the pan over medium-low heat, and warm until puffs of steam rise off its surface.

4 · Meanwhile, whisk the egg yolks, brown sugar, vanilla extract, and salt in a large bowl until grainy and pasty but well blended.

5 · Whisk about half the hot milk mixture into the egg yolk mixture in a slow, steady stream until smooth, then whisk this combined mixture into the remaining cream mixture in the pan. Set the pan over low heat and cook, stirring constantly, until the custard thickly coats the back of a wooden spoon and the temperature registers 170°F, 5 to 8 minutes.

6 · Strain through a fine-mesh sieve into a bowl, then refrigerate for at least 4 hours or up to 1 day, covering once the custard is cold.

TO FREEZE IT

7 · Prepare an ice-cream machine. Stir the cold custard, then pour it in the machine and freeze according to the manufacturer's instructions, until the gelato is smooth, somewhat firm, and definitely moundable. Store in a sealed container in the freezer for up to 1 month.

À LA MODE IT · If possible, balance a small scoop of gelato right on top of an apple cut side up in the serving bowl.

PRO TIP · For the creamiest gelato, skip the fine-mesh sieve in step 3. Line a colander with cheesecloth, then pour the walnut mixture through it. Gather up the walnuts in the cheesecloth; gently squeeze it over the pan to remove as much of the liquid as possible.

APPLE-ALMOND STRUDEL

—◆—

RUM-NUTMEG FROZEN CUSTARD

—————————————————————————————

Now we turn to more Continental fare. This one's not a traditional strudel but rather a free-form log stuffed with almonds and apples. You'll make two, quite a bit, perhaps best for crowds. Or you can freeze one of the baked logs. Together, this strudel with this frozen custard is about like pouring eggnog on apple pie and sprinkling it with toasted almonds. Get a bib.

APPLE-ALMOND STRUDEL

· YIELD: TWO 8- TO 9-INCH STRUDELS ·

—·◆·—

Making strudel can be a pain in the neck, but we simplified the matter, merely using sheets of phyllo stacked on each other. For a more home-spun look, we roll the stack but leave the ends somewhat open. Press and crumple them closed but don't seal them. The filling will leak out, a rustic look on the baking sheet. It will also shard like mad. You're probably best off cutting and serving these yourself, rather than letting your friends or family dig in on a platter.

I cup sliced almonds

2 tablespoons packed light brown sugar

¼ teaspoon salt

8 cups thinly sliced, peeled, and cored semitart apples, such as Northern Spy (about 6 large apples)

¾ cup granulated white sugar

6 tablespoons all-purpose flour

I½ teaspoons ground cinnamon

20 sheets frozen 9 x 13-inch phyllo dough, thawed according to the package directions

I½ cups almond oil

OVEN RACK · center | OVEN TEMPERATURE · 350°F
PREP · Line a large rimmed baking sheet with parchment paper.

TO ASSEMBLE THE STRUDELS

1 · Grind the almonds, brown sugar, and salt in a food processor until the mixture resembles coarse, somewhat wet sand. Set aside. Mix the apples, white sugar, flour, and cinnamon in a large bowl. Set aside as well.

2 · Unwrap and unfold the stack of phyllo sheets, then set them on your clean, dry countertop. Peel off one sheet and lay it on another part of the countertop, then lay a clean, dry kitchen towel on top of the rest of the sheets. Pour the almond oil into a small bowl. Brush the phyllo sheet with a little almond oil and sprinkle evenly with about ½ tablespoon of the ground almond mixture. Lay another sheet of phyllo on top and repeat this process—brushing and sprinkling—with that sheet plus 8 more (or 10 sheets total).

3 · Spoon half the apple mixture onto the sheet at one short side, about 1 inch from the end. Beginning with this short side, roll the phyllo packet up into a rustic log and transfer it seam side down to one side of the prepared baking sheet. Crumple the openings so they're closed but not sealed. Brush the entire roll with a little almond oil, then sprinkle the top with about 2 teaspoons of the almond mixture.

4 · Repeat this whole process (steps 2 and 3) to create a second phyllo roll-up.

TO FINISH UP

5 · Bake the strudels until brown and crisp, until the apple juices are running out, about 25 minutes. Transfer the baking sheet to a wire rack and

cool to room temperature, about 1½ hours. If desired, use a large, thin, flat spatula to transfer the strudels to a serving platter. Slice the strudels into 2-inch pieces to serve. Once cooled, store tightly sealed in plastic wrap at room temperature for 2 days or in the freezer for 2 months. If frozen, reheat without thawing on a baking sheet in a 350°F oven for about 15 minutes.

PRO TIP · Be prepared for phyllo loss. The sheets will crack and tear. You need 20 for the recipe, but you probably actually need 10 more for insurance. Standard phyllo dough is a 9 x 13-inch rectangle. If you only find 8 x 13-inch phyllo, simply make smaller logs. But watch out for various nonstandard sizes, often sold at high-end supermarkets.

RUM-NUTMEG FROZEN CUSTARD

· YIELD: ABOUT 1 QUART ·

This autumnal spice duo is made to go with apples. We use a little cornstarch in the custard because of the added rum. In like manner, there are whole eggs here, not just egg yolks. Again, we needed the extra protein because of the increased liquid. The whites will also give the frozen custard a somewhat chewy texture, a nice contrast to the crisp strudel. For a mich milder flavor, use aged rum such as Plantation or Cruzan in place of the dark rum.

1½ cups heavy cream

1 cup whole milk

½ cup dark rum, such as Myers's

¾ cup granulated white sugar

2 large eggs, plus 3 large egg yolks, at room temperature

1½ tablespoons cornstarch

¼ teaspoon freshly grated nutmeg

⅛ teaspoon salt

TO MAKE THE CUSTARD

1 · Warm the cream, milk, and rum in a large saucepan set over medium heat until puffs of steam rise off its surface. Meanwhile, use an electric mixer at medium speed to beat the sugar, eggs, egg yolks, cornstarch, nutmeg, and salt in a large bowl until pale yellow and quite thick, about 4 minutes.

2 · Beat about half the hot milk mixture into the egg yolk mixture until smooth, then beat this combined mixture into the remaining milk mixture in the pan. Set the pan over low heat and cook, stirring constantly, until the custard thickly coats the back of a wooden spoon and the temperature registers 170°F, 4 to 7 minutes.

3 · Pour the mixture through a fine-mesh sieve into a bowl. Refrigerate for at least 4 hours or up to 1 day, covering once the custard is cold.

TO FREEZE IT

4 · Prepare an ice-cream machine. Stir the custard and freeze it in the machine according to the manufacturer's instructions, until you can spoon up a mound with edges that do not immediately melt. Store in a sealed container in the freezer for up to 1 month.

À LA MODE IT · Set a slice cut side up on the plate and top directly with a scoop of frozen custard.

PRO TIP · You can barely overbeat the eggs in step 1. Yes, if you take a phone call and come back 10 minutes later, the mixture will have broken, little threads of egg in a watery mess. Barring that, just keep beating until quite thick. Make sure the cornstarch has thoroughly dissolved.

MIXED BERRY SUMMER PUDDING

— ✦ —

WHITE CHOCOLATE FROZEN CUSTARD

If you've ever wanted to put ice cream on bread and jam—and who hasn't?—you've come to the right place. A summer pudding is a British dessert, a no-bake cake (not really a "pudding" except in the Downton Abbey sense of the word) made with a fast-cooked berry mixture and sliced sandwich bread. We pair it with white chocolate, mostly because we can't imagine a better flavor match to the raspberries and the black currant flavor of the crème de cassis.

MIXED BERRY SUMMER PUDDING

· YIELD: ONE 8-INCH ROUND PUDDING ·

— ✦ —

Choose several types of berries: start with blueberries, then add raspberries or blackberries—or both—and perhaps one other. Once you're assembling the dessert, don't get too fussy. You want to make layers of bread and jam, but the overall cake should come out spotted and mottled, red with white bits throughout. Use a country-style white bread, the sort of sliced bread you'd use to make school lunches—not whipped bread but good ol' American sandwich slices.

8 cups mixed, stemmed and/or trimmed berries, such as blueberries, raspberries, blackberries, or gooseberries (if you mention salmonberries, you're just showing off)

1½ cups granulated white sugar

2 tablespoons crème de cassis

One 1½-pound loaf sliced white bread, crusts trimmed

TO ASSEMBLE THE SUMMER PUDDING

1 · Line the inside of a 2-quart round high-sided soufflé or baking dish with plastic wrap.

2 · Mix the berries, sugar, and crème de cassis in a large saucepan set over medium heat. Cook, stirring occasionally, until bubbling, almost like warmed, melted jam, about 5 minutes. Remove from the heat and cool for 5 minutes.

3 · Dip a couple of bread slices in the berry mixture and set them colored side down in the prepared dish, covering the bottom with the slices by cutting and squishing them together to make an even fit. Spoon a thick layer of the berries over the bread, then repeat this bread-then-berry process (without dipping any more slices), making even, compact layers (and always cutting and squishing the bread to fit). End with a layer of bread.

4 · Cover the top of the pudding with plastic wrap, sealing it against the bread. Set a small plate on top, then set a large can (like a 28-ounce can of tomatoes) on top of the plate. Set the bowl on a plate and refrigerate for at least 24 or up to 72 hours.

TO FINISH UP

5 · Remove the can, peel off the top layer of plastic wrap, and invert the baking dish over a serving platter. Use the plastic wrap inside the dish to help pull the pudding free from the dish. Peel off the plastic wrap. Slice the pudding into wedges like an angel food cake. To store, put the remainder of the summer pudding back in its baking dish, cover with plastic wrap, and keep in the refrigerator for up to 3 days.

PRO TIP · If you're unsure about the set, cook the berries a little longer, until the liquid in the pan is thick enough to coat the back of a spoon and you can make a line in it with your finger that doesn't immediately flow back together.

WHITE CHOCOLATE FROZEN CUSTARD

—·◈·—

White chocolate is cocoa butter with stabilizers and usually vanilla but without dark cocoa solids. Or that's what it's supposed to be. Some less expensive versions are little more than flavored vegetable shortening. If possible, look for non-deodorized white chocolate, such as that made by Icoa or Askinosie. These will have more of the flavor of the cocoa solids left in the creamy white cocoa butter.

8 ounces white chocolate

1¼ cups heavy cream

1 cup whole milk

6 large egg yolks, at room temperature

⅔ cup granulated white sugar

TO MAKE THE CUSTARD

1 · Finely chop the white chocolate and put it in a large bowl. Set aside.

2 · Heat the cream and milk in a large saucepan over medium heat until small bubbles fizz around the interior perimeter of the pan. Meanwhile, beat the egg yolks and sugar in a second large bowl with an electric mixer at medium speed until pale yellow and quite thick, until ribbons slide off the turned-off beaters, about 4 minutes.

3 · Beat about half the cream mixture into the egg yolk mixture in a slow, steady stream until smooth, then beat this combined mixture into the remaining cream mixture in the pan. Set the pan over low heat and cook, stirring constantly, until the custard thickly coats the back of a wooden spoon and the temperature registers 170°F, 4 to 7 minutes.

4 · Strain the mixture through a fine-mesh sieve into the bowl with the white chocolate. Stir until the chocolate has melted. Refrigerate for at least 4 hours or up to 2 days, covering the custard once it's cold.

TO FREEZE IT

5 · Prepare an ice-cream machine. Stir the cold custard and freeze it in the machine according to the manufacturer's instructions, until you can spoon up a mound without edges that instantly start to melt. Store in a sealed container in the freezer for up to 2 months.

À LA MODE IT · Although we're fans of warm desserts and cold ice creams, there's really no way to make that happen with this pairing. Use the frozen custard directly from the machine or let it stand at room temperature for 10 minutes to soften up.

COFFEE-POACHED PEARS

— ⬥ —

HAZELNUT GELATO

One final fruit dessert before we hit the cookies and cakes. We poach these pears in coffee to give them a downtown flavor, a wonderful mix among their natural aromatics and the bitter notes in the coffee, all bound together best with this nutty-laced gelato, earthy and sweet. It's hard to think of a more sophisticated pairing.

COFFEE-POACHED PEARS
· YIELD: 6 POACHED PEARS WITH SAUCE ·
— ⬥ —

The best pears will be firm but sweet-smelling. If they're too soft, they'll begin to dissolve when poached. Don't use espresso but rather a drip or pour-over coffee from a strong dark roast, using perhaps twice as many coffee grounds as you might under normal, morning circumstances.

3 cups very strong coffee

I cup granulated white sugar

I teaspoon pure vanilla extract

6 medium Bosc pears, peeled but with the
    stems still intact

TO POACH THE PEARS

1 · Stir the coffee, sugar, and vanilla extract in a 4- to 5-quart saucepan set over medium heat until the sugar dissolves. Bring to a simmer, stirring once in a while.

2 · Add the pears, making a snug fit. Add more water to the pan until the pears are submerged. Bring to a simmer over medium-high heat. Cover, reduce the heat to low, and simmer slowly until the pears are tender, about 40 minutes.

TO FINISH UP

3 · Use a slotted spoon to transfer the pears to a bowl and set in the refrigerator. Increase the heat to medium-high and bring the sauce in the pan to a full boil. Cook, stirring often, until the liquid has been reduced to half its original volume (from when you removed the pears), 10 to 15 minutes. Set aside off the heat to cool to room temperature, about 1 hour.

4 · Pour the reduced liquid over the pears and refrigerate for at least 6 hours, covering the bowl once the mixture is cold. Store in their liquid in a tightly covered bowl in the refrigerator for up to 4 days.

PRO TIP · If you slice about ¼ inch off the bottom of each pear, you can stand them up on the plates when you serve them.

HAZELNUT GELATO
· YIELD: ABOUT I QUART ·
— ⬥ —

There's no doubt this is a rich gelato: the hazelnuts add a lot of their natural oils, turning it silky and smooth. Toast the nuts until they're quite fragrant. They'll need all the flavor they can muster to stand up to six egg yolks—and the coffee syrup with the pears.

One IO-ounce package chopped hazelnuts
    (about 2 cups)

3 cups whole milk

½ cup heavy cream

6 large egg yolks, at room temperature

⅔ cup granulated white sugar

½ teaspoon pure vanilla extract

¼ teaspoon salt

TO PREPARE THE NUTS

1 · Heat the oven to 350°F with an oven rack positioned at the center. Spread the hazelnuts out on a large, rimmed baking sheet. Toast in the oven, stirring occasionally, until lightly browned, 5 to 7 minutes. Cool on the baking sheet for 10 minutes.

TO MAKE THE CUSTARD

2 · Put 1½ cups of the hazelnuts and the milk in a large saucepan set over medium heat; warm until just beginning to simmer. Cover and set aside off the heat for 30 minutes.

3 · Pour the contents of the pan into a blender, cover, remove the center knob from the lid, and blend until fairly smooth, scraping down the inside of the canister at least once.

4 · Strain the contents of the canister through a fine-mesh sieve or a cheesecloth-lined colander into a clean, large saucepan. Gently press down on the nutty residue in the sieve or cheesecloth to extract every drop of liquid. Stir in the cream and set over medium-low heat. Warm until puffs of steam come up off the surface.

5 · Meanwhile, use an electric mixer at medium speed to beat the egg yolks and sugar in a large bowl until thick and pale yellow, until wide ribbons slide off the turned-off beaters, about 4 minutes. Beat in the vanilla extract and salt.

6 · Beat about half the hot milk mixture into the egg yolk mixture until smooth. Beat this combined mixture into the remaining milk mixture in the pan. Set the pan over low heat and cook, stirring constantly, until the custard thickly coats the back of a wooden spoon and the temperature registers 170°F, 4 to 7 minutes.

7 · Strain the mixture through a fine-mesh sieve into a clean bowl. Refrigerate for at least 4 hours or up to 2 days, covering once the custard is cold.

TO FREEZE IT

8 · Chop the remaining toasted hazelnuts (about ½ cup before chopping). Set aside.

9 · Prepare an ice-cream machine. Stir the cold custard and freeze it in the machine according to the manufacturer's instructions, until the gelato is smooth and glossy, until it can mound on a spoon. Add the chopped hazelnuts and let the machine's dasher stir them into the gelato during the final few turns. Store in a sealed container in the freezer for up to 1 month.

À LA MODE IT · Stand a pear up on a small plate; set a large scoop of gelato to the side. Drizzle the syrup in the bowl over the pears and gelato.

PRO TIP · Don't stint on pressing against the nut mixture in the strainer. Extract every drop of liquid you can.

BAKE SHOP TREATS:

COOKIES, BARS, BEAR CLAWS, & MORE

SHOULDN'T EVERY BAKERY SERVE ICE CREAM? Then you could dip fresh biscotti in frozen custard. Or make a sorbet sandwich with two big sugar cookies. Or take baklava over the top with gelato.

What are you waiting for? They're all here—and more. You may not know it, but you haven't lived until you've put mocha ice cream on babka. Or goat cheese ice cream in a flaky ganache turnover. Or a fudgy brownie under marshmallowy semifreddo.

We're turning away from pies, tarts, pandowdies, and their kin to what many consider the heart of American desserts: baked goods. Thus, in terms of what we're looking for, we're turning from set and toward crumb—that is, the tender bits of cookies and cakes that shear off a slice or break apart with a bite, not flakes or drips, but discrete morsels, the ones that fall loose from a properly leavened and baked treat.

Crumb is the reason ice cream loves cake: those tiny morsels get bound up in the melt, softening to become irresistible. Sure, many pies take well to ice cream but some don't. Except for only the fussiest creations, like French macarons, we can't think of a cookie, biscotti, bar, brownie, or scone that doesn't welcome a scoop.

· BASIC BAKING TIPS ·

We're about to get a little more serious. Yes, we're mostly talking about cookies and the like in this section; but there are a couple of yeast-raised treats as well as one pretty intense pastry that mimics so-called "lamination," the technique used to get a zillion layers in croissant dough. Given all that, it's appropriate to offer a few more hints to help you turn your kitchen into a bakery.

1 · NOTE THE FLOUR TYPES AND MAKE NO SUBSTITUTIONS.
You'll see not only all-purpose flour in this chapter but also graham flour, cake flour, and even Southern biscuit flour. We'll get to the rationale and explanation for each in its turn. For now, just keep in mind that you must stick with what's written. Substituting one flour for another can lead to tough, gummy, or overly dense baked goods. We once spent an evening teaching some-one how to make a classic pie pastry. The next day, she tried it on her own, substituting corn-starch for flour. ("They're both white!") The results weren't good. And she blamed us.

2 · USE HIGH-QUALITY CHOCOLATE.
If we're turning away from fruit desserts, we're also turning toward chocolate. So keep this in mind: not all the flour and sugar in the world can cover the taste of inferior chocolate. Choose a bar you would eat on its own. If you use those squares designed for baking, read the label to make sure you've got real chocolate in hand, not something artificial. (Remember, too, that almost all real chocolate includes a stabilizer like lecithin.)

3 · TREAT ALL TIMINGS AS TRAFFIC LIGHTS IN MANHATTAN: MERE SUGGESTIONS.
As you know, there are manifold variables when it comes to determining when a baked good is ready to come out of the oven: your flour could have more residual moisture than ours, it could have a slightly higher protein content than ours, your sugar could have a higher residual liquid content than ours, your baking soda may be newer (or older) than ours, your pans may conduct heat more quickly (or more slowly) than ours, and on and on and on. Sheesh! To stymie the confusion, first go by the visual cues in a recipe, then by the suggested timing.

Our best advice is to set the oven timer for 5 to 10 minutes shy of where we suggest, then start checking from that point on. Indeed, we've always wanted to write a recipe that goes like this: "Set the timer and bake for 20 minutes, then start checking for when the cookies are lightly browned and firm to the touch, another 5 to 10 minutes." But it seems onerous and outside the pale of clear writing. Still, note our sentiment and follow its spirit.

Finally, use your intuition about the sort of baked good you'd like to create. Perhaps you prefer more "well done" cookies than we do. Or perhaps you like gooier, fudgier, less-done brownies. You'll need to adjust the timings based on your own visual cues. Keep a pencil in the kitchen and mark up this book to your liking.

· A WORD (OR SEVERAL) ABOUT YEAST ·

We used active, dry yeast throughout. The recipes were not calibrated to work with cake yeast, quick-rise yeast, or so-called instant yeast. If you know what you're doing, you can indeed make substitutions. If not, they can be tricky and time-consuming.

Check the expiration date on the yeast. Even if the day still lies a month or two in the offing, the yeast could have been compromised by heat, cold, and/or humidity. Don't take a chance. Replace it—but not necessarily with a big jar of yeast. Unless you bake with yeast on a regular basis, buy the small packets. At the store, they're often kept under refrigeration in the dairy case. A packet will yield about 2¼ teaspoons.

Make sure the bowls and utensils are just about room temperature to the touch, not cold (even from air conditioning). If possible, rinse a bowl with warm (not hot) water, then dry it out before using it. If you warm the milk or water in the microwave, stir it before you measure its temperature. It will have hot and cold pockets that must be blended for an accurate reading.

When the dough is rising, check it often. Not all yeast is of the same strength. The dough may rise in 40 minutes, 50 minutes, or an hour. If it starts to rise, even toward the end of our suggested timing, be patient and give it more time. The yeast may have been sluggish or your temperatures off. If the dough hasn't risen a whit in an hour, you're probably out of luck. You'll need to start over.

Sure, baking is chemistry, a more exacting science. Maybe you're wondering where your creativity comes in. Here: by now you've seen a lot of pairings in this book. Maybe ours aren't to your liking. Maybe you'd rather have chai frozen custard with soft vanilla bean cookies. Or popcorn ice cream with cream scones. Or marzipan gelato with bear claws. We hope you'll start mixing and matching to your heart's (and stomach's) content. That's how to run a bake shop!

· IN PRAISE OF PATIENCE ·

Cooking is guts, flame, and devil-may-care testosterone (at least in our house). But baking is an art: slow and mindful. You have to get your (cleaned!) hands right into it. You have to feel the dough. You have to hold the eggs. And you have to forget your phone. Ever tried to wipe butter off the screen? Impossible.

We once complained on Facebook that U. S. baking recipes are still written in volume amounts, not weight. "Why not grams?" we hollered. Jeanne Sauvage, a gluten-free baking maven from the other coast, replied that she finds the sounds and smells of dipping flours, sugars, and other ingredients incredibly comforting. "I'd miss that," she replied.

We've come to know her point. As we tested and developed these recipes, we often found ourselves in a quiet place, one we don't often discover when we're knocking out braises and sautés. So slow down and take baking as it comes. A warm kitchen, a wonderful dessert ahead, pure excess and pleasure: there can't be any rush.

BIG SOFT VANILLA BEAN COOKIES

—⬦—

CHOCOLATE—PEANUT BUTTER SORBET

Yes, you could enjoy these cookies on their own with a cup of tea or a glass of red wine. And you could make this creamy, decadent sorbet on its own for a summer gathering or even a winter dinner party. But at least once, try these two as we designed them: as sandwich cookies, almost like tender vanilla cake surrounding a frozen candy bar.

BIG SOFT VANILLA BEAN COOKIES

· YIELD: 16 COOKIES ·

—·⬦·—

These cakey cookies are pretty simple, certainly not heroic. We didn't even use butter because we wanted a cleaner palette. (The big flavors are found in the sorbet.) That said, for the most tender cookies, beat as much air as possible into the shortening and sugar, making sure the mixture is fluffy and light before you add the eggs. As they bake, the cookies will spread quite a bit; you'll only be able to put a few on each baking sheet. And don't line the baking sheets with silicone baking mats. Those will insulate the dough and make the cookies spread even more, causing them to crisp at the edges and remain too soft at their centers.

2 cups all-purpose flour

1/2 teaspoon baking powder

1/2 teaspoon baking soda

1/4 teaspoon salt

I vanilla bean

I cup granulated white sugar

3/4 cup solid vegetable shortening

I large egg, plus I large egg white, at room temperature

1/4 cup whole or low-fat milk

OVEN RACKS · top and bottom | OVEN TEMPERATURE · 350°F
PREP · Line two large, rimmed baking sheets with parchment paper.

TO MAKE THE COOKIE-DOUGH BATTER

1 · Mix the flour, baking powder, baking soda, and salt in a large bowl until uniform. Set aside.

2 · Split the vanilla bean in half lengthwise. Use the edge of a paring knife to scrape the tiny seeds into a second large bowl or the bowl of a stand mixer; reserve the pod halves (see Pro Tip on page 26). Using a hand electric mixer or a stand mixer fitted with the paddle attachment at medium speed, beat the vanilla seeds, sugar, and shortening until creamy and almost fluffy, about 4 minutes.

3 · Beat in the egg until smooth, scrape down the inside of the bowl, and beat in the egg white. Beat in the milk until creamy, then dump in the flour mixture and beat at low speed just until you have a fairly wet cookie-dough batter. Scrape down and remove the beaters or paddle.

TO FINISH UP

4 · Scoop up about 3 tablespoons of the dough and set it down as a mound on a prepared baking sheet. With damp, clean fingers, press it into a 1/2-inch-thick disk. Make a few more on the sheet, spacing them 6 inches apart. Then make more on the second baking sheet; you'll probably get 4 to 6 cookies per sheet. Cover the bowl and the remaining batter with a clean kitchen towel.

5 · Set one baking sheet on each oven rack; bake the cookies for 8 minutes. Reverse the sheets top to bottom and rotate each back to front. Continue baking until the cookies are pale beige, a little brown at the edges, and definitely set with no jiggle at their centers, about 10 minutes.

6 · Transfer the baking sheets to wire racks and cool the cookies on the sheets for 10 minutes. Transfer the cookies directly to the wire racks and cool completely, about 1½ hours. Cool the baking sheets for 15 minutes before lining again and making more cookies. Store in a sealed container between sheets of wax paper at room temperature for up to 3 days.

PRO TIP · If you have a convection oven, you can make three or four sheets at once on three or four racks, making sure the bottom rack is at least 5 inches from the heat source. Reduce the oven temperature to 325°F and rotate the baking sheets in a random way halfway through baking, turning them all back to front. Reduce the overall baking time to around 15 minutes.

CHOCOLATE–PEANUT BUTTER SORBET

· YIELD: ABOUT 1 QUART ·

— · ◆ · —

Because sorbet has a somewhat firmer texture than ice cream, it offers a better bite in the cookie sandwiches. But is this a sorbet? Well, we left out any dairy—so in the modern sense of sorbet, yes, it is. We wanted the peanut butter alone to carry the creaminess without interference. We also blended the ingredients into a homogenous whole, rather than having a ribbon of peanut butter in the sorbet. We wanted the taste of chocolate and peanut butter in every bite.

2¼ cups water

¾ cup granulated white sugar

9 tablespoons (½ cup plus 1 tablespoon) unsweetened natural-style cocoa powder

4½ ounces dark chocolate, between 70% and 80% cocoa solids, chopped

⅓ cup smooth, natural-style peanut butter

TO START THE SORBET

1 · Whisk the water, sugar, and cocoa powder in a large saucepan over medium heat until smooth; then cook, whisking quite often, until bubbling and somewhat thickened, about 4 minutes. Remove the pan from the heat, add the chocolate, and whisk until smooth.

2 · Pour and scrape the contents of the pan into a blender; add the peanut butter. Cover but remove the center knob from the lid. Cover the lid with a clean kitchen towel and blend until smooth, scraping down the inside of the canister at least once. Set the knob back in the blender's lid, then refrigerate for at least 4 hours or up to 2 days.

TO FREEZE IT

3 · Prepare an ice-cream machine. Blend the contents of the canister one more time, then freeze the mixture in the machine according to the manufacturer's instructions, until the sorbet is creamy and smooth, until it can hold its shape on a spoon. To store, wrap the sorbet sandwiches individually in plastic wrap and freeze for up to 1 month.

À LA MODE IT · If the sorbet has been in the freezer, first soften it at room temperature for a few minutes. Spoon about ¼ cup onto the flat side of half the cookies. Top with a second cookie flat side down. Dust with confectioners' sugar, if desired.

PRO TIP · For a more intense flavor, look for dark-roasted, natural-style creamy peanut butter at high-end grocery stores or even some health-food stores.

BROWNED BUTTER GRAHAM CRACKERS

BROWNED BUTTER-BUTTER PECAN ICE CREAM

Here's the right way to end a dinner party. It'll bring out the kid in everyone. Set a platter of homemade graham crackers in the middle of the table, pass out bowls of ice cream, and watch your guests get giddy! The browned butter in the pairing sets both apart from the standards: a nutty, slightly bitter finish in the sugary treats.

BROWNED BUTTER GRAHAM CRACKERS

· YIELD: 16 GRAHAM CRACKERS ·

Once you make crunchy, sweet graham crackers, you may never go back to store-bought! Graham flour is a whole-wheat flour, popularized by nineteenth-century dietary reformers. The flour is made by grinding the wheat's endosperm about as one would for all-purpose flour; the gram and the germ are then ground more coarsely and added back to the white flour to create the familiar texture that gives baked goods a crackly crunch.

6 tablespoons (³/₄ stick) unsalted butter

1¹/₂ cups graham flour

¹/₂ cup all-purpose flour

¹/₂ cup packed dark brown sugar

¹/₂ teaspoon baking soda

¹/₂ teaspoon salt

¹/₄ teaspoon baking powder

¹/₄ teaspoon ground cinnamon

At least ¹/₄ cup whole or low-fat milk, plus more as needed

2 tablespoons honey

1 teaspoon pure vanilla extract

OVEN RACK · center | OVEN TEMPERATURE · 350°F

TO MAKE THE BATTER

1 · Melt the butter in a small saucepan set over low heat, then stir and continue cooking until light amber brown, 2 to 3 minutes. Remove from the heat (the butter will continue to brown in the pan) and cool to room temperature, about 45 minutes.

2 · Mix the graham flour, all-purpose flour, brown sugar, baking soda, salt, baking powder, and cinnamon in a large bowl until uniform.

3 · Whisk ¹/₄ cup milk, honey, and vanilla extract in a second, smaller bowl until smooth. Stir both this milk mixture and the browned butter (including its separated solids) into the flour mixture to form a soft, moist dough, adding more milk in 1-tablespoon increments until it can easily form a not-sticky dough.

4 · Trim a sheet of parchment paper to match an 11 x 17-inch rimmed baking sheet; set the parchment paper on your work surface. Dust the parchment paper with flour, then set the dough on it. Use a lightly floured rolling pin to roll the dough into a 10 x 15-inch rectangle. Transfer the dough and parchment paper together to the baking sheet.

5 · Using a small, sharp knife, cut the dough in half lengthwise without pressing all the way through to the parchment paper—in other words, cut through the dough but certainly not the paper. Slice into 16 smaller rectangles by making 7 equidistant cuts widthwise in the same manner. Prick each smaller rectangle several times with the tines of a flatware fork: in 3 parallel, diagonal lines (for a classic look) or

perhaps in your initials, a holiday pattern, or other sorts of parallel lines.

TO FINISH UP

6 · Bake until set, firm, and browned, about 25 minutes. Transfer the baking sheet to a wire rack and cool to room temperature, about 1 hour. Break the large cookie into its smaller graham crackers. Store in a sealed container at room temperature for up to 3 days or in the freezer for up to 2 months.

PRO TIP · Make sure the rolled-out rectangle of dough is an even thickness. Roll the dough in small, smooth pushes from its center, rather than long strokes across its length. Use your hands to squish it in from the sides, evening it up as you roll it. And work with a ruler for exact measurements. In the end, it's better to overwork the dough a bit than have thinner, burned edges on the cookies—or underdone, chewy centers.

BROWNED BUTTER-BUTTER PECAN ICE CREAM
· YIELD: ABOUT 1 QUART ·

We put the butter back in butter pecan ice cream! Or to be more specific, browned butter—thereby cutting down on the ice cream's sweetness so the pecans show through. What we want are those browned and burned solids in the butter, often lying on the bottom of the saucepan. The only way to get enough is to make too much browned butter. But you'll then have a generous amount of browned, clarified butter for frying eggs, making outrageous cinnamon toast, or preparing curries.

16 tablespoons (2 sticks) unsalted butter

3/4 cup pecan pieces

2 cups whole milk

3/4 cup heavy cream

1/2 cup packed light brown sugar

1/4 cup light corn syrup

1 1/2 tablespoons cornstarch

TO MAKE THE BROWNED BUTTER

1 · Melt the butter in a large saucepan over medium-low heat until it turns dark brown, 3 to 5 minutes. Gently pour the clear, brown liquid off the top into a small glass storage container, leaving the browned milk solids and blackened bits on the bottom of the saucepan. Reserve the browned, clarified butter, covered, in the fridge for another purpose. Set the pan with the solids and blackened bits aside to cool for 10 minutes.

TO START THE ICE CREAM

2 · Toast the pecans in a large, dry skillet set over medium-low heat, stirring occasionally, until lightly browned and fragrant, about 7 minutes. Pour onto a cutting board and chop into small bits. Set aside.

3 · Add the milk, cream, brown sugar, corn syrup, and cornstarch to the pan with the browned butter bits; set over medium-low heat and stir until the brown sugar and cornstarch have dissolved, scraping up those browned and blackened bits on the bottom of the pan. Continue cooking, whisking constantly, until thickened and bubbling, about 5 minutes. Pour into a large bowl and refrigerate for at least 4 hours or up to 1 day, covering after the mixture is cold.

TO FREEZE IT

4 · Prepare an ice-cream machine. Stir the browned butter mixture, then freeze in the machine according to the manufacturer's instructions, until it can mound on a spoon. Add the pecans and let the machine's dasher churn them in for the last few rotations. Store in a sealed container in the freezer for up to 1 month.

À LA MODE IT · Serve scoops of the ice cream with graham crackers stuck in them. Or make graham cracker ice cream sandwiches.

PRO TIP · Scraping up the blackened bits of butter in step 3 is not as easy as it sounds. You'll need to put some elbow grease into it, working over the heat to get them soft and then dissolved.

CHOCOLATE-PECAN OLIVE OIL BISCOTTI
— ◈ —
CHOCOLATE OLIVE OIL ICE CREAM

Olive oil adds a floral undertone and even a bright savoriness to otherwise sweet fare. As such, it's an especially good pairing with chocolate: earthy and bright flavors in each bite! Or it should be a good pairing, depending on the olive oil's quality. Look for a bottling that is first cold expeller pressed, a more expensive bottle you might also use for drizzling on salad greens or finishing a salmon fillet off the grill.

CHOCOLATE-PECAN OLIVE OIL BISCOTTI
· YIELD: ABOUT 40 COOKIES ·
— · ◈ · —

These twice-baked cookies may have once been an Italian specialty; now they're made all over the world—often with poor results, soft and cakey. No way! They should be hard and require dunking (in partially melted ice cream, natch). Cutting the baked dough logs can be tricky: there's a small window of opportunity. If the log is too hot, its insides will tear when cut; if it's too cold, the crust will crumble. The log should be warm to the touch, not hot but also not room temperature. It's better to start cutting too early than too late. If you find the cookies are too soft and are breaking apart, you can always hold back a few minutes before carrying on.

2 cups all-purpose flour, plus additional for dusting

³/₄ cup unsweetened cocoa powder, preferably natural-style cocoa powder

1 teaspoon baking soda

¹/₄ teaspoon salt

3 large eggs, at room temperature

³/₄ cup granulated white sugar

2 tablespoons extra-virgin, first cold-pressed olive oil

1 teaspoon pure vanilla extract

1 cup chopped pecans

OVEN RACK · center | OVEN TEMPERATURE · 350°F
PREP · Line a large, rimmed baking sheet with parchment paper or a silicone baking mat.

TO BEGIN THE COOKIES

1 · Stir the flour, cocoa powder, baking soda, and salt in a large bowl until uniform. Whisk the eggs, sugar, olive oil, and vanilla extract in a second large bowl until smooth. Stir the liquid ingredients and the pecans into the dry ingredients until you have a loose, somewhat dry, but still coherent dough.

2 · Dust a clean, dry work surface with flour. Clean and dry your hands, then lightly dust them with flour. Divide the dough in half, set one of these dough halves on your work surface, and form it into an 11-inch-long log. Flatten slightly, then transfer to the prepared baking sheet. Dust your hands again and repeat with the second half of the dough.

TO FINISH UP

3 · Bake the logs until puffed, cracked, and lightly browned, about 25 minutes. Transfer the baking sheet to a wire rack and cool for 15 minutes. Maintain the oven temperature.

4 · Use a large metal spatula to transfer the logs to a cutting board; slice each on the diagonal into ½-inch-thick cookies. Set the cookies cut side down on the baking sheet and bake for 10 minutes. Turn them over and continue baking for 10 minutes more, or until browned and crunchy.

5 · Cool on the baking sheet on a wire rack for 5 minutes, then transfer the biscotti directly to

the rack and continue cooling to room temperature, about 1 hour. Store in a sealed container at room temperature for up to 5 days or in the freezer for up to 2 months.

PRO TIP · A serrated knife will cut through the pecans without shredding the dough. If you position the blade at a 45-degree angle to the log, you'll end with wider biscotti and more exposed surface for toasting in the second baking.

CHOCOLATE OLIVE OIL ICE CREAM
· YIELD: ABOUT 1 QUART ·

Although this one rides the line between a frozen custard and an ice cream, it's probably more the latter than the former, not because its technique makes it so, but because the olive oil gives it a less dense texture, more in keeping with traditional ice cream. But there's no doubt about this: it's a chic mix, a savory edge underneath the dark chocolate. Although we like a little salt in almost all desserts, its addition here made the ice cream too savory.

6 ounces dark chocolate, preferably 70% to 80% cocoa solids

1⅓ cups whole milk

1 cup heavy cream

6 large egg yolks, at room temperature

1 cup granulated white sugar

6 tablespoons extra-virgin, first cold-pressed olive oil

TO START THE ICE CREAM
1 · Chop the chocolate on a cutting board into small bits; scrape and pour these into a large bowl. Set aside.

2 · Heat the milk and cream in a large saucepan over medium-low heat until puffs of steam rise off its surface. Meanwhile, use an electric mixer at medium speed to beat the eggs and sugar in a large bowl until pale yellow and thick, until wide ribbons slide off the turned-off beaters, about 4 minutes.

3 · Beat about half the hot milk mixture into the egg yolk mixture in a slow, steady stream until smooth, then beat this combined mixture into the remaining milk mixture in the saucepan. Set the pan over low heat and cook, stirring constantly, until it thickly coats the back of a wooden spoon and the temperature registers 170°F, 4 to 7 minutes.

4 · Pour the custard through a fine-mesh sieve onto the chocolate in the bowl; stir until the chocolate dissolves. Stir in the olive oil until smooth. Refrigerate for at least 4 hours or up to 1 day, covering once the custard is cold.

TO FREEZE IT
5 · Prepare an ice-cream machine. Stir the cold custard and freeze it in the machine according to the manufacturer's instructions, until you can spoon up a mound of the ice cream with edges that do not immediately melt. Store in a sealed container in the freezer for up to 1 month.

À LA MODE IT · For a fancier presentation, crumble the biscotti over ice cream scoops on dinner plates. If desired, drizzle with a little fragrant olive oil.

RASPBERRY OAT BARS

---◆---

SORGHUM FROZEN CUSTARD

Here's the deal: take bar cookies with a shortbread crust, a jam filling, and a crunchy topping, then serve them with a malty, caramel-noted frozen custard. What could be bad? Well, perhaps you don't like raspberry jam. If so, feel free to substitute another flavor—but only jam, not jelly, preserves, nor all-fruit spread. Blackberry and apricot jam work particularly well with the buttery topping and the frozen custard.

RASPBERRY OAT BARS

· YIELD: A 9-INCH SQUARE PANFUL ·

---•◆•---

These bar cookies are in fact a hybrid among shortbread, blondies, granola bars, and a linzer tart. We know: we can't figure them out either. But they're impossible to resist. We've made them for book groups across our part of New England. Nobody seems interested in the books.

16 tablespoons (2 sticks) cool unsalted butter, cut into small bits, plus more for greasing

2/3 cup packed light brown sugar

1/2 cup granulated white sugar

1 large egg white, at room temperature

1 1/2 cups all-purpose flour

1 1/2 cups rolled oats (do not use steel-cut or quick-cooking)

1 cup sliced almonds

1/2 teaspoon ground cinnamon

1/2 teaspoon salt

1 cup raspberry jam

OVEN RACK · center | **OVEN TEMPERATURE** · 350°F
PREP · Butter the inside of a 9-inch square baking pan

TO MAKE THE CRUST

1 · Use an electric mixer at medium speed to beat the butter and the brown and white sugars in a large bowl until creamy, light, and fluffy, 5 to 6 minutes, scraping down the inside of the bowl occasionally. Beat in the egg white until smooth.

2 · Add the flour, oats, almonds, cinnamon, and salt. Beat at low speed just until a crumbly, grainy dough forms with no bits of dry flour anywhere.

3 · Press two-thirds of the dough into the prepared pan, making an even crust that rises about 1/2 inch up the sides. Spread the jam over this mixture, then crumble and dot with the remaining dough, creating an even, nubbly crust. Press gently to flatten slightly without causing the jam to squish up into the top crumble.

TO FINISH UP

4 · Bake until browned and set, about 45 minutes. Cool in the baking pan on a wire rack for 30 minutes or to room temperature. Cut into 6 or 9 bar cookies to serve. Once cut up, store the bars between sheets of wax paper in a sealed container at room temperature for up to 2 days.

PRO TIP · Invert the pan onto a cutting board, remove the pan, and invert the whole cake-and-cutting-board kit and caboodle onto a second cutting board so the cake is crumble side up. Now you can cut the bars without worrying about the sides of the pan.

SORGHUM FROZEN CUSTARD

· YIELD: ABOUT 1 QUART ·

—— · ◆ · ——

Long a favorite breakfast condiment in the South, sorghum syrup is an evaporated syrup made from the juice of sweet sorghum cane. The syrup has a savory, floral edge with malty, hoppy notes about like those in an IPA. Sorghum syrup is also thicker and denser than most maple syrup or some honey. If you spray a measuring cup with nonstick spray before using it, the syrup will fall right out. The egg whites combine with the syrup to create a rather chewy frozen custard.

1½ cups heavy cream

1 cup whole milk

½ cup sorghum syrup

3 large eggs, at room temperature

¼ cup granulated white sugar

¼ teaspoon salt

TO MAKE THE CUSTARD

1 · Heat the cream, milk, and syrup in a large saucepan over medium-low heat, stirring until the syrup dissolves and small puffs of steam rise off its surface. Meanwhile, use an electric mixer at medium speed to beat the eggs, sugar, and salt in a large bowl until pale yellow and quite thick, until wide ribbons slide off the turned-off beaters, about 4 minutes.

2 · Beat about half the hot milk mixture into the egg mixture in a slow, steady stream until smooth, then beat this combined mixture into the remaining milk mixture in the pan. Set the pan over low heat and cook, stirring constantly, until it can thickly coat the back of a wooden spoon, until its temperature reaches 170°F, 4 to 7 minutes.

3 · Pour the mixture through a fine-mesh sieve into a bowl; refrigerate for at least 4 hours or up to 2 days, covering once the custard is cold.

TO FREEZE IT

4 · Prepare an ice-cream machine. Stir the cold custard and freeze it in the machine according to the manufacturer's instructions, until it can mound on a spoon without instantly melting. Store in a sealed container in the freezer for up to 2 months.

À LA MODE IT · The bars should be slightly warm to melt the frozen custard. If they're not warm from the oven, they'll stand up well to a 15-second reheat on high in the microwave.

FUDGY BROWNIES

—◆—

MARSHMALLOW SEMIFREDDO

We designed these treats to go on top of each other as two stacked, 9-inch squares. On the bottom, there's a chewy, rich brownie; on the top, the softest, "meltiest" frozen treat. Wait until the last minute to put them together, then slice them into bars or squares.

FUDGY BROWNIES

· YIELD: A 9-INCH SQUARE PANFUL ·

—·◆·—

Sure, there's a lot of chopped chocolate here, but it's mostly for an intense flavor. The ratio of cocoa powder and butter makes these brownies dense and chewy. As you melt the chopped chocolate, keep the heat low so the water barely simmers. Steam can cause the chocolate to seize, even with butter in the mix. The recipe asks you to bake the brownies until they're of a uniform consistency, completely set up. However, if you underbake them by 2 or 3 minutes, you'll end up with soft, gooey centers—not to everyone's liking but an even more decadent match to the semifreddo.

1¹/3 cups all-purpose flour

2¹/2 tablespoons unsweetened cocoa powder, preferably natural-style cocoa powder

¹/2 teaspoon salt

10¹/2 tablespoons (1 stick plus 2¹/2 tablespoons) unsalted butter, cut into small bits, plus additional for greasing

8 ounces semisweet chocolate, chopped; or semisweet chocolate chips

2¹/2 ounces unsweetened chocolate, chopped

1 cup granulated white sugar

¹/2 cup packed dark brown sugar

4 large eggs, at room temperature

2 teaspoons pure vanilla extract

OVEN RACK · center | OVEN TEMPERATURE · 350°F
PREP · Butter the inside of a 9-inch square baking pan.

TO START THE BROWNIES

1 · Whisk the flour, cocoa powder, and salt in a medium bowl until uniform. Set aside.

2 · Set up a double boiler and bring about 1 inch of water to a simmer in the bottom half over low heat—or fit a heat-safe bowl over a medium saucepan with about the same amount of simmering water. Add the butter and both types of chocolate to the top half of the double boiler and cook, stirring often, until about two-thirds of the chocolate has melted. Remove the top half of the double boiler or the bowl from the heat (watch out for escaping steam!) and continue stirring until all the chocolate has melted. Whisk in the white and brown sugars until smooth. Set aside for 10 minutes to cool.

3 · Whisk in all the eggs and vanilla extract until smooth. Now stir in the flour mixture with a wooden spoon just until there are no dry bits of flour remaining in the batter. Pour and spread the batter into the prepared baking pan.

TO FINISH UP

4 · Bake the brownies until a toothpick inserted into the center comes out with a few moist crumbs attached, about 30 minutes. Cool in the baking pan on a wire rack for at least 30 minutes or to room temperature. Store the baked brownies in a sealed container between sheets of wax paper at room temperature for up to 2 days.

PRO TIP · You can't overwhisk the chocolate mixture until you add the flour; before that, the smoother, the better. Once the flour gets in, stir gently and evenly just until moistened to keep from elongating the glutens (and toughening the brownies).

MARSHMALLOW SEMIFREDDO

· YIELD: A HALF FULL 9-INCH SQUARE PAN ·

Unfortunately, semifreddo has morphed into "ice cream in a loaf pan," not at all like its origins. We started taking it back years ago with our second frozen-dessert book. Our technique is now a three-step fandango: a cooked meringue plus a zabaglione plus whipped cream. The loaf is soft, even right out of the freezer. Serve it the moment you cut it. And make sure the brownie cake is at room temperature, not warm.

1½ cups heavy cream

6 large egg yolks, at room temperature

⅔ cup granulated white sugar

¼ cup vanilla liqueur, such as Cuarenta Y Tres or Tuaca

⅛ teaspoon marshmallow flavoring extract, optional

2 large egg whites, at room temperature

¼ teaspoon salt

¼ teaspoon cream of tartar

PREP · Line a 9-inch square baking pan with plastic wrap.

TO MAKE THE COMPONENTS OF THE SEMIFREDDO

1 · Use an electric mixer at high speed to beat the cream in a large bowl until the turned-off beaters can lift up soft mounds of the stuff. Set the bowl in the fridge. Clean and dry the beaters.

2 · Set up a double boiler and bring about 1 inch of water to a simmer over low heat in the bottom half or set a heat-safe bowl over a medium saucepan with about the same amount of simmering water. Using an electric mixer at medium speed, beat the egg yolks, ⅓ cup sugar, the liqueur, and the marshmallow flavoring, if using, in the top of the double boiler or the bowl, scraping down the inside of the bowl occasionally with a rubber spatula, until a thick, foamy custard forms, about tripled in volume from its original state,

4 to 5 minutes. Scrape the contents of the top half of the double boiler into a second bowl and set aside at room temperature—or remove the bowl from the saucepan and set aside at room temperature.

3 · Clean and dry the beaters as well as the top half of the double boiler, if using. Again, set up that double boiler or a medium saucepan with the same amount of simmering water. Beat the egg whites, salt, cream of tartar, and the remaining ⅓ cup sugar at high speed in the top half of the double boiler or another heat-safe bowl until the mixture has doubled in volume, until it's thick and marshmallowy, about 3 minutes. Remove the top half of the double boiler or the bowl; continue beating, off the heat, at medium speed until cool and shiny, about 5 minutes more.

TO PUT IT TOGETHER

4 · Fold the egg yolk mixture into the egg white mixture, using a rubber spatula and long, even strokes to create a uniform but not deflated combo. Fold in the whipped cream in the same way until smooth.

5 · Pour and scrape this mixture into the prepared baking pan. Freeze for at least 12 hours, covering fully once cold. (Lay plastic wrap directly on its surface to prevent freezer burn and cross-contamination of food odors.) Store tightly covered in the freezer for up to 2 weeks.

À LA MODE IT · Invert the brownies in their pan onto a cutting board and remove the pan. To flip the cake right side up again, set a second cutting board on top, invert the whole thing, and remove the now-top cutting board. Uncover the semifreddo in its pan. Turn it over onto the brownies and use any overhanging plastic to get it loose from the pan. Remove the pan; peel off the wax paper. Slice into squares to serve.

PRO TIP · Both the bowl and the beaters should be cold to get the best loft out of the whipped cream. Also make sure the cooked meringue has returned to room temperature in step 4 or it will melt the whipped cream and the semifreddo's texture will be compromised.

BAKLAVA CUPS

— ◈ —

HONEY GELATO

Here's the baklava equation: phyllo + nuts + honey + butter. We split that formula into its components and morphed it into a dramatic dessert. Buttery phyllo dough is sprinkled with walnuts and turned into serving cups in a muffin pan. These aren't all that sweet. Instead, we let the honey gelato complete the profile. There are only two desserts in this book of pairings that are not in themselves stand-alones: this one and the vacherin to come. Chances are, you'd never serve these baklava cups on their own; but you could skip the gelato and serve them with a honey-sweetened ricotta and mascarpone mix.

BAKLAVA CUPS

· YIELD: 6 DESSERT CUPS ·

— ◈ —

A standard, one-pound box of frozen phyllo contains two sleeves of dough sheets. This recipe calls for about half of one of those sleeves. However, you'll also need more than 12 sheets of phyllo dough since they easily tear and shard, even when kept under a kitchen towel. Remember: the sheets don't have to be perfect in the pan's indentations. Fold and crimp them to fit, always keeping in mind that you're making a cup to hold gelato. Because of the way the cups' edges overhang the indentations, you'll need to space the phyllo cups one indentation apart—and thus you'll need to use either a 12-indentation muffin pan or two 6-indentation muffin pans.

I cup walnut pieces

2 tablespoons packed light brown sugar

1/2 teaspoon ground cinnamon

1/4 teaspoon salt

Twelve 9 x 13-inch sheets frozen phyllo dough, thawed according to the package instructions

12 tablespoons (1 1/2 sticks) unsalted butter, melted and cooled

OVEN RACK · center | **OVEN TEMPERATURE** · 375°F

TO START THE CUPS

1 · Put the walnuts, brown sugar, cinnamon, and salt in a food processor. Cover and process until finely ground. Set aside.

2 · Stack the phyllo sheets on your work surface, covering them with a clean, dry kitchen towel. Peel off a sheet and set it on a dry, clean part of the work surface. Brush fairly generously with butter and sprinkle 1 rounded tablespoon of the nut mixture evenly over the sheet. Fold the sheet the short way, then fold it again the short way. Brush lightly with butter and set into the standard, 2/3- to 3/4-cup indentation in the muffin pan, pressing it to conform into a cup.

3 · Lay a second sheet of phyllo on your work surface, cover the stack, and treat this one exactly as you did the first. Once folded, place, press, and conform it in the same indentation as the last but turning it 90 degrees so the ends point in different directions, still creating a cup in the pan.

4 · Spacing the cups one indentation apart, repeat steps 2 and 3 again and again, making 5 more phyllo cups.

TO FINISH UP

5 · Bake until browned and flaky-crisp, about 15 minutes. Transfer the pan (or pans) to a wire rack and cool for 10 minutes. Gently pry the cups out of the indentations, place the cups directly on the rack, and cool to room temperature, about 1 hour. Store uncovered at room temperature for up to 4 hours.

PRO TIP · Phyllo sheets are bigger than the indentations of a muffin pan. The sheets will come up the sides, stand up, and even flap over like dog ears. You want a rise to create the prettiest cups.

HONEY GELATO
· YIELD: 1 SCANT QUART ·

Use a high-quality, thick honey, perhaps even a dark honey from trees like chestnuts or oaks. For a slightly milder flavor, use orange-blossom or star thistle honey. The orange flower water, while not necessary, will give the gelato a distinct nose, best with the walnuts and butter. But if you're making this gelato on its own without the cups, we suggest omitting it.

2 cups whole milk

1/4 cup heavy cream

1/2 cup honey

6 large egg yolks, at room temperature

1/4 teaspoon salt

2 drops orange flower water, optional

TO MAKE THE CUSTARD

1 · Heat the milk and cream in a large saucepan set over medium-low heat until small bubbles fizz around the pan's inner perimeter. Meanwhile, use an electric mixer at medium speed to beat the honey, egg yolks, and salt in a large bowl until thick and a bit pasty, about 4 minutes.

2 · Beat about half the hot milk mixture into the honey mixture in a slow stream until smooth, then beat this combined mixture into the remaining milk mixture in the pan until smooth. Set the pan over low heat and cook, stirring constantly, until the mixture thickly coats the back of a wooden spoon and the temperature registers 170°F, 4 to 7 minutes.

3 · Stir in the orange flower water, if using. Pour through a fine-mesh sieve into a bowl; refrigerate for at least 4 hours or up to 2 days, covering once the custard is cool.

TO FREEZE IT

4 · Prepare an ice-cream machine. Stir the cold custard one more time and freeze it in the machine according to the manufacturer's instructions, until the gelato is smooth, glossy, and moundable. Store in a sealed container in the freezer for up to 2 months.

À LA MODE IT · Set one large or two smaller scoops of gelato in each phyllo cup. If desired, drizzle with honey and/or sprinkle with finely chopped walnuts.

CREAM SCONES WITH PEAR COMPOTE
STRACIA-FIOR DI LATTE

This one's a trio: tender, cakey scones; a buttery, rum-laced compote; and a riff on two Italian ice creams, morphed into one creamy treat. You can even make the three components in advance and assemble the dessert at the last minute. If so, warm the compote a few minutes in a saucepan, not until bubbling again, just until warm to the touch.

CREAM SCONES WITH PEAR COMPOTE
YIELD: 8 SCONES; ABOUT 3 CUPS COMPOTE

We make scones with Southern biscuit flour, milled from soft, low-protein wheat. It yields the most tender crumb. It also can be tough to find since many Southern cooks prefer the self-rising version. Look for the "plain" flour at high-end markets or online. In a pinch, substitute cake flour. By the way, there's not a lot of sugar in these scones. We're anticipating the compote and ice cream. If you're making them on their own, they'll need lots of jam.

FOR THE SCONES

2 cups Southern biscuit flour (do not use self-rising flour), plus additional for dusting

1 tablespoon baking powder

4 teaspoons granulated white sugar

1 teaspoon salt

1 to 1¼ cups heavy cream

2 tablespoons unsalted butter, melted and cooled, plus additional for greasing

FOR THE COMPOTE

4 tablespoons (½ stick) unsalted butter

4 medium Comice or Anjou pears, peeled, halved, cored, and thinly sliced

6 tablespoons packed muscavado or dark brown sugar

2 tablespoons gold or even aged rum (but not dark rum)

1½ teaspoons cornstarch

1 teaspoon water

OVEN RACK · center | **OVEN TEMPERATURE** · 425°F
PREP · Butter the inside of a 12-inch oven-safe skillet, preferably cast-iron.

TO MAKE THE SCONES

1 · Mix the flour, baking powder, 2 teaspoons of the sugar, and salt in a large bowl until uniform. Pour in just enough cream to make a soft, smooth dough, adding about ¾ cup cream at first and then additional cream in 1- to 2-tablespoon increments.

2 · Dust a clean, dry work surface with flour. Turn the dough onto it, gently gather it together, and pat it into a fairly rustic, 10-inch circle. Cut into 8 triangular wedges. Transfer to the prepared pan, placing the wedges in their original circle but slightly apart (about ¼ inch). Brush the tops with the melted butter; sprinkle with the remaining 2 teaspoons sugar.

3 · Bake until browned, puffed, and dry to the touch, about 15 minutes. Cool in the baking pan on a wire rack for 10 minutes, then break the wedges apart and continue cooling the scones directly on the rack for at least another 15 minutes or to room temperature, about 1½ hours.

TO MAKE THE PEAR COMPOTE

4 · Melt the butter in a large skillet set over medium heat. Add the pears and cook, stirring often, until slightly softened and lightly browned, about 4 minutes.

5 · Add the sugar, stir well, and add the rum. Cook, stirring often, until the sugar has melted and the sauce is bubbling. Whisk the cornstarch and water in a small bowl; add this slurry to the pear mixture. Cook, stirring all the while, until bubbling and thickened, about 1 minute. Set aside off the heat for at least 20 minutes to cool.

6 · The scones can be kept in a sealed container at room temperature for 1 day or in the freezer for up to 2 months. The compote can be stored in a sealed container in the fridge for up to 3 days.

PRO TIP · Gently work the scone dough. Once the cream has been added, stir as little as possible, just until the flour is wet. Form it into shape with as little pulling as possible.

STRACIA-FIOR DI LATTE
· YIELD: A LITTLE MORE THAN 1 QUART ·

——— · ◆ · ———

We've fused two classics into one recipe. First, fior di latte (*FEE-ohr dee LAH-tay* or the "flower of the milk") is about the purest ice cream in Italy: a mix of cream and sugar, vanilla rarely included. It's not cooked; there are no eggs. It's delectable, straightforward ice cream. Second, stracciatella (*STRAH-chee-ah-TELL-ah*, something like "little torn-up bits) is an egg-rich gelato with shaved chocolate. We fused them, adding the shaved chocolate to that pure fior di latte. Chocolate and cream on pears and scones? What's not to like?

2½ cups heavy cream

1 cup whole milk

¾ cup granulated white sugar

½ teaspoon salt

1 ounce dark chocolate, between 70% and 80% cocoa solids, shaved

TO BEGIN THE ICE CREAM

1 · Stir the cream, milk, sugar, and salt in a large saucepan set over medium heat until the sugar dissolves. Continue heating just until whiffs of steam rise off its surface. Pour into a bowl and refrigerate for at least 4 hours or up to 2 days, covering once the mixture is cold.

TO FREEZE IT

2 · Prepare an ice-cream machine. Stir the milk mixture again and freeze it in the machine according to the manufacturer's instructions, until the ice cream can mound on a spoon without melting edges, like a firm soft-serve.

3 · Add the shaved chocolate and let the machine's dasher fold it in for just the last few turns. Store in a sealed container in the freezer for up to 2 weeks.

À LA MODE IT · For a slightly more elegant presentation, split the scones in half lengthwise and open them onto a plate. Spoon the pear compote on top, then add scoops of the ice cream.

PRO TIP · To shave chocolate, use a vegetable peeler or a cheese plane, running it along the smooth sides of the chocolate block to create small curls and chips.

CHOCOLATE CHIP–HAZELNUT SCONES

CHOCOLATE SEMIFREDDO

Once we took semifreddo back to its traditional roots—and yes, it's more work than packing ice cream into a loaf pan—we knew we had to create desserts that were simple enough to highlight that incredible, soft texture. We wouldn't put semifreddo with cake or pie—it's just too much! But these scones fit the bill.

CHOCOLATE CHIP–HAZELNUT SCONES
· YIELD: 8 SCONES ·

Because of the chocolate chips and nuts, we wanted to craft a light scone to keep the flavors from being weighed down by the texture. So this one's not your typical, biscuitlike dough. It's soft, sort of like a cross between an unbaked shortbread dough and a traditional scone. The results have lots of loft—and so are a good match to the powerhouse frozen dessert.

10 ounces hazelnuts (about 1 cup)

1 cup all-purpose flour, plus additional for dusting

1/4 cup granulated white sugar

1 tablespoon baking powder

1/2 teaspoon salt

4 tablespoons (1/2 stick) cold unsalted butter, cut into small bits

3/4 cup heavy cream

1/2 cup milk chocolate chips

OVEN RACK · center | OVEN TEMPERATURE · 375°F

TO PREPARE THE HAZELNUTS

1 · Spread the nuts out on a large, rimmed baking sheet and toast, stirring occasionally, until lightly browned and fragrant, about 5 minutes. Pour the nuts into a clean kitchen towel and cool for a few minutes. Gather the towel together and rub the hazelnuts together to remove their skins (or as much as you can). Open the towel, pick the hazelnuts out, and transfer them to a food processor. Cover and process until finely ground, like coarse meal. (Maintain the oven temperature.)

PREP · Line a large, rimmed baking sheet with parchment paper.

TO MAKE THE SCONES

2 · Add the flour, sugar, baking powder, and salt to the food processor; cover and pulse until evenly distributed. Add the butter, cover, and pulse until the mixture resembles coarse cornmeal. Pour into a large bowl and stir in the cream just until incorporated. Add the chocolate chips and stir until uniform throughout.

3 · Flour your cleaned, dried hands, gather the dough into a mass, and divide it into 8 even pieces, each about 1/3 cup. Flouring your hands as necessary, shape each piece into a ball. Set these on the prepared baking sheet and flatten them to about 1/2-inch-thick disks.

4 · Bake until lightly browned and firm, about 20 minutes. Transfer the baking sheet with the scones to a wire rack and cool for 5 minutes, then transfer the scones directly to the rack and cool for at least 20 minutes or to room temperature, about 1 hour. Store in a sealed container at room temperature for up to 2 days or in the freezer for up to 2 months.

PRO TIP · The less flour used for dusting and such, the more tender the scones.

CHOCOLATE SEMIFREDDO

· YIELD: ONE 9 X 5-INCH LOAF ·

This recipe uses the same technique as that for the Marshmallow Semifreddo—that is, cooked meringue, zabaglione, and whipped cream, all folded together. But the results are richer, thanks to 6 ounces of dark chocolate.

I cup heavy cream

4 large egg yolks, at room temperature

I cup granulated white sugar

¼ cup whole milk

6 ounces dark chocolate, between 70% and 80%, chopped

I teaspoon pure vanilla extract

2 large egg whites

¼ teaspoon salt

PREP · Line a 9 x 5-inch loaf pan with plastic wrap.

TO MAKE THE COMPONENTS

1 · Use an electric mixer at high speed to beat the cream in a large bowl until the turned-off beaters create soft mounds throughout. Set in the fridge.

2 · Clean and dry the beaters. Set up a double boiler and bring about 1 inch of water to a simmer in the bottom half over low heat or jury-rig a double boiler with a medium saucepan with about the same amount of simmering water. Add the egg yolks, ½ cup sugar, and the milk to the top half of the double boiler or a heat-safe bowl. Set it over the water and beat with an electric mixer at medium speed, scraping and stirring almost constantly, until thickened and pale, until the mixture forms wide ribbons that slide off the turned-off beaters, about 6 minutes.

3 · Remove the top half of the double boiler or the bowl from the heat. (Maintain the water's simmer.) Add the chocolate and vanilla extract; whisk until smooth. Scrape the contents of the double boiler, if using, into a bowl; clean and dry the top part of the double boiler. If you've used a jury-rigged bowl, just set it aside.

4 · Clean and dry the beaters. Set the top half of the double boiler or another heat-safe bowl over the simmering water. Add the egg whites, salt, and the remaining ½ cup sugar; beat with an electric mixer at medium speed, stirring and scraping constantly, until fluffy and marshmallowy, 3 to 4 minutes. Remove the top half of the double boiler or the bowl from the heat and continue beating to room temperature until shiny, about 5 minutes.

TO PUT THE COMPONENTS TOGETHER

5 · Fold the egg yolk mixture into the egg white mixture, using a rubber spatula and long, even strokes, just until uniform. Fold in the whipped cream, taking care not to deflate its air but getting it well combined throughout.

6 · Pour and scrape this mixture into the prepared loaf pan. Cover with plastic wrap and freeze for at least 12 hours. Store covered in the freezer for up to 2 weeks.

À LA MODE IT · Turn the semifreddo out onto a cutting board and unwrap it. Slice off ½-inch-thick pieces, like slices of bread. Split a scone widthwise and set it in a bowl with a slice of semifreddo on top.

PRO TIP · The egg yolks and whites must be at room temperature or they'll take too long to set over the heat and begin to scramble. And the egg white mixture must be at room temperature when you fold all the semifreddo components together or it will deflate the whipped cream you've worked hard to create.

YEAST-RAISED GRAHAM WAFFLES

—◆—

BLACK CURRANT JAM SWIRL ICE CREAM

There's a vast divide among waffle mavens—and in our home, too. One of us (the chef) likes softer waffles with lots of lighter beige spots on the surface; the other (the writer, who is clearly right) likes waffles that can best be compared to shingles, ones that shard on the plate. He leaves them in the machine for two complete cycles at the highest setting. Still, no matter which you prefer, you'll end up with a perfect platform for this soft, sweet ice cream.

YEAST-RAISED WAFFLES

· YIELD: 8 WAFFLES

—◆—

These waffles are denser than you might think, a little cakier than the breakfast standard. There's also not as much sugar since we wanted them to be a fit vehicle for ice cream. You need to start them the day before so they rise in the fridge. The yield depends on the size of the waffle maker. We tested with a 6½-inch-diameter machine.

2 cups warmed whole milk, between 100°F and 110°F

1 tablespoon packed light brown sugar

One .25-ounce package active dry yeast

1½ cups all-purpose flour

1 cup graham flour

¼ teaspoon baking soda

¼ teaspoon salt

8 tablespoons (1 stick) unsalted butter, melted and cooled

2 large eggs, lightly beaten in a small bowl

½ teaspoon pure vanilla extract

TO MAKE THE BATTER

1 · Stir the milk, sugar, and yeast in a large bowl until the brown sugar dissolves. Set aside to proof until foamy, about 5 minutes. Meanwhile, mix both flours, the soda, and salt in a medium bowl until uniform.

2 · Stir the melted butter, beaten eggs, and vanilla extract into the yeast mixture. Add the flour mixture and stir just until a wet batter forms, until there's no dry specks of flour. Cover the bowl with plastic wrap and set in the fridge overnight, for at least 8 hours but not more than 12 hours, until bubbly, foamy, and doubled in bulk—or set the bowl aside at room temperature for 3 hours until that same consistency.

TO MAKE THE WAFFLES

3 · Prepare a waffle iron according to the manufacturer's instructions. Uncover the bowl and stir down the batter. Bake the waffles according to the size and timing specifications of your machine, setting the finished waffles on a wire rack while you make more. Completely cooled waffles may be sealed in plastic wrap and stored in the freezer for up to 1 month. To reheat, place them frozen on the oven rack and warm in a 325°F oven for up to 10 minutes.

PRO TIP · These days, every waffle maker claims to be a "Belgian waffle maker." We're not sure what happened: how the standard American morphed into the international wannabe. That said, machines that yield many pockets, none excessively deep and spongy, will make the best waffles for this dessert.

BLACK CURRANT JAM
SWIRL ICE CREAM

· YIELD: ABOUT 1 QUART ·

— · ◈ · —

This ice cream is sort of like the Italian classic fior di latte (see page 134) since this one doesn't even include vanilla extract. We wanted a purer flavor for the jam. However, we did add potato starch, the dehydrated starch from potatoes. It's an Old World thickener, prized for the smooth consistency it brings to soups and sauces. It gives the ice cream a slightly firmer chew. But in the end, the taste here is all about the jam. Buy the best you can comfortably afford.

2 cups heavy cream

1¼ cups whole milk

½ cup granulated white sugar

3 tablespoons potato starch

¼ teaspoon salt

⅓ cup black currant jam

TO BEGIN THE ICE CREAM

1 · Whisk the cream, milk, sugar, potato starch, and salt in a large saucepan set over medium-low heat until the sugar dissolves. Continue cooking, whisking often (more and more, in fact) until the mixture is thick and bubbling, about 6 minutes.

2 · Pour the mixture into a bowl and refrigerate for at least 4 hours or up to 2 days, covering once the mixture is cold.

TO FINISH UP

3 · Prepare an ice-cream machine. Stir the cream mixture, then freeze it in the machine according to the manufacturer's instructions, until you can spoon up a mound with edges that do not instantly start melting.

4 · Spoon some of the ice cream into a loaf pan, top with a thin layer of the jam, add more ice cream, more jam, and on and on, until it's all in, finishing up with a layer of ice cream. When you scoop it up, you'll make ribbons in the ice cream. Store in a sealed container in the freezer for up to 1 month.

À LA MODE IT · Set a waffle on a plate and top with (lots of) ice cream. Dust with confectioners' sugar, if desired.

PRO TIP · Most North American loaf pans are about 1½-quart pans. They'll work fine for this layering techniques, but you'll get many more layers in a more esoteric 1-quart loaf pan because it isn't so wide.

CHOCOLATE BABKA

◆

MOCHA FROZEN CUSTARD

Back when we lived in New York, we got on an ice cream/babka kick—but were always dissatisfied. See, the babka we'd buy had too much filling. It didn't sit well with the ice cream. In the end, we wanted cake in babka form. So we developed this recipe to cake-i-fy the classic and make it a fit vehicle for an intense coffee/chocolate frozen dessert.

CHOCOLATE BABKA

· YIELD: ONE 9 X 5-INCH LOAF ·

◆

Babka is a rolled, shaped loaf with spirals of filling—in this case, chocolate. This one's a no-knead version, a take on the no-knead breads popularized by Jim Lahey and Nancy Baggett. You don't have to work it on the countertop or in a stand mixer. In fact, handle the dough as little as possible. You're making cake, after all. We don't want to elongate the glutens any more than we have to. You'll end up with a crumb that's halfway between cake and bread, the perfect pairing for a rich frozen custard.

FOR THE LOAF

2/3 cup warmed whole milk, between 100°F and 110°F

1/2 cup granulated white sugar

One .25-ounce package active dry yeast

16 tablespoons (2 sticks) unsalted butter, melted and cooled, plus additional for greasing

4 large eggs, at room temperature and lightly beaten in a small bowl

1 1/2 teaspoons salt

1 teaspoon pure vanilla extract

4 1/2 to 5 cups all-purpose flour, plus additional for dusting

FOR THE FILLING

1 cup semisweet chocolate chips

1 cup sliced almonds

1/4 cup packed dark brown sugar

2 tablespoons unsalted butter, melted and cooled if still slightly warm

1/2 teaspoon ground cinnamon

1 large egg, lightly beaten in a small bowl

FOR THE TOPPING

1/4 cup all-purpose flour

1/4 cup packed light brown sugar

2 tablespoons unsalted butter, melted and cooled

OVEN RACK · center | OVEN TEMPERATURE · 350°F
PREP · Butter the inside of a 9 x 5-inch loaf pan.

TO START THE BABKA

1 · Stir the warmed milk, sugar, and yeast in a large bowl until the sugar has dissolved. Set aside to proof until foamy, about 5 minutes.

2 · Stir the melted butter, eggs, salt, and vanilla extract into the yeast mixture. Add 4 cups of the flour and stir to form a soft, pliable, smooth dough, adding more flour in 1/4-cup increments as needed. The dough should be soft and supple, not sticky but also not stiff. Cover the bowl tightly with plastic wrap and set aside in a warm, draft-free place until doubled in bulk, about 1 hour.

3 · Lightly flour a clean, dry work surface. Turn the dough out onto it, then shape it into a cohesive mass. Use a lightly floured rolling pin to roll it into an 18 x 15-inch rectangle. Lay a clean kitchen towel on top and set aside.

TO MAKE THE FILLING AND SHAPE THE BABKA

4 · Mix the chocolate chips, almonds, brown sugar, melted butter, and cinnamon in a medium bowl. Remove the towel from over the dough and sprinkle this chocolate chip mixture evenly over the rectangle.

5 · Starting with one of the long sides, roll the dough rectangle into a fairly tight log. Bend this log into a "U" with the two ends facing you. Now twist the sides of the "U" over and around each other repeatedly to create a spiraled loaf. Set it in the prepared loaf pan. Brush the top of the loaf with the beaten egg.

TO FINISH UP

6 · Mix the flour, brown sugar, and butter in a small bowl until crumbly. Sprinkle and crumble evenly over the top of the loaf. Cover the loaf pan loosely but well with plastic wrap and set aside in a warm, draft-free place to rise until puffed up over the top of the loaf pan, about 30 minutes.

7 · Uncover and bake until browned, until the loaf sounds hollow when thumped, 35 to 45 minutes. Cool in the pan on a wire rack for 10 minutes before turning the loaf out and continuing to cool on the rack for at least 25 minutes or to room temperature before slicing or storing. Store tightly wrapped at room temperature for up to 2 days or in the freezer for up to 2 months.

PRO TIP · Make sure you cool the melted butter that goes into the loaf and the filling. If it's too hot, it can kill off the yeast and the loaf won't rise.

MOCHA FROZEN CUSTARD
· YIELD: ABOUT 1 QUART ·

—◦◈◦—

This one's not overly sweet. Nor is it overly chocolate-flavored. Rather, we wanted a coffee frozen custard with just a hint of the earthy notes chocolate affords. For the best flavor, use a dark-roast coffee, like a French or Viennese roast.

Grind the beans coarsely, as if you're using them in a French press. If the grind is much finer, you'll need to line the sieve with cheesecloth to get rid of every speck in the custard. For a bigger chocolate hit, add ½ cup chopped, chocolate-covered almonds just at the end of the ice cream's time in the machine, so the dasher stirs them in evenly with just a few turns.

1¾ cups heavy cream

1 cup whole milk

½ cup coarsely ground coffee beans

1 ounce unsweetened chocolate, chopped

5 large egg yolks, at room temperature

½ cup packed light brown sugar

¼ cup granulated white sugar

¼ teaspoon pure vanilla extract

⅛ teaspoon salt

TO MAKE THE CUSTARD

1 · Heat the cream, milk, and coffee in a large saucepan until little bubbles fizz around the pan's inner perimeter. Cover and set aside off the heat to steep for 15 minutes.

2 · Strain the mixture through a fine-mesh sieve to remove the coffee grounds. Discard the coffee grounds, pour the cream mixture back into the saucepan, and add the chocolate. Whisk over low heat until the chocolate has melted. Drop the heat to very low and keep warm.

3 · Use an electric mixer at medium speed to beat the egg yolks, both sugars, the vanilla extract, and salt in a large bowl until quite thick and wide ribbons slide off the turned-off beaters, about 4 minutes.

4 · Beat about half the hot cream mixture into the egg yolk mixture until smooth, then beat this combined mixture into the remaining cream mixture in the pan. Set over low heat and cook, stirring constantly, until the custard thickly coats the back of a wooden spoon and the temperature registers 170°F, 4 to 7 minutes.

5 · Strain the mixture through a fine-mesh sieve into a bowl, then refrigerate for at least 4 hours or up to 1 day, covering once the custard is cold.

TO FREEZE IT

6 · Prepare an ice-cream machine. Stir the cold custard and freeze it in the machine according to the manufacturer's instructions, until you can spoon up a mound with edges that do not instantly start melting. Store in a sealed container in the freezer for up to 2 months.

À LA MODE IT · Slice the babka into ½-inch-thick pieces and set the scoops of frozen custard just to the side on the plates so you can drag bits of the bready cake right into the melty goodness.

PRO TIP · When unsweetened chocolate melts, it can first turn into tiny specks, like coffee grounds. Whisk over the heat to melt these thoroughly and produce a smooth combo for the custard.

ALMOND BEAR CLAWS

—◆—

CHERRY CHEESECAKE ICE CREAM

This pairing may be the richest in the book: almonds, cream cheese, cherries, and buttery pastry. In fact, these bear claws are probably best served as a half portion. That way, you can eat more of the ice cream! Save any leftover bear claws in a sealed bag in the freezer; set them still frozen on a baking sheet and warm them in a 300°F oven for 10 minutes or so.

ALMOND BEAR CLAWS

· YIELD: 8 BEAR CLAWS ·

—◆—

Our version of bear claws is a tad less sweet than the bake-shop classics. The dough rises in the fridge so the butter stays cold and is ready for repeated rollings—aka laminating, the method used to give hundreds of flaky layers to croissants. Ours is a somewhat easier version of the technique. Somewhat.

FOR THE DOUGH

1/2 cup warmed milk, between 100°F and 110°F

1/4 cup granulated white sugar

One .25-ounce package active dry yeast

At least 3 1/2 cups all-purpose flour

1/2 teaspoon salt

1/2 cup heavy cream

2 large eggs, at room temperature

24 tablespoons (3 sticks) cold unsalted butter, cut into little bits

FOR THE FILLING

One 7-ounce tube almond paste

1/4 cup granulated white sugar

1/4 cup unsweetened shredded coconut

I large egg, at room temperature

2 tablespoons unsalted butter, melted and cooled

1/2 teaspoon ground cinnamon

TO MAKE THE PASTRY

1 · Stir the milk, sugar, and yeast in a large bowl until the sugar has dissolved. Set aside to proof about 5 minutes, until foamy. Meanwhile, mix 3 1/2 cups flour and salt in a second large bowl. Use a pastry cutter or a fork to cut in the butter until the mixture resembles coarse, dry sand.

2 · Stir the cream and eggs into the milk mixture. Pour in the flour mixture and stir to form a crumbly, somewhat dry dough. Gather the dough into a ball (it should come together fairly easily.) Cover the bowl tightly with plastic wrap and refrigerate for 4 hours or up to 8 hours, until just about doubled in bulk.

3 · Dust a clean, dry work surface with flour. Turn the dough out onto it and dust with flour. Use a rolling pin to roll the dough into a 16 x 20-inch rectangle. Be precise! Fold the rectangle into thirds, one short side toward and then over the middle, then the other short side over the middle, overlapping the sections completely. Turn the dough 90 degrees and roll it again into a 16 x 20-inch rectangle. Once again, fold it in thirds, as before. Set in the fridge while you complete the next step.

TO MAKE THE FILLING

4 · Put the almond paste, sugar, coconut, egg, butter, and cinnamon in a food processor. Cover and pulse until pasty, like very wet sand.

OVEN RACK · center | OVEN TEMPERATURE · 400°F
PREP · Line a large rimmed baking sheet with parchment paper.

TO FILL AND SHAPE THE BEAR CLAWS

5 · Dust your work surface one more time with flour and set the dough on it. Using a rolling pin, roll it one more time into a (precise!) 16 x 20-inch rectangle. Making one cut lengthwise and three widthwise, slice the dough into eight 5 x 8-inch rectangles. Separate them so you can work with them individually.

6 · Spread about 2½ tablespoons of the filling on each rectangle. Starting with a long side, roll one into a fairly tight tube (but don't let the filling squish out). Bend the tube into a curve, sort of like a half-moon. Make four cuts along the outside edge of the curve, exposing the filling a bit and making the "toes" (as it were). Transfer to the prepared baking sheet and make the remainder of the claws.

TO FINISH UP

7 · Bake the bear claws until browned and puffed, about 18 minutes. The filling will ooze out a bit between the slits. Cool on the baking sheet for a couple of minutes, then use a metal spatula to transfer the bear claws to a wire rack and cool for at least 20 minutes or to room temperature, about 1 hour. Store between sheets of wax paper in a sealed container at room temperature for up to 2 days.

PRO TIP · You've got to work with a ruler. And make sure the ends are not thinner than the middle. Roll from the center out.

CHERRY CHEESECAKE ICE CREAM
· YIELD: ABOUT 1 QUART ·

Cream cheese and lemon zest give ice cream a taste very much like cheesecake. Sweet cherry jam—rather than sour—will work best against the slightly sour flavors of the cream cheese.

1¼ cups whole milk

¾ cup heavy cream

⅔ cup granulated white sugar

6 ounces regular cream cheese (do not use low-fat or fat-free)

3 large egg yolks, at room temperature

½ tablespoon pure vanilla extract

½ teaspoon finely grated lemon zest

⅔ cup sweet cherry jam

TO BEGIN THE ICE CREAM

1 · Heat the milk and cream in a medium saucepan over medium heat until puffs of steam rise off the surface.

2 · Put the sugar, cream cheese, egg yolks, vanilla extract, and lemon zest in a food processor. Cover and pulse a few times to combine well. With the machine running, pour the warmed milk mixture in through the feed tube. Process until smooth, scraping down the inside of the canister at least once. Pour the mixture into a bowl and refrigerate for at least 4 hours or up to 2 days, covering once the mixture is cold.

TO FINISH UP

3 · Prepare an ice-cream machine. Stir the custard and freeze it in the machine according to the manufacturer's instructions, until you can spoon up a mound without its edges immediately melting.

4 · Spoon some of the ice cream into a loaf pan, spread a little cherry jam on top, and then keep making these alternating layers, ending with ice cream. As you scoop it up, you'll make ribbons of jam in the ice-cream balls. Store in a sealed container in the freezer for up to 1 week.

À LA MODE IT · We advocate serving these separately, the bear claw on a plate and the ice cream in a nearby bowl, so the melting cream doesn't ruin the zillions of flaky layers.

PRO TIP · The eggs may not come up to a safe temperature in this method—and so may be a tad "raw" in the final mix. Use farm-fresh organic eggs from a local farmers' market or search out pasteurized eggs at your supermarket if you're concerned.

GANACHE TURNOVERS

—◆—

GOAT CHEESE ICE CREAM

Our last bake-shop treat uses a terrific combo: dark chocolate ganache and goat cheese. We started combining the two in truffles years ago when we wrote the first-ever all-goat cookbook (meat, milk, and cheese). Here, we've pulled them apart to include the flaky crust of a classic turnover. The ice cream is a bit hard if it's been stored in the freezer. Set it out on the countertop for a few minutes for better scoopability.

GANACHE TURNOVERS

· YIELD: 8 TURNOVERS ·

—◆—

You know what's wrong with apple turnovers? The apples. They take up all the real estate so there's no room for ganache, a chocolate confection that bakes up into a melty, soft, warm wonder inside.

8 ounces semisweet chocolate, chopped; or semisweet chocolate chips

2/3 cup heavy cream

All-purpose flour, for dusting

One 17.3-ounce package frozen puff pastry, thawed according to the package directions

2 large eggs, well beaten in a small bowl

1½ tablespoons coarse-grained white sugar

TO START THE TURNOVERS

1 · Put the chocolate in a medium bowl. Heat the cream in a small saucepan set over medium heat until puffs of steam rise off its surface; do not simmer. Pour the hot cream over the chocolate in the bowl and stir until smooth. Refrigerate until the mixture can be formed into mounds, 2 to 3 hours.

OVEN RACK · center | **OVEN TEMPERATURE** · 400°F
PREP · Line an 11 x 17-inch rimmed baking sheet with parchment paper.

2 · Dust a clean, dry work surface with flour. Place one sheet of puff pastry on top. Cut into 4 squares. Place about 2 tablespoons of the chocolate ganache in the center of each square; flatten the ganache a bit, about like a thick coin. Brush the edges of each square with the beaten egg, then fold each square into a triangle, opposite corner to opposite corner. Seal the edges by pressing with the tines of a fork and transfer the turnover to the prepared baking sheet. Repeat this process with the second sheet of puff pastry, making 4 more turnovers.

TO FINISH UP

3 · Brush the tops of the turnovers with the remaining beaten egg, then sprinkle evenly with sugar. Bake until puffed and browned, about 14 minutes. Cool on the baking sheet for 5 minutes, then continue cooling the turnovers directly on a wire rack for at least 20 minutes or until just warm, about 45 minutes. Serve after cooling. The turnovers cannot be stored; the pastry goes soggy fast.

PRO TIP · Coarse-grained sugar, sometimes called "sanding sugar," is a baker's specialty, a way to get a glistening crunch on a baked good without melting. You can use colored sanding sugar, of course—but the clear stuff looks better on these turnovers.

GOAT CHEESE ICE CREAM

· YIELD: A LITTLE LESS THAN 1 QUART ·

— · ◈ · —

The best goat cheese isn't tangy. It's earthy with a savory edge. Don't cheap out and buy the downscale stuff. You want soft, creamy chèvre, preferably bought from a cheese counter where you can actually smell what you're getting. (No barnyard odor, please.)

2 cups whole milk

1¼ cups heavy cream

1 cup granulated white sugar

1½ tablespoons cornstarch

6 ounces soft, plain, fresh goat cheese

TO START THE ICE CREAM

1 · Stir the milk, cream, sugar, and cornstarch in a medium saucepan set over medium heat until the sugar has dissolved. Continue cooking, whisking often (and more and more) until the mixture thickens and bubbles, 5 to 6 minutes.

2 · Remove from the heat and whisk in the goat cheese until dissolved. Pour the mixture into a bowl and refrigerate for at least 4 hours or up to 2 days, covering once the mixture is cold.

TO FREEZE IT

3 · Prepare an ice-cream machine. Stir the goat cheese mixture and freeze it in the machine according to the manufacturer's instructions, until you can spoon up a mound with edges that do not instantly start melting. Store in a sealed container in the freezer for up to 1 month. The flavor will become increasingly intense.

À LA MODE IT · Split open the warm turnovers and set a large scoop of ice cream right in the center, right on top of the ganache. Or for a less messy dessert, cool the turnovers more fully and set some softened ice cream to the side of each.

CAKES:
SPONGE, POUND, SHEET, BUNDT,
&
MORE

IF, AS WE'VE MENTIONED, CRUMB IS THE NEXT BEST THING

to (or with) ice cream, we're about to get way more serious about it. While tiered layer cakes are yet to come, here's a collection of single layer cakes. Some are iced, some are glazed, but most stand on their own. Some are reinventions of classics; some are whimsy. A cranberry kefir Bundt with eggnog ice cream? Pine nut pound cake toasted in butter and topped with marmalade frozen custard? A deconstruction of hummingbird cake, that Southern favorite, into a banana and coconut sheet cake, cream cheese icing, toasted pecans, and pineapple ice cream? See: more serious. But also more fun.

As always, each cake was designed to pair with a frozen concoction. Yes, we worked on flavor matches, inherent balance, and textural contrasts. But in the end, one thing became clear: a good cake's crumb demands extra richness. So there are many more frozen custards in this section than ice creams or gelati.

OUR BEST TIP: DIP THE FLOUR, THEN LEVEL IT

Volume measurements still rule the day in U.S. recipes. Given that stricture, every baker should reveal his or her method for measuring flour since the weight can vary wildly with the method. Here's ours: dip the measuring cup into the flour, overfill it without compacting it against the side of the bag or the canister, lift the measuring cup up, and level it off with a flatware knife, letting the excess fall back into the bag or canister.

THREE MORE TIPS FOR SUCCESS

Now that we've gotten the flour out of the way, here are a few more things to keep in mind.

1 · IF ASKED, GREASE AND FLOUR THE INSIDE OF THE WHOLE PAN. Yes, the inside. Sigh. We once got a letter—not an e-mail, a letter—from someone who said he didn't understand how you could hold onto the baking pan with butter all over it. So in a bid for specificity: the inside of the pan.

And all of it. Although you don't want to leave chunks of butter or shortening in the crooks or corners, make sure you give the thing a thin, even coating, right up to the rim. Cut off a small chunk of butter and grab it with a little wax paper—or dip wax paper into shortening to pick up a few dabs. Use the paper to protect your fingers as you coat the pan evenly and thoroughly.

If required, add a fairly generous amount of flour to the pan—say, 2 tablespoons. Tilt the pan this way and that to coat it, then tap out the excess flour. You'll see if you missed any spots. Grease (and then flour) them again.

2 · UNLESS OTHERWISE INSTRUCTED, DON'T LEAVE CAKES IN THEIR PANS FOR VERY LONG. Yes, sheet cakes almost always stay in their sheet pans: the cakes are too large and too thin to get out without breaking. But others should some out of the pan after only a few minutes of cooling on the wire rack. That pan is hot enough to continue to bake the cake. Plus, some cakes fuse to the pan as they cool.

3 · IF IN DOUBT, CHANGE OUT PANTRY STAPLES. Cinnamon loses its punch after about a year if stored in a dark, cool place. (It'll go dull much faster if it stands in a clear jar on the countertop.) Nutmeg? Even more quickly. Baking soda lasts about 1 year at its best quality; baking powder only about 6 months if you live in a humid place.

To test if baking soda still works, mix ½ cup hot tap water and ¼ teaspoon distilled white or apple cider vinegar in a small bowl; stir in ¼ teaspoon baking soda and look for fizzing. To test if baking powder still works, do the same but omit the vinegar and look for the fizzing.

HIGH-ALTITUDE CONCERNS

Your kitchen's distance from sea level will affect your success. If you live more than 5,000 feet above sea level, reduce the oven's temperature by 25°F (or by 15°F for chocolate cakes). Increase the liquid and the flour in the recipe by 1 tablespoon per cup—and then by ½ tablespoon for every 1,000 feet over 5,000 feet. In like measure, decrease the sugar (or other sweeteners like maple syrup) by 1 tablespoon per cup. Also cut any leavening in half—or more at even higher altitudes. And decrease the baking time by about 10 percent (or by more at higher altitudes).

These are ridiculously general guidelines. For more information, check out the online charts and graphs for baking at the Colorado State University Extension Resource Center.

ORANGE SPONGE CAKE

— ⬦ —

CHOCOLATE FROZEN YOGURT

Orange and chocolate make a great match! That prized glint from the citrus is a little duller than, say, that from lemons, so it doesn't ride up over the earthy undertones in chocolate. Oranges also contain a subtle vanilla tone that complements dark chocolate's slight bitterness. However, we have one caveat: those flavor accents and overtones dull quickly. This cake and yogurt are truly best the day you make them. Wait to fill the cake until you're ready to serve it so the crème fraîche mixture doesn't turn the crumb soggy.

ORANGE SPONGE CAKE
· YIELD: ONE 10-INCH ROUND TUBE CAKE ·

— ⬦ —

Let's start with a basic sponge cake, sort of like an angel-food cake but with egg yolks (as well as whites) for a denser texture. We use orange juice concentrate here, not fresh juice, to offer a bit more punch, given the fairly assertive flavors of the frozen yogurt to come. The filling is runny; we didn't want to thicken it. We wanted a rich "sauce" right inside the cake.

FOR THE CAKE

Unsalted butter, for greasing

Flour, to prep pan

6 large eggs, separated and at room temperature

1/4 teaspoon salt

1/2 teaspoon cream of tartar

I cup granulated white sugar

2 tablespoons finely minced orange zest (from about 2 medium oranges)

I tablespoon frozen orange juice concentrate, thawed

I cup cake flour

FOR THE FILLING

3/4 cup crème fraîche

1/3 cup orange marmalade

Confectioners' sugar, for garnishing

OVEN RACK · center | **OVEN TEMPERATURE** · **350°F**
PREP · Butter and flour the inside of a 10-inch angel-food cake or tube pan.

TO START THE CAKE

1 · Use an electric mixer at low speed to beat the egg whites and salt in a large bowl until foamy. Add the cream of tartar and continue beating first at medium speed, then at high speed until the mixture forms soft, droopy peaks when the turned-off beaters are dipped into it.

2 · Clean and dry the beaters. Beat the egg yolks and granulated white sugar at medium speed in a second large bowl until pale yellow, thick, wide ribbons slide off the turned-off beaters, about 5 minutes. Beat in the zest and concentrate; scrape down and remove the beaters.

3 · Using a rubber spatula, fold the flour into the egg yolk mixture just until there are no pockets of undissolved flour in the mix. Add half the beaten egg whites and fold gently but efficiently until fairly uniform. Add the remaining egg whites; fold slowly and more gently just until combined but with some streaks of egg white remaining in the batter. Pour and spread the batter into the prepared pan.

TO BAKE THE CAKE

4 · Bake until a toothpick or cake tester inserted into the cake comes out clean, about 35 minutes. Cool the cake in its pan on a wire rack for 5 minutes; then invert it, remove the pan, and turn the

cake top side up on the rack. Continue cooling to room temperature, about 1½ hours. If desired, store tightly covered at room temperature for 2 days before filling.

TO FILL THE CAKE

5 · Use a long serrated knife to split the cake horizontally into two even sections. Carefully remove the top half and set it aside. Mix the crème fraîche and marmalade in a small bowl until smooth. Spread it on the cut portion of the cake—the crème fraîche mixture will run. Set the top back on the cake. Dust the cake with confectioners' sugar before slicing into wedges—or dust the individual wedges with confectioners' sugar on the serving plates.

PRO TIP · Beating egg whites can be a chore. Use a deep bowl with a rounded bottom. A copper bowl is the pastry chef's choice, although not necessary; avoid aluminum or wooden bowls. Make sure the whites are, indeed, at room temperature—or very close to it. And stop beating when you get them fluffy and "peak-able." They can appear to dry out a bit and then maddeningly reliquefy with further beating.

CHOCOLATE FROZEN YOGURT
· YIELD: 1 SCANT QUART ·

What's with these new-fangled frozen yogurt shops? The stuff they sell doesn't taste like yogurt. Where's the zip, the tang, the creamy smoothness? We want that characteristic yogurt flavor in every bite, even with lots of chocolate. Use a high-quality yogurt—but do not use Greek (or strained) yogurt: its moisture content will be too low to make a successful frozen dessert.

1 cup heavy cream

¼ cup unsweetened cocoa powder, preferably natural-style cocoa powder

3 ounces chopped semisweet chocolate (or semisweet chocolate chips), melted and cooled

2 cups plain, full-fat yogurt

¾ cup granulated white sugar

1 teaspoon pure vanilla extract

⅛ teaspoon salt

TO BEGIN THE FROZEN YOGURT

1 · Whisk the cream, cocoa powder, and chocolate in a medium saucepan set over medium-low heat until the chocolate has melted and the mixture is warm and smooth. Do not simmer.

2 · Put the yogurt, sugar, vanilla extract, and salt in a blender. Pour and scrape every drop of the chocolate mixture into the canister. Cover but remove the center knob from the lid. Cover the lid with a clean kitchen towel, then blend until smooth, scraping down the inside of the canister at least once. Set the knob back in the lid and refrigerate covered for at least 4 hours or up to 2 days.

TO FREEZE IT

3 · Prepare an ice-cream machine. Blend the chocolate mixture one more time and freeze it in the machine according to the manufacturer's instructions, until the frozen yogurt can mound on a spoon without the edges immediately melting. Store in a sealed container in the freezer for up to 1 month.

À LA MODE IT · Slice the cake into wedges (the filling will run). Either set the scoops next to the slices or push the top layer partly askew in the servings and set the scoops on (and to the side of) the exposed filling.

PRO TIP · When it comes to chopping chocolate for melting, the best tool is a chocolate chipping fork, available at specialty kitchenware stores.

PINE NUT POUND CAKE

—◆—

ORANGE MARMALADE FROZEN CUSTARD

Here, we took an American dessert—pound cake and ice cream—and morphed the flavors with those of the southern Mediterranean to give the combo a chic twist with bitter and savory notes, thanks mostly to the orange marmalade and pine nuts. Because the ice cream is sweet, toast the pine nuts until they've browned a bit, giving them spiky flavors to further balance the pairing.

PINE NUT POUND CAKE

· YIELD: ONE 9-INCH LOAF CAKE ·

—◆—

Yes, pound cake is all about the butter. But we've included a little sour cream to balance the earthy sweetness of the pine nuts. We also opt for a more traditional version of pound cake without any leavening. You'll end up with a dense loaf—which you can then slice and fry in butter.

½ cup pine nuts

16 tablespoons (2 sticks) cool unsalted butter, cut into small bits, plus additional for greasing

1¼ cups granulated white sugar

5 large eggs, at room temperature

¼ cup regular or low-fat sour cream

1½ teaspoons pure vanilla extract

½ teaspoon salt

1¾ cups all-purpose flour

OVEN RACK · center | OVEN TEMPERATURE · 325°F
PREP · Butter the inside of a 9 x 5-inch loaf pan.

TO MAKE THE BATTER

1 · Toast the pine nuts by placing them in a dry skillet over low heat, stirring occasionally, until fragrant and lightly browned, about 5 minutes. Pour into a bowl, cool for at least 20 minutes, and then chop into smaller bits.

2 · Beat the butter and sugar in a large bowl with an electric mixer at medium speed until fluffy and light, about 5 minutes, occasionally scraping down the inside of the bowl. Beat in the eggs one at a time, adding the next only after the previous one has been incorporated. Beat in the sour cream, vanilla extract, and salt.

3 · Turn off the beaters; add the flour and toasted pine nuts. Beat at a very low speed until there are no dry pockets of flour, until you have a fairly stiff batter. (You may need to use a rubber spatula to fold the last few turns.) Scrape down and remove the beaters. Pour and spread the batter into the prepared loaf pan.

TO FINISH UP

4 · Bake until a toothpick or cake tester inserted into the center of the cake comes out clean, about 1 hour 20 minutes. If the cake begins to brown too deeply, cover it loosely with aluminum foil for the remainder of the baking time. Cool the cake in its pan on a wire rack for 10 minutes; then turn it out of the pan, right it on the rack, and cool to room temperature, about 1 hour. Store tightly covered at room temperature for 2 days or in the freezer for up to 2 months.

PRO TIP · You can barely overbeat this batter. Keep beating in step 2 until you truly have a light, airy consistency. Even in step 3 when you add the flour, don't get carried away but don't worry about beating the flour into the batter. The more air, the better.

ORANGE MARMALADE FROZEN CUSTARD

— ◆ —

The addition of the extra sugar in the marmalade causes this frozen custard to be quite soft, even after it's been stored in the freezer. Yes, it has an irresistible texture but it's also prone to developing ice crystals during storage, given its softer set. You just need to eat it up! Choose a marmalade that has chunks of fruit in the mix. Bitter orange marmalade is often made from Seville oranges, which have a particularly bright and sophisticated flavor, more complex than standard orange marmalade. However, if you buy a high-end version with thin orange slices stacked in the jar, you'll need to chop these into smaller bits.

1¾ cups heavy cream

¾ cup whole milk

4 large egg yolks, at room temperature

3 tablespoons granulated white sugar

I cup orange marmalade, preferably bitter orange marmalade

I½ tablespoons cornstarch

TO MAKE THE CUSTARD

1 · Heat the cream and milk in a large saucepan set over medium heat until puffs of steam rise off its surface. Meanwhile, beat the egg yolks and sugar in a large bowl with an electric mixer at medium speed until thick and pale yellow, about 4 minutes, occasionally scraping down the inside of the bowl. Beat in the marmalade and cornstarch.

2 · Beat about half the hot cream mixture into the egg yolk mixture in a slow, steady stream until smooth; then beat this combined mixture into the remaining cream mixture in the pan. Set over low heat and cook, stirring constantly, until the custard thickly coats the back of a wooden spoon and the temperature registers 170°F, 4 to 7 minutes.

3 · Pour the mixture into a bowl and refrigerate for at least 4 hours or up to 2 days, covering once the custard is cold.

TO FREEZE IT

4 · Prepare an ice-cream machine. Stir the cold custard once more and freeze it in the machine according to the manufacturer's instructions, until you can spoon up a mound without edges that instantly melt. Store in a sealed container in the freezer for up to 1 month.

À LA MODE IT · Melt some unsalted butter in a skillet over medium heat, then add several pound cake slices. Fry until lightly browned on both sides. Transfer to plates and top with scoops of the frozen custard.

SPICED CRANBERRY KEFIR BUNDT WITH LEMON BUTTERMILK GLAZE

EGGNOG ICE CREAM

Don't wait for the winter holidays to try this: a cake stocked with warm spices and loads of cranberries, a vehicle for a boozy ice cream. Kefir is a cultured, yogurtlike drink, prized for its sourness. Look for it in the dairy case of large supermarkets. It will keep the cake grounded, not too airy the way buttermilk might, and so a better match to the smooth and assertive ice cream.

SPICED CRANBERRY KEFIR BUNDT WITH LEMON BUTTERMILK GLAZE

· YIELD: ONE 10-INCH ROUND BUNDT CAKE ·

We wanted just enough cake batter to hold all those berries in place. The cake itself is fairly sweet, given how tart those cranberries are. If you don't want to buy buttermilk just for the glaze, whisk ½ tablespoon plain kefir and ½ tablespoon milk in a small bowl until smooth, then use this as a substitute. The resulting glaze will be a bit murkier (and tarter).

FOR THE CAKE

2½ cups all-purpose flour

2 teaspoons baking powder

I teaspoon ground cinnamon

¾ teaspoon salt

¼ teaspoon ground cardamom

¼ teaspoon freshly grated nutmeg

⅛ teaspoon ground cloves

¾ cup plus I tablespoon granulated white sugar

½ cup plus I tablespoon packed dark brown sugar

13 tablespoons (I stick plus 5 tablespoons) cool unsalted butter, cut into small bits

3 large eggs, at room temperature

2 teaspoons fresh lemon juice

1½ teaspoons finely grated lemon zest

¾ cup plain, regular kefir

4 cups fresh or frozen cranberries (about 14 ounces)

FOR THE GLAZE

Up to I cup confectioners' sugar

I tablespoon regular buttermilk

2 teaspoons fresh lemon juice

¼ teaspoon pure vanilla extract

OVEN RACK · center | OVEN TEMPERATURE · 350°F
PREP · Butter and flour the inside of a 10-inch Bundt pan.

TO START THE CAKE

1 · Whisk the flour, baking powder, cinnamon, salt, cardamom, nutmeg, and cloves in a medium bowl until uniform. Set aside.

2 · Beat the granulated white sugar, brown sugar, and butter in a large bowl with an electric mixer at medium speed until fluffy, light, and thick, about 6 minutes, occasionally scraping down the inside of the bowl. Beat in the eggs one at a time, making sure the previous one is thoroughly incorporated before adding the next.

3 · Beat in the lemon juice and zest, then beat in about ½ cup of kefir until smooth. Beat in half the flour mixture at low speed until incorporated. Beat in the remaining ¼ cup kefir until smooth. Scrape down and remove the beaters. Fold in the cranberries and the remaining flour mixture just until there are no dry specks of flour in the batter. Pour and scrape the batter into the prepared pan.

TO BAKE IT

4 · Bake until a toothpick inserted into the center of the cake comes out clean, about 1 hour 10 minutes. Cool the cake in its baking pan on a wire rack for 10 minutes, then invert it onto the rack and remove the pan. Set the cake top side up. Cool to room temperature before glazing, about 2 hours.

TO MAKE THE GLAZE

5 · Whisk ¾ cup of the confectioners' sugar, the buttermilk, lemon juice, and vanilla extract in a small bowl. Continue adding more confectioners' sugar in 1-tablespoon increments until you have a smooth, thin glaze. Drizzle off the tines of a fork all over the cake. Store tightly wrapped at room temperature for 2 days. Or wrap the cool, unglazed cake in plastic wrap and store in the freezer for up to 2 months; thaw before glazing.

PRO TIP · Cranberries are seasonal. You can sometimes find them in the freezer section during the warm months. The best bet is to snatch up packages in the fall, then store them right in the bags in your own freezer. Thaw them on the countertop for 10 or 15 minutes before adding them to the batter.

EGGNOG ICE CREAM
· YIELD: A LITTLE MORE THAN 1 QUART ·

This one's really a custard with whipped cream folded into it. For that reason, it's not exactly a frozen custard in the traditional sense of the word. We've punted and called it an "ice cream" for simplicity's sake. That whipped cream will give the frozen dessert a lighter, airier consistency, a great textural contrast to the dense cake. The brandy and dark rum are folded in at the last minute so their flavors do not mellow but remain rather present, even a tad stark, about as they are in good eggnog.

1¾ cups whole milk

6 large egg yolks, at room temperature

⅓ cup granulated white sugar

1½ tablespoons cornstarch

½ teaspoon freshly grated nutmeg

¼ teaspoon ground cloves

2 tablespoons brandy

2 tablespoons dark rum, such as Myers's

1¼ cups heavy cream

TO START THE ICE CREAM

1 · Heat the milk in a medium saucepan set over medium-low heat until puffs of steam come off its surface. Meanwhile, beat the egg yolks and sugar in a large bowl with an electric mixer at medium speed until pale yellow and quite thick, about 4 minutes. Beat in the cornstarch, nutmeg, and cloves.

2 · Beat about half the hot milk into the egg yolk mixture in a thin, steady stream until smooth; then beat this combined mixture into the remaining milk mixture in the pan. Set over low heat and cook, stirring constantly, until the custard thickly coats the back of a wooden spoon and the temperature registers 170°F, 4 to 7 minutes.

3 · Strain the mixture through a fine-mesh sieve into a bowl; refrigerate for at least 4 hours or up to 2 days.

TO FINISH UP

4 · Stir the brandy and rum into the milk mixture. Beat the cold cream in a large, chilled bowl with an electric mixer at high speed until the whipped cream can be spooned into very soft mounds; do not overbeat. Fold the mixture into the custard.

5 · Prepare an ice-cream machine. Stir the milk mixture, then freeze the custard in it according to the manufacturer's instructions, until the ice cream can be mounded on a spoon with the edges immediately melting. Store in a sealed container in the freezer for up to 1 week.

À LA MODE IT · Slice the cake into wedges and serve with the ice cream on the side. Or skip the glaze on the cake and drizzle the glaze over both the cake slices and the ice cream when serving.

CHOCOLATE NUT CAKE

—✦—

VIETNAMESE COFFEE FROZEN CUSTARD

Our initial concept for this pairing was an Old World, Viennese pastry shop. Imagine a slice of nut cake, a cup of coffee, and a long afternoon with little to do. We then tweaked the scene, morphing the coffee frozen custard into a rendition of southeast Asian coffee. Its cinnamon and extra sweetness unexpectedly seemed to lift the nut cake's flavors, to bring them more in line with a sunny afternoon.

CHOCOLATE NUT CAKE

· YIELD: ONE 9-INCH ROUND CAKE ·

—·✦·—

Don't underbake this cake. If you do, it will collapse in the center as it cools (since those nuts are heavy). And don't poke it to test its doneness—it will deflate (since it's made from a meringue). Instead, tap the pan at the sides. There should be no jiggle whatsoever and the top should be slightly rounded at the center.

I cup walnut pieces

I cup pecan pieces

1/2 cup sliced or slivered almonds

6 large eggs, separated, plus 6 large egg whites,
    all at room temperature

1/2 teaspoon salt

I cup granulated white sugar

1/2 cup packed dark brown sugar

I teaspoon ground cinnamon

1/4 cup toasted walnut oil

1/3 cup unsweetened natural-style cocoa powder

3 tablespoons all-purpose flour

Confectioners' sugar, for garnishing

OVEN RACK · center | OVEN TEMPERATURE · 325°F
PREP · Butter and flour the inside of a 9-inch
springform baking pan.

TO MAKE THE BATTER

1 · Spread the nuts on a large, rimmed baking sheet. Toast in the oven until lightly browned, stirring often, about 7 minutes. Transfer to a wire rack; cool for 15 minutes. Pour into a food processor and grind to the consistency of sand.

2 · Beat the 12 egg whites and the salt in a large bowl with an electric mixer at low speed until foamy; then beat at medium speed for less than a minute; and finally beat at high speed until they make soft, droopy, peaks when you dip the turned-off beaters into them, 5 to 7 minutes in all.

3 · Clean and dry the beaters. Beat the egg yolks, granulated white sugar, brown sugar, and cinnamon in a second large bowl until smooth and creamy, about 3 minutes. Scrape down the inside of the bowl and beat in the oil until smooth. Turn off the beaters; add the cocoa powder and flour. Beat at low speed just until incorporated. Add half the beaten egg whites and beat at low speed just until the mixture loosens up a bit. Scrape down and remove the beaters.

4 · Add the ground nuts and use a rubber spatula to fold them into the stiff batter. Add the remaining beaten egg whites and fold gently and smoothly just until they are even throughout the batter; there will be some white streaks. Pour and spread it into the prepared pan.

TO FINISH UP

5 · Bake until the cake is puffed and set, with no jiggling at its center, about 50 minutes. Cool in its pan on a wire rack for 15 minutes, then unlatch the sides and remove the pan's collar. Cool for at least 1 hour or to room temperature, about 1½ hours. Dust with confectioners' sugar

before serving. Store tightly covered at room temperature for up to 2 days or in the freezer for up to 2 months.

PRO TIP · If you want to transfer the cake from the pan's bottom to a serving platter, run a long, thin knife, like a fileting knife, under the cake, loosening it from the pan. Now with the courage of your convictions, tilt the cake and pan over the platter and slide the cake onto it.

VIETNAMESE COFFEE FROZEN CUSTARD

· YIELD: 1 SCANT QUART ·

Coffee across southeastern Asia is given sugary heft with sweetened condensed milk; in Vietnam, there's often a touch of cinnamon. We've crafted this frozen custard to mimic those flavors but beware: the final result is very soft. It won't even be firm after sitting in the freezer. Consider this a frozen sauce for the cake with just a slight firmness in the texture.

2 cups heavy cream

½ cup dark-roasted coffee beans, preferably low-acid beans

One 2-inch cinnamon stick

½ teaspoon salt

One 14-ounce can sweetened condensed milk (do not use low-fat or fat-free)

4 large egg yolks, at room temperature

TO MAKE THE CUSTARD

1 · Heat the cream, coffee beans, cinnamon stick, and salt in a large saucepan set over medium heat until bubbles fizz around the pan's inner perimeter. Cover and set aside off the heat to steep for 30 minutes.

2 · Strain the mixture through a fine-mesh sieve into a bowl (discard the coffee beans and cinnamon stick). Stir in the sweetened condensed milk and return the mixture to the saucepan. Set it over low heat and warm the mixture until puffs of steam come off its surface. Meanwhile, beat the egg yolks in a large bowl with an electric mixer at medium speed until creamy and smooth, about 1 minute.

3 · Beat in about half the hot cream mixture in a slow, steady stream until smooth; then beat this combined mixture into the remaining cream mixture in the pan. Set the pan over low heat and cook, stirring constantly, until the custard thickly coats the back of a wooden spoon and the temperature registers 170°F, 4 to 7 minutes.

4 · Strain the mixture through a fine-mesh sieve into a bowl. Refrigerate for at least 4 hours or up to 2 days, covering the bowl once the custard is cold.

TO FREEZE IT

5 · Prepare an ice-cream machine. Stir the cold custard one more time and freeze it in the machine according to the manufacturer's instructions, until you can spoon up a mound of the ice cream without its edges immediately melting. Store in a sealed container in the freezer for up to 1 month.

À LA MODE IT · Because the frozen custard is so soft, make sure the cake is at room temperature before you slice it.

PRO TIP · The cream needs to be hot enough to begin to release the coffee beans' oils and infuse their flavors. It should definitely begin to bubble at its edges before you remove it from the heat.

LEMON POLENTA BUNDT

◆

POPPY SEED FROZEN CUSTARD

Remember the '80s? The shoulder pads? The big hair? And lemon poppy seed everything? Some trends need a revival. (Others, not so much.) Problem was, poppy seeds seemed little more than coloring back then, a few sprinkled in the mix, turning anything lemon spotted. That's hardly a way to taste the earthy muskiness of poppy seeds! We wanted to highlight that sophisticated flavor, so we crafted this ice cream to have loads of them, now a true and formidable match to the sour spark of the lemons in the cake.

LEMON POLENTA BUNDT
· YIELD: ONE 10-INCH ROUND BUNDT CAKE ·

◆

This cake has a dense texture, sort of like a pound cake. There's no leavening in the mix. We didn't want anything to get in the way of the slightly grainy texture and sweet corn flavor the polenta brings to the cake. Polenta comes in various grinds. The standard variety sold in North America is generally coarser than will work in this batter. Even a moderately ground polenta will keep the batter from coming together. Check the package to determine the grind—or grind standard polenta in a food processor until the consistency of very fine sand.

1¾ cups all-purpose flour

1 cup finely ground polenta

2 teaspoons baking powder

1½ teaspoons baking soda

½ teaspoon salt

16 tablespoons (2 sticks) cool unsalted butter, cut into small bits, plus more for greasing

1¼ cups granulated white sugar

4 large eggs, at room temperature

1 tablespoon finely grated lemon zest

¾ cup plain, full-fat yogurt (do not use Greek yogurt)

Up to ½ cup fresh lemon juice

2 cups confectioners' sugar

OVEN RACK · center | OVEN TEMPERATURE · 350°F
PREP · Butter and flour the inside of a 10-inch Bundt pan.

TO MAKE THE BATTER

1 · Whisk the flour, polenta, baking powder, baking soda, and salt in a medium bowl until uniform. Set aside.

2 · Use an electric mixer at medium speed to beat the butter and sugar in a large bowl until creamy and thick, about 5 minutes, occasionally scraping down the inside of the bowl. Beat in the eggs one at a time, adding the next only after the previous one has been thoroughly incorporated.

3 · Scrape down the inside of the bowl, then beat in the lemon zest. Beat in the yogurt and ¼ cup of lemon juice until smooth. Scrape down and remove the beaters. Add the flour mixture and fold with a rubber spatula until thoroughly moistened (but no more!). Pour and spread the batter into the prepared pan.

TO FINISH UP

4 · Bake until a toothpick or cake tester inserted into the center of the cake comes out clean, about 45 minutes. Cool the cake in its pan on a wire rack for 10 minutes, then invert it onto the rack and remove the pan. Continue cooling to room temperature, about 1½ hours.

5 · When you're ready to serve the cake, stir the confectioners' sugar and 2 tablespoons of the

remaining lemon juice in a small bowl. Stir in more lemon juice in 1-teaspoon increments until you have a thick, smooth glaze that will almost hold its shape (but not quite). Drizzle off a spoon or the tines of a fork all over the cake before slicing and serving. Store tightly sealed at room temperature for up to 2 days.

PRO TIP · When glazing the cake, line your work surface with paper towels and set the rack with the cake on top. Now drizzle away! Any drips that miss the cake will fall onto the paper towels for easier cleanup. (Yes, you'll still have to wash the rack).

POPPY SEED FROZEN CUSTARD
· YIELD: ABOUT 1 QUART ·

Crushing the poppy seeds releases more of their inherent savoriness—and even gives the ice cream a slightly blue-gray tint. If you want even more flavor and color, crush them more finely. Poppy seeds are high in fat, so they go rancid quickly. Take a whiff of yours to make sure they carry no acrid bite. Store any sealed jars in the freezer to preserve the seeds' freshness. We stir the vanilla into the ice cream at the last minute so it's never cooked or even warmed and thus retains more of its characteristic flavor to balance all those poppy seeds.

2¼ cups heavy cream

1 cup whole milk

2 tablespoons lightly crushed poppy seeds

4 large egg yolks, at room temperature

⅔ cup granulated white sugar

¼ teaspoon salt

½ teaspoon pure vanilla extract

TO MAKE THE CUSTARD

1 · Heat the cream, milk, and poppy seeds in a large saucepan set over medium heat until bubbles fizz around the inner perimeter. Meanwhile, use an electric mixer at medium speed to beat the egg yolks, sugar, and salt in a large bowl until pale yellow and thick, until wide ribbons slide off the turned-off beaters, about 4 minutes.

2 · Beat about half the hot cream mixture into the egg yolk mixture in a slow, steady stream until smooth; then beat this combined mixture into the remaining cream mixture in the pan. Set over low heat and cook, stirring constantly, until the custard coats the back of a wooden spoon and the temperature registers 170°F, 4 to 7 minutes.

3 · Pour into a bowl and refrigerate for at least 4 hours or up to 1 day, covering the bowl once the custard is cold.

TO FREEZE IT

4 · Prepare an ice-cream machine. Stir the vanilla extract into the custard and freeze it in the machine according to the manufacturer's instructions, until the frozen custard can mound without its edges instantly melting. Store in a sealed container in the freezer for up to 1 week.

À LA MODE IT · Serve slices of the cake with the frozen custard to the side. Either enjoy the cake slightly warm or set the frozen custard on the countertop for 10 minutes to soften it before serving.

PRO TIP · Poppy seeds can go everywhere when you try to crush them under a heavy saucepan. Pour about 1¾ tablespoons in a plastic bag, seal well, and then crush them on your work surface by gently but firmly pressing down on the bag with the bottom of a heavy pot.

CHOCOLATE WHISKEY BUNDT
WITH A GINGER GLAZE

—◆—

GINGERSNAP ICE CREAM

This one's all about the complex rivalry of whiskey and ginger: a bit woody, a bit spicy, very aromatic and satisfying. We actually started making this cake a few years ago with solid vegetable shortening, thinking that its cleaner palette let the whiskey and ginger shine through. Then we tried butter. With the chocolate, it softens the basic pairing of the dessert.

CHOCOLATE WHISKEY BUNDT
WITH A GINGER GLAZE

· YIELD: ONE 10-INCH ROUND CAKE ·

—◆—

Make sure you butter and flour that Bundt pan in every nook and cranny so the tender cake doesn't stick and tear. Look for ginger marmalade or jam that includes lots of bits of ginger. When you make the glaze, those will look like sparkling jewels on the cake. Glaze the cake on a rimmed serving plate; the glaze will run down the sides and onto the plate. The cake will also absorb some of the sticky glaze.

FOR THE CAKE

3 tablespoons unsweetened natural-style cocoa powder

I cup boiling water

I cup whiskey

2 cups all-purpose flour, plus additional for dusting

I teaspoon baking soda

1/4 teaspoon salt

16 tablespoons (2 sticks) unsalted butter, cut into small bits, plus additional for greasing

2 cups granulated white sugar

3 large eggs

5 ounces unsweetened chocolate, chopped, melted, and cooled

I tablespoon pure vanilla extract

FOR THE GLAZE

2/3 cup packed light brown sugar

1/3 cup water

1/3 cup ginger jam or ginger marmalade

OVEN RACK · center | OVEN TEMPERATURE · 325°F
PREP · Butter and flour the inside of a 10-inch Bundt pan.

TO START THE CAKE

1 · Stir the cocoa, boiling water, and whiskey in a large bowl until smooth. Set aside for 30 minutes to cool. Meanwhile, whisk the flour, baking soda, and salt in a medium bowl until uniform. Set aside as well.

2 · Beat the butter and white sugar in a large bowl with an electric mixer at medium speed until pale yellow and quite fluffy, about 5 minutes. Don't stint. The combo should be light and airy. Beat in the eggs one at a time, occasionally scraping down the inside of the bowl and making sure the previous egg is incorporated before adding the next. Beat in the melted chocolate and vanilla extract until smooth.

3 · Beat in about half the cocoa mixture until smooth, then beat in half the flour mixture at low speed until uniform. Beat in the remaining cocoa mixture, then scrape down the inside of the bowl. Scrape down and remove the beaters. Add the remaining flour mixture and stir just until there are no dry specks of flour remaining in the batter. Pour and spread the batter evenly into the prepared pan.

TO FINISH UP

4 · Bake until a cake tester or toothpick inserted into the center of the cake comes out with a

few moist crumbs attached, about 1 hour. Cool the cake in its pan on a wire rack for 5 minutes, then turn it out onto the rack and remove the pan. Cool for at least 10 minutes but no more than 30 minutes before transferring to a rimmed serving platter.

5 · While the cake is warm, mix the brown sugar, water, and jam or marmalade in a small saucepan set over medium heat; bring to a simmer, stirring occasionally. Boil for 2 minutes, then pour this hot syrup over the still-warm cake. Cool for at least 30 minutes or to room temperature, about 1½ hours, before slicing into wedges to serve. Store tightly sealed at room temperature for up to 2 days.

PRO TIP · The butter in the Bundt pan can leave small discolored patches on the chocolate cake. Shave these off with a sharp paring knife for better aesthetics.

GINGERSNAP ICE CREAM
· YIELD: ABOUT 1 QUART ·

Use crunchy, buttery, boxed gingersnap cookies rather than the cakey ones often sold in the bakery section of your supermarket. These crisp ones will better hold their consistency in the ice cream. For a bigger flavor, layer this ice cream with bottled chocolate sauce in a loaf pan (make three full layers, starting and ending with ice cream—that is, four layers of ice cream and three much thinner layers of chocolate sauce.) Cover and freeze for at least 4 hours before scooping up into balls with ribbons of chocolate in them.

1½ cups heavy cream

1 cup whole milk

2 tablespoons minced peeled fresh ginger

3 large eggs, at room temperature

¾ cup granulated white sugar

½ teaspoon pure vanilla extract

⅔ cup crushed gingersnap cookies

TO START THE ICE CREAM

1 · Mix the cream, milk, and ginger in a medium saucepan and set over medium heat until puffs of steam rise off its surface. Cover and set aside off the heat to steep for 30 minutes.

2 · Strain the mixture through a fine-mesh sieve into a bowl. Discard the solids and return the cream mixture to the saucepan. Set it over medium-low heat and warm until small bubbles fizz around its inside perimeter.

3 · Meanwhile, beat the eggs and sugar in a large bowl with an electric mixer at medium speed until thick and pale yellow, until wide ribbons slide off the turned-off beaters, about 4 minutes.

4 · Beat half the hot milk mixture into the egg mixture in a thin, steady stream until smooth; then beat this combined mixture into the remaining milk mixture into the pan. Stir in the vanilla extract. Set the pan over low heat and cook, stirring constantly, until the mixture thickly coats the back of a wooden spoon and the temperature registers 170°F, 4 to 7 minutes.

5 · Pour the mixture into a bowl and refrigerate for at least 4 hours or up to 12 hours, covering once the custard is cold.

TO FREEZE IT

6 · Prepare an ice-cream machine. Stir the cold milk mixture again and freeze it in the machine according to the manufacturer's instructions, until the ice cream can be mounded on a spoon but is still a tad soft.

7 · Add the gingersnap cookies and let the dasher stir them into the cold custard for the final turns, until a spoonful of the ice cream doesn't immediately melt at the edges. Store in a sealed container in the freezer for up to 1 month.

À LA MODE IT · To go all out, layer slices of the cake with ice-cream scoops and whipped cream in a trifle bowl.

PRO TIP · While there's plenty of preminced ginger at supermarkets, the best flavor will come from grating your own.

APPLE-TOFFEE UPSIDE-DOWN CAKE

—— ◈ ——

BOURBON-RAISIN FROZEN CUSTARD

This pairing hearkens to the style of American bistros: big flavors, nothing too subtle, an updated version of comfort fare. We nixed the pineapple in the standard upside-down cake so we could develop deeper, more complex caramelized notes, the better to pair with a frozen custard spiked with bourbon. You're going to need something to drink. You've got the bourbon open. You know what to do.

APPLE-TOFFEE UPSIDE-DOWN CAKE
· YIELD: ONE 9-INCH ROUND CAKE ·
—— ◈ ——

Here's a cross between an upside-down cake and a tart Tatin, that classic pastry with loads of buttery apples. Work with tongs and a heat-safe rubber spatula to get the apple slices in place in the hot toffee. These will begin to melt into the cake as it cooks, a little softer than the standard pineapple rings in the '50s version of this dessert.

14½ tablespoons (I stick plus 6½ tablespoons) cool unsalted butter, plus additional for greasing

6 tablespoons packed dark brown sugar

3 tablespoons honey

2 medium firm, moderately sweet baking apples, such as Honeycrisps, peeled, halved, cored, and thinly sliced

1½ cups all-purpose flour

½ teaspoon baking powder

½ teaspoon baking soda

½ teaspoon salt

I cup plus I tablespoon granulated white sugar

2 large eggs plus I large egg yolk, at room temperature

½ cup buttermilk

2½ teaspoons pure vanilla extract

**OVEN RACK · center | OVEN TEMPERATURE · 350°F
PREP ·** Butter the inside of a 9-inch round cake pan with 2-inch sides.

TO PREPARE THE APPLES

1 · Melt 6 tablespoons of the butter in a large skillet set over medium-low heat. Add the brown sugar, stir well, and cook until bubbling, about 1 minute. Remove from the heat and stir in the honey until smooth. Pour the mixture into the bottom of the prepared pan. Using tongs and a heat-safe rubber spatula, arrange the apple slices in a decorative pattern like overlapping, concentric circles in this (very hot!) toffee. Set aside.

TO MAKE THE BATTER

2 · Whisk the flour, baking powder, baking soda, and salt in a medium bowl until uniform. Set aside.

3 · Use an electric mixer at medium speed to beat the remaining 8½ tablespoons butter and the white sugar in a large bowl until creamy and light, almost fluffy, about 5 minutes, occasionally scraping down the inside of the bowl. Beat in the eggs, one at a time, then beat in the egg yolk. Add the buttermilk and vanilla extract; beat until smooth. Stop the beaters, add the flour mixture, and beat at low speed just until no dry bits of flour remain in the batter. Pour, scrape, and smooth the batter over the apples in the pan.

TO FINISH UP

4 · Bake until a toothpick or cake tester inserted into the center of the cake without going through to the bottom comes out clean, about 45 minutes. Transfer to a wire rack and cool for just 5 minutes. Set a platter over the cake, invert the whole thing, and remove the (hot!) pan,

letting the (hot!) toffee run down the sides. Cool a bit but serve warm if possible. The cake can be stored at room temperature for a few hours.

PRO TIP · Some apple slices may get stuck in the pan or jostled out of your pattern when the cake is unmolded. No problem: pick them up with tongs (again, they're hot) and put them in place, nudging them this way and that.

BOURBON-RAISIN FROZEN CUSTARD
· YIELD: ABOUT 1 QUART ·

Bourbon twists the classic frozen dessert into something that better pairs with that toffee-laced cake. Bourbon also has those woody, oaky notes that match so well with apples. Soaking the raisins in the bourbon softens them and drops their freezing point so they stay somewhat chewy in the frozen dessert, rather than icy bits.

³/₄ cup raisins

³/₄ cup bourbon, plus a little more if needed

1³/₄ cups heavy cream

1 cup whole milk

2 large eggs plus 2 large egg yolks, at room temperature

²/₃ cup granulated white sugar

1¹/₂ tablespoons cornstarch

¹/₈ teaspoon salt

TO MAKE THE CUSTARD

1 · Mix the raisins and bourbon in a small bowl, cover, and soak at room temperature for at least 8 hours or up to 12 hours.

2 · Strain the raisins in a fine-mesh sieve, catching the bourbon in a bowl below. Measure the amount of bourbon; add more to make it come to 3 tablespoons. Reserve the raisins.

3 · Mix this bourbon with the cream and milk in a large saucepan. Set over medium heat until puffs of steam rise off its surface. Meanwhile, beat the eggs, egg yolks, sugar, and salt with an electric mixer at medium speed until very thick and pale yellow, until wide ribbons slide off the turned-off beaters, about 4 minutes.

4 · Beat about half the hot cream mixture into the egg yolk mixture in a thin, steady stream until smooth; then beat this combined mixture into the remaining cream mixture in the pan. Beat in the cornstarch until smooth. Set over low heat and cook, stirring constantly, until the mixture thickly coats the back of a wooden spoon and the temperature registers 170°F, 4 to 7 minutes.

5 · Pour the mixture through a fine-mesh sieve into a bowl. Refrigerate for at least 4 hours or up to 1 day, covering once the custard is cold.

TO FREEZE IT

6 · Prepare an ice-cream machine. Stir the cold custard and freeze it in the machine according to the manufacturer's instructions, until you can spoon up the ice cream into a mound.

7 · Add the raisins and let the dasher stir them into the frozen custard for the final few turns, just until evenly distributed. Store in a sealed container in the freezer for up to 2 weeks.

À LA MODE IT! · Since the cake will still be warm, make sure the frozen custard is very cold.

PRO TIP · Cheap bourbon can give the frozen custard a distinctly unpleasant bite, almost metallic.

CINNAMON ROLL CAKE

—◆—

MAPLE FROZEN CUSTARD

One day we asked ourselves what would happen if we packed a bunch of cinnamon rolls in a pan and baked them together like a cake, not side by side, but all scrunched on top of each other. It didn't work. But it sounded good. So we kept at it until we left the dough in a single log. We let the dough rise and had yeasty cinnamon rolls turned into a cake. It just needed maple frozen custard. Make sure you save some back. You need breakfast, don't you?

CINNAMON ROLL CAKE
· YIELD: ONE 8-INCH ROUND CAKE ·

— · ◆ · —

This dough is not like that for a coffee cake, nor like that for bread. It's fairly stiff and not at all sticky. We've kept the cake dense, rather than light and airy like the traditional morning pastry. The tube of dough will not fill the pan, but will rise up in a big bubble along one side of the pan. We serve it plain, with no glaze or icing, because it's waiting for that frozen custard.

FOR THE CAKE

3/4 cup warmed milk, between 100°F and 110°F

3 tablespoons granulated white sugar

One .25-ounce package active dry yeast

1 teaspoon salt

3 tablespoons unsalted butter, melted and cooled, plus additional for greasing

1 large egg, lightly beaten in a small bowl, at room temperature

2 3/4 cups all-purpose flour, plus additional for dusting

FOR THE FILLING

3 tablespoons unsalted butter, softened to room temperature

1/4 cup granulated white sugar

1 1/2 tablespoons ground cinnamon

Confectioners' sugar, for garnishing

TO START THE CAKE

1 · Stir the warmed milk, white sugar, yeast, and salt in a large bowl. Set aside to proof until foamy, about 5 minutes. Stir in the melted butter and egg, then stir in the flour to form a soft, pliable, smooth dough.

2 · Dust a clean, dry work surface with flour, gather the dough into a ball, and set it on top. Knead for 10 minutes, until smooth, a little glossy, and quite soft. Lightly butter the inside of a bowl; set the dough in it. Turn the dough over to coat it in butter, cover, and set aside in a warm, draft-free place until doubled in bulk, about 1 hour.

OVEN RACK · center | OVEN TEMPERATURE · 350°F
PREP · Butter the inside of an 8-inch round layer cake pan.

3 · Clean and dry your work surface. (Dust it with flour only if the dough sticks—the less flour, the better.) Turn the dough out onto it and form it into a cohesive mass. Use a rolling pin to roll the dough into a 11 x 15-inch rectangle.

TO FILL IT

4 · Spread the butter evenly over the rectangle of dough. Mix the white sugar and cinnamon in a small bowl; sprinkle evenly over the dough. Starting at one of the long sides, roll the dough into a tube. Wind the tube of dough into a coil and transfer it to the prepared pan. It will not fill the pan; set it off-center, keeping the dough's seam against the side of the pan. Cover loosely with plastic wrap and set aside in a warm,

draft-free place until the dough rises enough to almost fill the pan, about 45 minutes.

TO FINISH UP

5 · Uncover and bake until browned, until the cake sounds hollow when thumped, about 35 minutes. Transfer to a wire rack, then immediately turn the cake out of the pan. Right it on the rack and cool to room temperature, about 1½ hours. If desired, set the cake on a serving platter. Put the confectioners' sugar in a fine-mesh sieve and sift it over the cake. Store sealed in plastic wrap (without the confectioners' sugar) at room temperature for up to 1 day or in the freezer for up to 3 months.

PRO TIP · Keeping the dough tube's seam against the baking pan will ensure that the tube stays closed as the dough rises.

MAPLE FROZEN CUSTARD
· YIELD: ABOUT 1 QUART ·

If you love maple syrup, you've come to the right place. Make sure you use a full-flavored syrup: the darker, the better. Don't think about light amber syrup—or so-called "pancake syrup." You want the most floral, aromatic flavor in this treat.

1½ cups whole milk

1 cup heavy cream

½ teaspoon pure vanilla extract

½ teaspoon salt

5 large egg yolks, at room temperature

1 cup maple syrup, preferably dark amber or Grade B or 2

1½ tablespoons cornstarch

TO MAKE THE CUSTARD

1 · Heat the milk, cream, vanilla extract, and salt in a large saucepan set over medium heat until little puffs of steam rise off its surface. Meanwhile, use an electric mixer at medium speed to beat the egg yolks, maple syrup, and cornstarch in a large bowl until thick and pale yellow, about 4 minutes.

2 · Beat about half the hot cream mixture into the egg yolk mixture in a slow, steady stream until smooth; then beat this combined mixture into the remaining cream mixture in the pan. Set the pan over low heat and cook, stirring constantly, until the custard thickly coats the back of a wooden spoon and the temperature registers 170°F, 4 to 7 minutes.

3 · Strain the mixture through a fine-mesh sieve into a bowl. Refrigerate for at least 4 hours or up to 2 days, covering once the custard is cold.

TO FREEZE IT

4 · Prepare an ice-cream machine. Stir the cold custard and freeze it in the machine according to the manufacturer's instructions, until you can spoon up the frozen custard into a little mound with edges that do not immediately melt. Store in a sealed container in the freezer for up to 1 month.

À LA MODE IT! · If you're interested in even more flavor, drizzle a little maple syrup, bourbon, or even chocolate syrup over servings of the cake and frozen custard.

PRO TIP · Beating egg yolks and maple syrup will not produce thick, wide ribbons the way egg yolks and sugar will, Instead, watch for a definite thickening, a sticky and dense mixture.

CHOCOLATE SHEET CAKE WITH FUDGY ICING

—◆—

SALT CARAMEL FROZEN CUSTARD

Sheet cakes are a Texas tradition, a favorite at potlucks and family reunions, card games and church socials. We suspect the whole attraction to these things is that you get as much icing as cake in every bite. You'll need an 11 x 17-inch sheet pan, preferably a nonstick one. You'll also make more cake than a quart of frozen custard will match. So make a double batch. Or make two flavors.

CHOCOLATE SHEET CAKE WITH FUDGY ICING

· YIELD: ONE 11 X 17-INCH SHEET CAKE ·

—◆—

Here's a dense cake with a rich icing. Listen, something needs to stand up to the salt caramel. The cake is actually a fairly thin layer once baked, almost like a giant, fudgy brownie. To ice it, use an offset spatula; a long, narrow, metal spatula with a step-down ledge in the blade.

FOR THE CAKE

1 cup whole or low-fat milk

2/3 cup sifted unsweetened natural-style cocoa powder

2 cups plus 2 tablespoons all-purpose flour, plus more for dusting

1 teaspoon baking soda

1/2 teaspoon salt

12 tablespoons (1 1/2 sticks) cool unsalted butter, cut into small chunks, plus more for greasing

1 cup granulated white sugar

3/4 cup packed dark brown sugar

3 large eggs, at room temperature

1/2 cup regular sour cream

2 teaspoons pure vanilla extract

FOR THE ICING

6 tablespoons heavy cream

6 tablespoons (3/4 stick) unsalted butter, cut into small bits

1 pound finely chopped dark chocolate, preferably 70% cocoa solids

1 cup regular sour cream

At least 1 1/2 cups confectioners' sugar, plus more as needed

OVEN RACK · center | OVEN TEMPERATURE · 350°F
PREP · Butter and flour the inside of an 11 x 17-inch sheet pan.

TO START THE CAKE

1 · Pour the milk into a medium saucepan and set over medium heat until puffs of steam rise off its surface. Add the cocoa and whisk until dissolved. Set aside off the heat for at least 15 minutes or up to 30 minutes. Meanwhile, whisk the flour, baking soda, and salt in a medium bowl. Set aside.

2 · Using an electric mixer at medium speed, beat the butter and both sugars in a large bowl until velvety and thick, about 5 minutes. Beat in the eggs, one at a time, scraping down the inside of the bowl occasionally and only adding the next egg after the first has been fully incorporated. Beat in the sour cream and vanilla extract until smooth. Pour in the cocoa mixture and beat at low speed until smooth.

3 · Finally, add the flour mixture and beat at low speed just until the flour has been fully moistened, with no dry pockets anywhere. Pour, scrape, and smooth the batter evenly into the prepared baking sheet.

TO FINISH UP

4 · Bake until a toothpick inserted into the center of the cake comes out clean, about 25 minutes. Cool the cake in its baking sheet on a wire rack to room temperature, about 1½ hours.

TO ICE IT

5 · Warm the cream and butter in a medium saucepan set over medium heat until the butter has melted. Put the chocolate in a large bowl and pour the hot cream mixture on top. Stir until the chocolate has melted and the mixture is smooth.

6 · Stir in the sour cream, then stir in 1½ cups confectioners' sugar to make a soft, silky icing, adding more confectioners' sugar in 1-tablespoon increments until the icing is spreadable and holds its shape on a spoon. Set aside to cool for a few minutes, then spread evenly over the sheet cake. Set aside for at least 30 minutes before slicing into squares to serve. Store covered loosely with plastic wrap at room temperature for up to 1 day.

PRO TIP · It seems fussy to sift cocoa powder but it's necessary to get rid of the little lumps caused as the powder picks up ambient humidity. In this case, you need to measure the cocoa powder after sifting.

SALT CARAMEL FROZEN CUSTARD
· YIELD: ABOUT 1 QUART ·

—— · ◈ · ——

Sea salt will add a mineral complexity to this frozen custard, a complex flavor that table salt lacks. If you have fine sea salt (rather than coarse), use only 1 teaspoon. The salt will also keep the frozen custard pretty soft.

1⅓ cups whole milk

2 tablespoons unsalted butter, cut into little bits

1 cup granulated white sugar

1⅔ cups heavy cream

2 teaspoons coarse sea salt

1 teaspoon pure vanilla extract

5 large egg yolks, at room temperature

TO MAKE THE CUSTARD

1 · Warm the milk and butter in a large saucepan set over low heat until the butter has melted and puffs of steam rise off the surface. Keep warm without raising the mixture's temperature.

2 · Pour the sugar into a medium skillet and set it over medium heat. Cook, stirring a bit at first and then fewer and fewer times, until the sugar has melted and turned golden amber, about 5 minutes. Turn the heat off under the milk. Working steadily and carefully, whisk this caramel into the hot milk mixture in a slow, steady stream. Be careful: the milk will roil up dramatically.

3 · Set this combined mixture over medium heat and whisk until the sugar remelts and smooths out. Stir in the cream, salt, and vanilla extract. Set aside on a second burner turned to very low heat to keep warm without simmering.

4 · Use an electric mixer at medium speed to beat the egg yolks in a large bowl until very smooth and a bit paler in color, about 2 minutes. Beat about half the hot milk mixture into the egg yolks in a slow, steady stream until smooth; then beat this combined mixture into the remaining milk mixture in the saucepan. Set over low heat and cook, stirring constantly, until the mixture thickly coats the back of a wooden spoon and the temperature registers 170°F, 4 to 7 minutes.

5 · Strain the mixture through a fine-mesh sieve into a bowl; refrigerate for at least 4 hours or up to 1 day, covering the custard once it's cold.

TO FREEZE IT

6 · Prepare an ice cream machine. Stir the cold custard and freeze it in the machine according to the manufacturer's instructions, until the frozen custard can mound on a spoon without instantly melting at the edges. Store in a sealed container in the freezer for only a few days. (It will become saltier as it sits.)

À LA MODE IT · Since the frozen custard is so soft, you'll want to serve it to the side of the cake, rather than on top of it.

CARROT SHEET CAKE WITH SOUR CREAM AND CREAM CHEESE ICING

— ❖ —

HORCHATA ICE CREAM

Ever tried to eat rice pudding with carrot cake? Neither have we! And it admittedly doesn't sound too appetizing. But surprise, these two desserts work together! A moist cake with lots of warm spices is set next to an almond-scented, rice-flavored ice cream. The slightly sour icing on the cake actually balances the two.

CARROT SHEET CAKE WITH SOUR CREAM AND CREAM CHEESE ICING

· YIELD: ONE 11 X 17-INCH SHEET CAKE ·

— · ❖ · —

This sheet cake is thicker than the last one, a cakey base for the icing. Look for shredded carrots in the produce section—or even on the salad bar at your supermarket. If you choose, you can use low-fat sour cream and cream cheese in the icing, but then you'll probably have to add more confectioners' sugar to get the stuff to the right consistency. And with more confectioners' sugar, you've mitigated any calorie savings. So why bother?

FOR THE CAKE

2½ cups all-purpose flour, plus additional for dusting

1½ teaspoons baking powder

1½ teaspoons ground cinnamon

½ teaspoon baking soda

½ teaspoon freshly grated nutmeg

½ teaspoon salt

8 tablespoons (1 stick) cool unsalted butter, cut into small chunks, plus more for greasing

¾ cup granulated white sugar

¾ cup packed dark brown sugar

½ cup canola or vegetable oil

5 large eggs, at room temperature

3 cups grated carrots (about 5 medium carrots)

2 tablespoons finely grated orange zest (about 2 medium oranges)

FOR THE ICING

12 tablespoons (1½ sticks) unsalted butter, cut into small bits, at room temperature

12 ounces regular cream cheese, at room temperature

¾ cup packed light brown sugar

¾ cup regular sour cream, at room temperature

1 tablespoon pure vanilla extract

8 to 10 cups confectioners' sugar

OVEN RACK · center | OVEN TEMPERATURE · 350°F
PREP · Butter and flour the inside of an 11 x 17-inch sheet pan.

TO START THE CAKE

1 · Whisk the flour, baking powder, cinnamon, baking soda, nutmeg, and salt in a large bowl until uniform. Set aside.

2 · Use an electric mixer at medium speed (preferably a stand mixer) to beat the butter, the white and brown sugars, and the oil in a large bowl until creamy, light, and even fluffy, about 5 minutes. Scrape down the inside of the bowl at least once.

3 · Beat in the eggs one at a time, scraping down the inside of the bowl and adding the next egg only after the previous one has been incorporated. Beat in the carrots and orange zest until uniform. Turn off, scrape down, and remove the beaters. Fold in the flour mixture in even, wide strokes with a rubber spatula until there's no dry flour remaining in the batter. Pour, scrape, and spread the batter into the prepared pan.

TO FINISH UP

4 · Bake until a toothpick or cake tester inserted into the center comes out with a few moist crumbs attached, about 28 minutes. Cool the cake in its baking sheet on a wire rack until room temperature, about 1½ hours.

TO ICE IT

5 · Use an electric mixer at medium speed to beat the butter, cream cheese, and brown sugar in a large bowl until creamy and smooth, about 4 minutes. Scrape down the inside of the bowl, then beat in the sour cream and vanilla extract until smooth. Add 6 cups of the confectioners' sugar and beat at low speed until incorporated. Continue adding confectioners' sugar in ½-cup increments until you have a smooth icing that will hold its shape on a spoon. Spoon and spread the icing over the cake. Store loosely covered with plastic wrap in the refrigerator for up 2 days.

PRO TIP · The icing's consistency is a matter of humidity, temperature, and even the age of the ingredients. There's no real way to tell how much confectioners' sugar you'll use. Once you've got 8 cups in the bowl, add it by smaller and smaller amounts as you try to get the right consistency.

HORCHATA ICE CREAM
· YIELD: ABOUT 1 QUART ·

—·◆·—

Horchata is the name for a whole set of thickened beverages made across Latin America and in Spain. Ours is a mix of rice and nut syrup (instead of the usual ground nuts). You'll end up with something like "almondy" rice pudding. As the ice-cream mixture chills in the fridge, it will thicken quite a bit as the rice absorbs more and more liquid. Stir it with a fork to loosen it up before you scrape it into the ice-cream machine.

2 cups whole milk

¼ cup orgeat (almond-flavored syrup)

¼ cup long-grain white rice, such as basmati rice

2 large eggs, at room temperature

6 tablespoons granulated white sugar

¼ teaspoon salt

¼ teaspoon ground cinnamon

1 cup heavy cream

TO START THE ICE CREAM

1 · Stir the milk, orgeat, and rice in a medium saucepan set over medium heat; bring to a simmer. Cover, reduce the heat to low, and simmer slowly until the rice is well beyond tender, even mushy, about 35 minutes.

2 · Put the eggs, sugar, salt, and cinnamon in a blender. Cover but remove the center knob from the lid. With the machine running, pour in the hot rice mixture in a slow steady stream. Blend until smooth, scraping down the inside of the canister at least once. Add the cream and blend until smooth. Return the knob to the lid and refrigerate for at least 4 hours or up to 2 days.

TO FREEZE IT

3 · Prepare an ice-cream machine. Blend the contents of the canister one more time, then freeze this mixture in the machine according to the manufacturer's instructions, until the ice cream can mound on a spoon without immediately melting at the edges. Store in a sealed container in the freezer for up to 1 week.

À LA MODE IT · We cut the eggs down in the ice cream to make the almond flavor more present. However, the ice cream can get icy as it sits in the freezer. Set it out on the countertop for at least 10 minutes before serving with squares of the cake.

SPICED BANANA SHEET CAKE WITH CREAM CHEESE BUTTERCREAM

— ✦ —

PINEAPPLE ICE CREAM

Every Southerner knows about hummingbird cake: a banana/coconut/pecan/pineapple wonder with cream cheese frosting. Here's our (deconstructed) take. We start with a cinnamon-laced banana and coconut sheet cake in an 11 x 17-inch sheet pan. We cover that, not with a cream cheese icing, but in fact with a cream cheese buttercream with toasted pecans. And we serve it with pineapple ice cream. Potlucks just got better.

SPICED BANANA SHEET CAKE WITH CREAM CHEESE BUTTERCREAM

· YIELD: ONE 11 X 17-INCH SHEET CAKE ·

— ✦ —

Mind the cake as it bakes. It needs to be fully set at the center but it can be easily overbaked, turning dry at its edges. The butter and cream cheese need to be at room temperature to create a smooth, silky buttercream. If possible, leave them out on the countertop overnight.

FOR THE CAKE

2¼ cups all-purpose flour, plus additional for dusting

1 teaspoon baking soda

1 teaspoon ground cinnamon

¼ teaspoon freshly grated nutmeg, optional

1 teaspoon salt

1½ cups granulated white sugar

¾ cup pecan oil, plus additional for greasing

3 large eggs, at room temperature

4 medium ripe bananas, peeled and cut into chunks

1 cup shredded sweetened coconut

¾ cup chopped pecans

1 teaspoon pure vanilla extract

FOR THE ICING

1 cup whole milk

1 cup granulated white sugar

¼ cup all-purpose flour

½ teaspoon pure vanilla extract

16 tablespoons (2 sticks) unsalted butter, at room temperature

12 ounces regular cream cheese (do not use low-fat or fat-free), at room temperature

1 cup finely chopped pecans

OVEN RACK · center | OVEN TEMPERATURE · 350°F
PREP · Generously oil and flour the inside of an 11 x 17-inch sheet pan.

TO START THE CAKE

1 · Whisk the flour, baking soda, cinnamon, nutmeg (if using), and salt in a medium bowl until uniform. Set aside.

2 · Use an electric mixer at medium speed to beat the sugar and oil in a large bowl until smooth, about 2 minutes. Beat in the eggs one at a time, scraping down the inside of the bowl and adding the next egg only after the previous one has been incorporated. Beat in the bananas (the batter may look "broken" at this point), then beat in the coconut, pecans, and vanilla extract at low speed.

3 · Turn the mixer off, scrape down the bowl, and remove the beaters. Add the flour mixture and fold it in with a rubber spatula just until there are no dry bits of flour remaining in the batter. Pour, scrape, and spread the batter into the prepared sheet pan.

TO FINISH UP

4 · Bake until a toothpick or cake tester inserted into the center of the cake comes out clean, about 23 minutes. Cool the cake in the baking sheet on a wire rack to room temperature, about 1½ hours.

TO ICE IT

5 · Whisk the milk, sugar, flour, and vanilla extract in a medium saucepan set over medium heat until thick and bubbling, about 4 minutes. Set aside off the heat and cool to room temperature, about 1 hour.

6 · Use an electric mixer at medium speed to beat the butter and cream cheese in a large bowl until smooth and light, about 3 minutes, scraping down the inside of the bowl occasionally. Beat in the milk mixture until smooth. Spread the icing evenly over the cooled cake. Sprinkle with pecans. Cool for at least 20 minutes before slicing into squares to serve. Store loosely covered in plastic wrap in the refrigerator for up to 1 day.

PRO TIP · There's really no point in trying to invert a sheet cake and remove it from the baking sheet. Who has a platter that large? These things are most often served right in their sheet pans. Cut with a nonstick-safe knife to avoid nicking the pan's surface.

PINEAPPLE ICE CREAM
· YIELD: ABOUT 1 QUART ·
—— · ◆ · ——

You can't make pineapple ice cream with fresh pineapple. It will curdle the milk. But you can used canned crushed pineapple; the troubling enzymes are rendered ineffective with the heating in the canning process. However, canned crushed pineapple lacks a bit of that characteristic flavor. So we add pineapple jam. It gives the ice cream a ridiculously smooth texture.

1½ cups heavy cream

1 cup whole milk

1½ tablespoons cornstarch

⅔ cup pineapple jam (not preserves)

½ cup drained crushed canned pineapple in syrup

¼ cup turbinado sugar, such as Sugar in the Raw, or light brown sugar

2 large egg yolks, at room temperature

TO START THE ICE CREAM

1 · Warm the cream, milk, and cornstarch in a medium saucepan over medium heat, whisking until thickened and bubbling, about 5 minutes.

2 · Put the jam, pineapple, sugar, and egg yolks in a blender. Cover but remove the center knob from the lid. With the machine running, pour in the hot cream mixture in a thin, steady stream through the hole in the lid. Turn off the machine, scrape down the inside of the canister, and then blend until smooth. Return the knob to the lid and set in the refrigerator for at least 4 hours or up to 12 hours.

TO FREEZE IT

3 · Prepare an ice-cream machine. Blend the contents of the canister one more time, then freeze this mixture in the machine according to the manufacturer's instructions, until the ice cream will mound on a spoon without immediately melting at the edges. Store in a sealed container in the freezer for up to 2 months.

À LA MODE IT · You need good-sized plates for this pair. It's going to get messy.

PRO TIP · The canned crushed pineapple needs to be well-drained. Put it in a fine-mesh sieve or a strainer lined with paper towels and push down on the pineapple bits with the back of a wooden spoon to remove excess liquid. Note that the canned, crushed pineapple is measured after draining, not before. An 8-ounce can should do the trick.

GINGERBREAD SHEET CAKE WITH TOASTED MARSHMALLOW ICING

— ✦ —

PUMPKIN PIE FROZEN CUSTARD

Here's our tribute to Thanksgiving: plenty of warm spices, a moist cake for crowds, and an ice cream that tastes like the classic holiday dessert.

GINGERBREAD SHEET CAKE WITH TOASTED MARSHMALLOW ICING

· YIELD: ONE 9 X 13-INCH SHEET CAKE ·

— ✦ —

This spicy, sweet cake is not a true sheet cake (in the American potluck sense of the word). Instead, it's made in a 9 x 13-inch baking pan. It gets turned out and coated in a meringue that's like melted marshmallows. That meringue is then browned in the oven.

FOR THE CAKE

3 cups plus 2 tablespoons all-purpose flour, plus additional for dusting

I teaspoon baking soda

I teaspoon ground cinnamon

I teaspoon ground dried ginger

1/4 teaspoon ground allspice

1/4 teaspoon ground cloves

1/4 teaspoon salt

12 tablespoons (1 1/2 sticks) unsalted butter, cut into small bits, plus additional for greasing

I cup packed light brown sugar

I cup molasses

3 large eggs, at room temperature

1/4 cup grated peeled fresh ginger

I cup milk, warmed in a small saucepan over low heat

FOR THE ICING

4 large egg whites, at room temperature

I cup granulated white sugar

1/2 teaspoon cream of tartar

1/4 teaspoon salt

1/4 teaspoon marshmallow flavoring or pure vanilla extract

OVEN RACK · center | **OVEN TEMPERATURE** · 350°F
PREP · Butter and flour the inside of a 9 x 13-inch baking pan.

TO START THE CAKE

1 · Whisk the flour, baking soda, cinnamon, dried ginger, allspice, cloves, and salt in a medium bowl until uniform. Set aside.

2 · Use an electric mixer at medium speed to beat the butter and brown sugar in a large bowl until light and fluffy, about 5 minutes. Scrape down the inside of the bowl, then beat in the molasses until smooth. Beat in the eggs one at a time, making sure the previous one is incorporated before adding the next. Beat in the fresh ginger.

3 · Beat in about half the warm milk, then beat in about half the flour mixture at low speed until uniform. Beat in the remaining milk, then remove the beaters and stir in the remaining flour mixture with a rubber spatula until there are no dry bits of flour remaining in the batter. Pour and scrape the batter evenly into the prepared pan.

TO FINISH UP

4 · Bake until puffed and set, until a toothpick or cake tester inserted into the center of the cake comes out clean, about 40 minutes. Cool the cake in its baking sheet on a wire rack until room temperature, about 1 1/2 hours.

TO ICE THE CAKE

5 · Heat the oven to 425°F. Bring about 1 inch of water to a simmer in the bottom half of a double

boiler or a medium saucepan. Reduce the heat to low so the water simmers slowly. Put the egg whites, sugar, cream of tartar, and salt in the top half of the double boiler or a heat-safe bowl. Set over the simmering water and beat with an electric mixer at medium speed until hot and fluffy, until no sugar granules can be felt in the mixture, about 3 minutes.

6 · Remove the top half of the double boiler or the bowl from over the water. Set on the countertop—on a hot pad, if necessary—and add the flavoring or vanilla extract. Beat at medium speed until cool, thick, and shiny, sort of like Marshmallow Fluff, about 7 minutes.

7 · Unmold the cooled cake onto a rimmed baking sheet; remove the baking pan. (The cake is now upside down.) Spread the fluffy icing all over the cake, coating the top and sides evenly. Use a rubber spatula to make wavy peaks in the icing.

8 · Bake until lightly browned, about 8 minutes. Cool on a wire rack for at least 30 minutes or to room temperature, about 1 hour. Store loosely wrapped in plastic wrap in the refrigerator for 1 day. Bring to room temperature before serving.

PRO TIP · The warmed milk helps incorporate the molasses evenly in the batter. However, don't make it too hot or it can scramble the eggs.

PUMPKIN PIE FROZEN CUSTARD

· YIELD: ABOUT 1 QUART ·

Or call it "frozen pumpkin pie." Solid-pack canned pumpkin is just what it sounds like: cooked pumpkin in a can. Do not use overly sweet pumpkin pie filling or savory frozen pumpkin puree.

1¼ cups heavy cream

1 cup regular evaporated milk (do not use low-fat or fat-free)

5 large egg yolks, at room temperature

¾ cup packed dark brown sugar

½ teaspoon ground cinnamon

½ teaspoon ground dried ginger

⅛ teaspoon freshly grated nutmeg

⅛ teaspoon salt

⅔ cup canned solid-pack pure pumpkin, stored in the refrigerator for at least 4 hours before using

½ teaspoon pure vanilla extract

TO MAKE THE CUSTARD

1 · Warm the cream and evaporated milk in a large saucepan set over medium-low heat until little bubbles fizz around the inner perimeter of the pan. Meanwhile, beat the egg yolks, brown sugar, cinnamon, ginger, nutmeg and salt in a large bowl with an electric mixer at medium speed until pale brown and fluffy, about 6 minutes, scraping down the inside of the bowl once.

2 · Beat about half the milk mixture into the egg yolk mixture in a slow, steady stream until smooth; then beat this combined mixture into the remaining milk mixture in the pan. Set over low heat and cook, stirring constantly, until the custard thickly coats the back of a wooden spoon and the temperature registers 170°F, 4 to 7 minutes.

3 · Strain the mixture through a fine-mesh sieve into a bowl; refrigerate for at least 4 hours or up to 2 days.

TO FINISH UP

4 · Whisk the pumpkin puree and vanilla extract into the custard and refrigerate while you prepare an ice-cream machine. Freeze the canned pumpkin mixture in the machine according to the manufacturer's instructions, until the frozen custard can be mounded on a spoon without the edges immediately melting. Store in a sealed container in the freezer for up to 1 month.

À LA MODE IT · Put the frozen custard to the side of it!

PRO TIP · Almost every can of condensed milk has "shake well" embossed on the lid. No joke: milk solids fall out of suspension.

LAYER
CAKES
&
OTHER
CELEBRATIONS

SO WE'VE COME TO THE END—AND TO THE BIG DESSERTS.

These are probably not right for a weeknight . . . although who knows? Maybe you're prone to champagne on Tuesday nights. (In which case, we're jealous.) If so, you're probably the type who'll make even more layer cakes, vacherins, and steamed puddings than we do. (In which case, we're more jealous.)

We start off with five big layer cakes, every one of them a double-decker affair fit for a cake stand. We include both American (uncooked) and French (cooked) buttercreams and even make a bow to that old, Southern favorite, seven-minute frosting. Although most of these desserts can be saved a day or two in the fridge, they'll have suffered from exposure and time. There's really no way to sugarcoat this news: these desserts are best on the day you make them, with just enough time for the frosting to cool to room temperature.

With one exception (a creamy frozen yogurt), most of the accompanying frozen desserts are a bit more, um, ornate, too: modeled on Nutella or on hard sauce, laced with sour cream or Marshmallow Fluff. But by now you've already seen dozens of other recipes for ice creams, gelati, and the like. You could—no, should—mix and match. Think of the pairings like wine and food: match sour and earthy to sweet, savory and nutty to complex with bitter undertones (chocolate, ahem).

We end this section with three specialty desserts: a rich jelly roll/frozen custard combo, some pretty spectacular vacherins (or meringue shells), and a holiday steamed pudding with a frozen "sauce." In fact, those vacherins and their attendant Blackberry Sour Cream Sherbet were the first recipes we tested for this book. It was a warm summer evening. We were having a barbecue dinner with friends on our outdoor dining porch. We finished the meal with this sweet/sour combo just as a luna moth landed on one of the screens. It seemed a good omen for the book. In fact, it's hard to describe how happy it made us to spend a year bringing sixty à la mode pairings to the table. It's a sweet life. We wish the same for you.

CHOCOLATE SOUR CREAM LAYER CAKE WITH MILK CHOCOLATE BUTTERCREAM

MINT CANDY ICE CREAM

Our first layer cake is a doozy: an over-the-top confection with a buttery frosting and a pure, smooth ice cream. We didn't want to go with gelato or frozen custard because the buttercream is, well, buttercream. The ice cream has a cleaner finish, the better to complement the cake.

CHOCOLATE SOUR CREAM LAYER CAKE WITH MILK CHOCOLATE BUTTERCREAM

· YIELD: ONE 2-LAYER, 8-INCH ROUND LAYER CAKE ·

There are various types of buttercream frosting. This cake has an American buttercream—that is, one that's not "cooked" and includes no eggs. Yes, you have to melt the chocolate. But after that, it's just about getting enough butter into it to hold all that chocolate onto the cake. You'll end up with a two-toned layer cake: a dark chocolate cake coated in a milk chocolate frosting.

FOR THE CAKE

3/4 cup whole milk

3 ounces unsweetened chocolate, chopped

1/3 cup regular sour cream (do not use low-fat or fat-free)

1/4 cup unsweetened natural-style cocoa powder

1 1/3 cups cake flour, plus additional for dusting (do not use all-purpose flour)

1 1/2 teaspoons baking soda

1/2 teaspoon salt

8 tablespoons (1 stick) cool unsalted butter, cut into small chunks, plus additional for greasing

1 cup plus 2 tablespoons packed dark brown sugar

2 large eggs plus 1 large egg white, at room temperature

2 teaspoons pure vanilla extract

FOR THE BUTTERCREAM

6 ounces semisweet chocolate, chopped; or semisweet chocolate chips

6 ounces milk chocolate, chopped; or milk chocolate chips

1 cup plus 2 tablespoons confectioners' sugar

9 tablespoons unsweetened natural-style cocoa powder

24 tablespoons (3 sticks) unsalted butter, at room temperature

3 tablespoons heavy cream

1 teaspoon pure vanilla extract

1/4 teaspoon salt

OVEN RACK · center | **OVEN TEMPERATURE** · 350°F
PREP · Butter and flour the inside of two 8-inch round cake pans.

TO MAKE THE CAKE LAYERS

1 · Warm the milk in a small saucepan set over low heat, just until puffs of steam come off its surface. Meanwhile, melt the unsweetened chocolate in the top half of a double boiler set over about an inch of slowly simmering water or in a bowl in the microwave in 15-second bursts on high, stirring after each.

2 · Whisk the melted chocolate into the warmed milk until smooth; continue to whisk for 1 minute. Then whisk in the sour cream and cocoa powder until smooth. Set aside. Whisk the flour, baking soda, and salt in a medium bowl until uniform. Set aside as well.

3 · Use an electric mixer at medium speed to beat the butter and brown sugar in a large bowl until creamy, smooth, and even light, about 5 minutes, occasionally scraping down the inside of the bowl. Beat in the eggs, one at a time, then beat in the egg white and vanilla extract until smooth.

4 · Turn off the beaters, add the chocolate mixture, and beat at low speed until well incorporated. Turn off the beaters again, scrape down the inside of the bowl, add the flour, and beat at very low speed just until there are no dry specks of flour remaining in the batter. Pour and spread the batter into the prepared pans, dividing it equally.

TO BAKE IT

5 · Bake until firm and set, until a cake tester or toothpick inserted into the center of the rounds comes out clean, about 25 minutes. Cool the cakes in their pans on a wire rack for 10 minutes, then turn them out, remove the pans, and cool upside down to room temperature, about 1½ hours.

TO MAKE THE BUTTERCREAM

6 · Melt the semisweet and milk chocolate in the top half of a double boiler set over about 1 inch of slowly simmering water, stirring often; or melt them in a large bowl in a microwave in 15-second bursts on high, stirring after each. If using a double boiler, scrape the melted chocolate into a large bowl. In any event, set aside to cool for 20 minutes.

7 · Use an electric mixer at medium speed to beat the confectioners' sugar into the chocolate until smooth and creamy. Beat in the cocoa until well incorporated. Beat in the butter in 1-tablespoon increments, occasionally scraping down the inside of the bowl, until smooth, glossy, and a bit firm. Beat in the cream, vanilla, and salt until smooth.

TO FROST THE CAKE

8 · Lay rectangles of wax paper on a cake plate or stand to protect it. Set one of the cake layers top side up in the center. Dollop on about 1 cup buttercream and smooth it to the layer's edge, taking care that it doesn't mound at the center. Set the second layer of cake bottom side up (that is, the flatter side up) on top. Scoop up a little of the buttercream with a spatula and fill in at the edges between the two layers of cake.

9 · Dump the remainder of the buttercream on top of the cake. Using an offset spatula, spread the frosting, letting the excess ooze over the edges. Catch this excess and spread it along the side, taking more off the top as necessary. Gently pull out the sheets of wax paper. Store lightly covered in plastic wrap in the refrigerator for up to 2 days. Let the cake come back to room temperature before serving.

PRO TIP · We tend not to flour cake pans for chocolate cakes since the edges get unsightly as the cake bakes. However, since we're frosting this cake, we don't fear the flour! Unsightly edges will be covered up—and the cake layers will slip out of their pans more easily.

MINT CANDY ICE CREAM
· YIELD: ABOUT 1 QUART ·
—— · ◆ · ——

Mint chocolate chip ice cream is so yesterday! Why not fold in small mint candies for a chewy texture and a great hit of flavor. The candies are sticky; use kitchen shears to snip them into small pieces, rather than cutting them with a knife.

2 cups heavy cream

1 cup whole milk

⅔ cup granulated white sugar

1½ tablespoons cornstarch

2 tablespoons green crème de menthe liqueur

2 drops peppermint oil, optional

3 ounces chocolate mint candies, preferably After Eight Mints, chopped

TO START THE ICE CREAM

1 · Put the cream, milk, sugar, and cornstarch in a large saucepan set over medium heat. Cook, whisking often, until the mixture comes to a simmer and thickens, about 5 minutes. Remove the pan from the heat. Whisk in the crème de menthe and peppermint oil, if using. Pour into a bowl and refrigerate for at least 4 hours or up to 2 days, covering once cold.

TO FREEZE IT

2 · Prepare an ice-cream machine. Stir the cream mixture and freeze it in the machine according to the manufacturer's instructions, until the ice cream can be mounded on a spoon. Add the chopped candies and let the machine's dasher stir them into the custard for the final few turns. Store in a sealed container in the freezer for up to 1 month.

À LA MODE IT · You're not going to have enough ice cream for that cake. Make two batches.

ORANGE BUTTERCREAM LAYER CAKE
ORANGE SWIRL GELATO

This one is our go-to birthday cake combo: orange through and through, festive with bright flavors. It needs a little Eiswein on the side. We have been known to leave the swirl out of the gelato. But it's an ill-advised austerity measure.

ORANGE BUTTERCREAM LAYER CAKE
· YIELD: ONE 2-LAYER, 8-INCH ROUND CAKE ·

Here's a French buttercream, a buttery orange confection on layers of orange cake. When you add the sugar syrup to the bowl with the egg yolks, pour it very slowly and aim it between the beaters and the edge of the bowl so the beaters do not scatter the syrup. Stop occasionally and scrape down the inside of the bowl to get the still-hot sugar syrup into the buttercream.

FOR THE CAKE

2 cups cake flour, plus additional for dusting

I cup granulated white sugar

2¹/₂ teaspoons baking powder

¹/₂ teaspoon salt

¹/₂ cup whole milk

4 large egg yolks, at room temperature

I¹/₂ teaspoons pure vanilla extract

9 tablespoons (I stick plus I tablespoon) unsalted butter, melted and cooled, plus additional for greasing

2¹/₂ tablespoons frozen orange juice concentrate, thawed

FOR THE BUTTERCREAM

6 large egg yolks, at room temperature

³/₄ cup granulated white sugar

¹/₂ cup light corn syrup

I pound (4 sticks) unsalted butter, at room temperature

¹/₄ cup orange-flavored liqueur, such as Grand Marnier

I tablespoon finely grated orange zest

OVEN RACK · center | **OVEN TEMPERATURE** · 350°F
PREP · Butter and flour the inside of two 8-inch round cake pans.

TO BEGIN THE CAKE LAYERS

1 · Whisk the flour, sugar, baking powder, and salt in a medium bowl until uniform. Set aside.

2 · Beat the milk, egg yolks, and vanilla extract in a large bowl with an electric mixer at medium speed until smooth and creamy, about 2 minutes. Add the melted butter and continue beating until smooth. Turn off the beaters, add the flour mixture, and beat at low speed until all the flour has been moistened. Add the orange juice concentrate and beat until smooth. Pour and spread the batter into the two prepared pans, dividing it equally.

TO BAKE THEM

3 · Bake until lightly browned, slightly puffed at the center, and set to the touch, until a toothpick or cake tester inserted into the center of the cake comes out clean, 20 to 22 minutes. Cool the cakes in their pans on a wire rack for 10 minutes, then invert and continue cooling upside down on the wire rack until room temperature, about 1¹/₂ hours.

TO MAKE THE BUTTERCREAM

4 · Beat the egg yolks with an electric mixer at medium speed in a large bowl until creamy,

thick, and pale yellow, about 2 minutes. (A stand mixer is the best tool. Use the whisk attachment.) Set aside.

5 · Heat the sugar and corn syrup in a large skillet set over medium heat until boiling, stirring only until the sugar has dissolved. Bring to a boil undisturbed. The moment big bubbles cover the surface of the sugar mixture, pour it in a very slow, steady stream into the egg yolks, beating all the while with the electric mixer at medium speed until smooth. Once all the sugar syrup has been added, scrape down the inside of the bowl and continue beating until room temperature, about 10 minutes.

6 · Beat in the butter at high speed in 2-tablespoon increments until smooth. Continue beating until silky, glossy, and moundable. Beat in the liqueur and zest.

TO FROST THE CAKE

7 · Lay rectangles of wax paper on a cake plate or stand. Set one of the cake layers top side up in the center of the plate or stand. Add about 1 cup buttercream and smooth it to the edge, taking care that it doesn't mound at the center. Set the second layer of cake bottom side up (that is, the flatter side up) on top. Scoop up a little of the buttercream with a spatula and spackle between the two layers of cake.

8 · Dump the remainder of the buttercream on top of the cake. Using an offset spatula, spread the frosting, letting the excess ooze over the edges. Catch this excess and spread it along the sides, taking more off the top as necessary. Gently pull out the sheets of wax paper. Store lightly covered in plastic wrap in the refrigerator for up to 2 days. Let the cake come back to room temperature before serving.

PRO TIP · Lay candied orange slices or even chocolate-covered orange peel (orangettes) around the top of the cake.

ORANGE SWIRL GELATO
· YIELD: ABOUT 1 QUART ·

Low-acid orange juice concentrate yields a gentler orange flavor, the better to match the orange flavor in the cake. The swirl is pure childhood bliss: Marshmallow Fluff or Marshmallow Crème layered into the gelato. Either can be difficult to spread over the soft gelato. Spoon some up, dollop it on top, then use damp, cleaned fingers to spread it out a bit.

1¾ cups whole milk

¼ cup heavy cream

6 large egg yolks, at room temperature

⅔ cup granulated white sugar

1½ tablespoons cornstarch

One 6-ounce can frozen, pulp-free orange juice concentrate, thawed (¾ cup)

⅔ cup jarred Marshmallow Fluff or Marshmallow Crème

TO MAKE THE CUSTARD

1 · Warm the milk and the cream in a large saucepan set over medium-low heat until whiffs of steam come off its surface. Meanwhile, use an electric mixer at medium speed to beat the egg yolks and sugar in a large bowl until pale yellow and very thick, until wide ribbons slide off the turned-off beaters, about 5 minutes. Beat in the cornstarch until smooth.

2 · Beat about half the milk mixture into the egg yolk mixture in a slow, steady stream until smooth, then beat this combined mixture into the remaining milk mixture in the pan. Set over low heat and cook, stirring almost constantly, until the custard can thickly coat the back of a wooden spoon, until its temperature reaches 170°F, 4 to 7 minutes. Remove from the heat and stir in the orange juice concentrate until smooth.

3 · Strain through a fine-mesh sieve into a bowl. Refrigerate for at least 4 hours or up to 1 day, covering once the custard is cold.

TO FREEZE IT

4 · Prepare an ice-cream machine. Stir the custard and freeze it in the machine according to the manufacturer's instructions, until you can scoop up a mound with edges that do not instantly start melting.

5 · Layer about a third of the custard into a loaf pan, spread half the Marshmallow Fluff or Marshmallow Crème on top, then top with half

the remaining gelato, the rest of the Fluff or Crème, and the rest of the gelato. Fold one time with a rubber spatula to make thick ribbons. Smooth the top of the gelato before serving or storing. Store in a sealed container in the freezer for up to 1 week.

À LA MODE IT · The gelato is soft, even when set in the freezer for a long while. Store it in the freezer in between a first serving and seconds so it doesn't melt too much.

CHOCOLATE SOUR CHERRY LAYER CAKE
VANILLA FROZEN YOGURT

Not all layer cakes have to be extravaganzas. Here's our deconstruction of black forest cake: a chocolate layer with cherry jam in between, served with a fairly simple frozen yogurt. The chocolate curls on top will gussy the dessert up a bit, masking its essential simplicity.

CHOCOLATE SOUR CHERRY LAYER CAKE
· YIELD: ONE 2-LAYER, 8-INCH ROUND CAKE ·

You want a rustic look on this layer cake without frosting. The layers are a bit denser than in our previous layer cakes, sort of like a cross between a quick bread and a genoise. The jam should ooze out. However, if you miss the frosting, beat 1½ cups cold heavy cream with 3 tablespoons confectioners' sugar and ¼ teaspoon pure vanilla extract in a large cold bowl with an electric mixer at high speed until firm but not hard peaks form. Spread this whipped cream on the sides of the cake just before serving.

- 2 cups boiling water
- ¾ cup unsweetened natural-style cocoa powder
- 4 ounces semisweet chocolate, chopped; or semisweet chocolate chips
- 2¼ cups all-purpose flour
- 1½ teaspoons baking powder
- ½ teaspoon salt
- 16 tablespoons (2 sticks) cool unsalted butted, cut into small bits, plus additional for greasing

- 1 cup granulated white sugar
- ½ cup packed dark brown sugar
- 4 large eggs, at room temperature
- 1 tablespoon pure vanilla extract
- 1½ cups sour cherry jam
- One 1½- to 2-ounce dark chocolate block, preferably 70% to 80% cocoa solids

OVEN RACK · center | OVEN TEMPERATURE · 350°F
PREP · Generously butter the inside of two 8-inch round cake pans.

TO MAKE THE CAKE LAYERS

1 · Whisk the boiling water, cocoa, and chocolate in a medium bowl until smooth. Set aside at room temperature to cool for 15 minutes. Meanwhile, whisk the flour, baking powder, and salt in a second medium bowl until uniform. Set aside as well.

2 · Use an electric mixer at medium speed to beat the butter and the white and brown sugars in a large bowl until light and fluffy, about 6 minutes, occasionally scraping down the inside of the bowl. Beat in the eggs one at a time, making sure the previous one has been fully incorporated before adding the next.

3 · Beat in the chocolate mixture and the vanilla extract. Stop the beaters, add the flour mixture, and beat at low speed just until there are no dry specks of flour remaining in the batter. Pour and spread the batter into the prepared pans, dividing it equally.

TO BAKE THEM

4 · Bake until a bit puffed but definitely firm to the touch, until a toothpick or cake tester inserted into the center of one of the cakes comes out with a few moist crumbs attached, about 28 minutes. Cool the cakes in their pans on a wire rack for a few minutes; then turn them out, remove the pans, and invert the cakes to cool them to room temperature on the rack, about 1½ hours.

TO FINISH UP

5 · Set one layer top side up on a cake stand or serving plate. Spread 1 cup jam over the cake layer. Add the second layer bottom side up (that is, the flat side up). Spread the remaining ½ cup jam over the top.

6 · Just before serving, make chocolate curls by running a cheese plane or vegetable peeler over the chocolate with a bit of pressure, peeling off long thin strips that curl up at their edges. Sprinkle on top of the cake. Store at room temperature, uncovered, for up to 6 hours or loosely covered in the refrigerator for up to 1 day.

PRO TIP · Since the layers are not frosted, they may have some butter residue from the greased pans. You can cut off or even flick away discolored bits with a small knife.

VANILLA FROZEN YOGURT
· YIELD: 1 SCANT QUART ·

Here's a very simple frozen treat. We add heavy cream and corn syrup for the same reason: texture. Pure yogurt churned in the machine can turn grainy, no one's idea of a great frozen dessert.

2¼ cups plain, regular yogurt (do not use Greek yogurt or low-fat yogurt)

½ cup plus 1 tablespoon heavy cream

½ cup plus 1 tablespoon granulated white sugar

3 tablespoons light corn syrup

½ tablespoon pure vanilla extract

TO START THE FROZEN YOGURT

1 · Whisk all the ingredients in a big bowl until the sugar has dissolved. Set in the refrigerator for at least 4 hours or up to 2 days, covering once cold.

TO FREEZE IT

2 · Prepare an ice-cream machine. Whisk the cold yogurt mixture and freeze it in the machine according to the manufacturer's instructions, until the frozen yogurt can mound on a spoon. Store in a sealed container in the freezer for up to 2 months.

À LA MODE IT · For even more flavor, spoon a little warmed cherry preserves over large scoops of the frozen yogurt on the plate.

PRO TIP · Insipid vanilla will do this frozen yogurt no favors.

TOASTED COCONUT LAYER CAKE WITH SEVEN-MINUTE FROSTING

PASSION FRUIT FROZEN CUSTARD

The sour spark of passion fruit cuts through the otherwise rich cake with its marshmallowy frosting. Yes, it's all very tropical. Still, it's not made for a hot day after a workout. It's probably best in the evening when the lights are low and you've settled in.

TOASTED COCONUT LAYER CAKE WITH SEVEN-MINUTE FROSTING

· YIELD: ONE 2-LAYER, 8-INCH ROUND LAYER CAKE ·

Seven-minute frosting is a cooked confection, a riff on Italian meringues and something of a tradition in the South. It's marshmallowy and light, a little sticky on the lips. It makes a great contrast to this dense cake. But one warning: seven-minute frosting can crust if the humidity gods look askance. Get the toasted coconut on the cake while the frosting is still soft and sticky.

FOR THE CAKE

2 cups cake flour, plus additional for dusting

1½ teaspoons baking powder

¼ teaspoon salt

1¼ cups granulated white sugar

8 tablespoons (1 stick) cool unsalted butter, cut into small bits, plus additional for greasing

4 large eggs, at room temperature

¾ cup whole milk

½ teaspoon almond extract

½ cup shredded sweetened coconut

FOR THE FROSTING

2 cups shredded unsweetened coconut

3 large egg whites, at room temperature

2½ cups granulated white sugar

½ cup water

2 teaspoons light corn syrup

¼ teaspoon salt

2 teaspoons pure vanilla extract

OVEN RACK · center | OVEN TEMPERATURE · 350°F
PREP · Butter and flour the inside of two 8-inch round cake pans.

TO START THE CAKE LAYERS

1 · Whisk the flour, baking powder, and salt in a medium bowl. Set aside.

2 · Use an electric mixer at medium speed to beat the sugar and butter in a large bowl until creamy, fluffy, and light, about 5 minutes, occasionally scraping down the inside of the bowl. Beat in the eggs one at a time, adding the next only after the previous has been thoroughly incorporated.

3 · Beat in the milk and almond extract until smooth. Turn off the beaters, add the flour mixture, and beat at low speed just until it's incorporated. Scrape down the inside of the bowl, turning up any dry flour at the bottom; add the coconut and beat at low speed just until uniform. Pour and spread the batter into the two prepared pans, dividing it equally.

TO BAKE THEM

4 · Bake until lightly browned and set to the touch, until a cake tester or a toothpick inserted into the center of the cakes comes out clean, about 30 minutes. Cool the cakes in their pans on a wire rack for 10 minutes; then invert them, remove the pans, and cool upside down to room temperature, about 1½ hours. Maintain the oven temperature.

TO MAKE THE FROSTING

5 · Spread the coconut on a large, rimmed baking sheet and toast in the oven until lightly browned, stirring occasionally, about 10 minutes. Set aside to cool for at least 20 minutes.

6 · Meanwhile, bring about an inch of water to a boil in the bottom half of a double boiler or a similar amount of water in a medium saucepan. Reduce the heat so the water bubbles slowly. Put the egg whites, water, corn syrup, and salt in the top half of the double boiler or a heat-safe bowl that will fit securely over the saucepan. Set over the simmering water and use an electric mixer at medium speed to beat the egg white mixture until thick, moundable, and shiny, almost exactly 7 minutes, scraping down the inside of the pan or bowl almost constantly to keep the mixture from singeing. Remove the top half of the double boiler or the bowl from the heat; beat in the vanilla extract until smooth. Frost the cake at once.

TO FROST THE CAKE

7 · Lay rectangles of wax paper on a cake plate or stand. Set one of the cake layers top side up in the center of the plate or stand. Add about 1 cup frosting and smooth it to the edge, taking care that it doesn't mound at the center. Set the second layer of cake bottom side up (that is, the flatter side up) on top. Scoop up a little of the frosting with a spatula and fill in at the edges between the two layers of cake.

8 · Dump the remainder of the frosting on top of the cake. Using an offset spatula, spread out the frosting, letting the excess ooze over the edges. Catch this excess and spread it along the sides, taking more off the top as necessary. Gently pull out the sheets of wax paper. Cover the frosting with the toasted coconut. Store the cake at room temperature for up to 12 hours.

PRO TIP · As you beat the frosting, its texture will change instantly, right at the 7-minute mark at sea level (or a little before at higher elevations). The frosting becomes shiny and thick, as if it's turned from whipped cream into Marshmallow Fluff. You'll hear the mixer's beaters begin to have difficulty. When you can make peaks with a spoon, peaks that will hold their droop, it's ready.

PASSION FRUIT FROZEN CUSTARD
· YIELD: ABOUT 1 QUART; SEE NOTE BELOW ·

There's nothing quite like the sour, fragrant flare of passion fruit. Of course, the best taste in this tropical frozen custard is had by using fresh ones. However, you can also use ½ cup frozen passion fruit puree, thawed in the refrigerator for at least 24 hours.

6 to 8 large, ripe passion fruit

1²/₃ cups heavy cream

³/₄ cup whole milk

6 large egg yolks, at room temperature

³/₄ cup granulated white sugar

1 tablespoon cornstarch

¹/₄ teaspoon salt

2 teaspoons pure vanilla extract

TO MAKE THE CUSTARD

1 · Set up a fine-mesh sieve over a bowl. Halve the passion fruit over the sieve (to catch any drops of juice), then scrape the pulp into the sieve. Repeat with the remaining fruit. Then use a rubber spatula to wipe the seeds and their pulp against the mesh, letting the juice fall into the bowl below. Use enough passion fruit to get ½ cup of juice. Discard the seeds and set the juice aside.

2 · Heat the cream and milk in a large saucepan set over medium-low heat until whiffs of steam rise off its surface. Meanwhile, beat the egg yolks and sugar in a large bowl with an electric mixer at medium speed until quite thick and pale yellow, until wide ribbons slide off the turned-off beaters, about 4 minutes. Beat in the cornstarch and salt until smooth.

3 · Beat about half the hot cream mixture into the egg yolk mixture in a thin, steady stream until smooth; then beat this combined mixture into the remaining cream mixture in the pan. Set over low heat and cook, stirring constantly, until the custard thickly coats the back of a wooden spoon and the temperature registers 170°F, 4 to 7 minutes.

4 · Strain the mixture through a fine-mesh sieve into a bowl. Stir in the passion fruit juice and vanilla extract. Refrigerate for at least 4 hours or up to 1 day, covering once the custard is cold.

TO FREEZE IT

5 · Prepare an ice cream machine. Stir the custard and freeze it in the machine according to the manufacturer's instructions, until you can spoon up a mound that doesn't instantly melt. Store in a sealed container in the freezer for up to 1 month.

À LA MODE IT · Once again, you may not have enough frozen custard for a big layer cake. Either make two batches or cut bigger pieces of cake!

PRO TIP · Look for withered, shriveled passion fruit with some dark spots on the skin. Ones that are too shriveled have little pulp left. Hold them over the sieve and cut off about 1/2 inch off the top with a pair of kitchen shears, catching any juice below. Scoop the seeds and pulp into the sieve with a serrated spoon.

WALNUT LAYER CAKE
WITH SPICED BUTTERCREAM

— ◆ —

BACIO ICE CREAM

This is probably the richest pairing in the book: lots of nuts, butter, and cream. There's no going back. Imagine a dense layer cake, an egg-rich buttercream with tons of spices, and an ice cream that's almost like a frozen version of Nutella. Or don't imagine it. Just make it.

WALNUT LAYER CAKE WITH SPICED BUTTERCREAM
· YIELD: ONE 2-LAYER, 8-INCH ROUND CAKE ·

— ◆ —

This one's our layer-cake version of a Mexican wedding cookie, a spicy little cookie made from ground nuts and coated in confectioners' sugar. The cake itself is a cross between a génoise (French, *zjen-WAHZ*), a whole-egg sponge cake, and a traditional nut cake. Do not use cake flour. It won't have enough oomph to stand up to the ground nuts. The frosting is a true French buttercream: a cooked frosting with eggs for body and tons of butter. The warm spices cut some of the richness. But only some. Since you're working with a very hot sugar syrup, a stand mixer is your best option for making the frosting.

FOR THE CAKE

1/2 cup all-purpose flour, plus more for dusting

1/4 teaspoon baking soda

1/4 teaspoon salt

4 large eggs, at room temperature

1/4 cup granulated white sugar

I teaspoon pure vanilla extract

I cup finely ground walnuts

8 tablespoons (I stick) unsalted butter, melted and cooled, plus more for greasing

FOR THE BUTTERCREAM

I large egg plus 2 large egg yolks, at room temperature

1/4 teaspoon salt

I cup granulated white sugar

1/4 cup water

I tablespoon light corn syrup

24 tablespoons (3 sticks) unsalted butter, at room temperature

2 teaspoons ground cinnamon

1 1/2 teaspoons pure vanilla extract

1/4 teaspoon freshly grated nutmeg, plus additional for garnishing

1/8 teaspoon ground cloves

OVEN RACK · center | **OVEN TEMPERATURE · 350°F**
PREP · Butter and flour the inside of two 8-inch round cake pans.

TO START THE CAKE LAYERS

1 · Whisk the flour, baking soda, and salt in a medium bowl until uniform. Set aside.

2 · Beat the eggs and sugar in a large bowl with an electric mixer at medium speed until thick and pale yellow, until wide ribbons slide off the turned-off beaters, about 4 minutes. Beat in the vanilla extract until smooth, light, and airy, almost foamy. Scrape down and remove the beaters. Fold in the flour mixture with a rubber spatula, working gently and efficiently so as not to deflate the batter. Then fold in the ground nuts in the same manner.

3 · Add the melted butter and fold in gently until smooth, making sure you get the spatula down to the bottom of the bowl where the butter might collect. Pour and spread the batter into the prepared pans, dividing it equally.

TO BAKE THEM

4 · Bake until lightly browned and set to the touch, until a toothpick or cake tester inserted into the center of one of the cakes comes out clean, about 20 minutes. Cool the cakes in their pans on a wire rack for 5 minutes; then turn them out onto the wire rack, remove the pans, and cool upside down to room temperature, about 1½ hours.

TO MAKE THE BUTTERCREAM

5 · Using clean and dry beaters, beat the egg, egg yolks, and salt in a large bowl until smooth and creamy, about 1 minute. Set aside.

6 · Stir the sugar, water, and corn syrup in a skillet set over medium-high heat until the sugar has dissolved. Bring to a boil, stirring once or twice. Boil, undisturbed, for 3 minutes (or 2 minutes at or above 5,000 feet above sea level).

7 · With the beaters running at medium speed, drizzle the sugar syrup into the beaten egg yolk mixture in a slow, steady stream, scraping down the inside of the bowl repeatedly. Continue beating at medium speed until light and creamy, until the mixture is at room temperature to the touch (see Pro Tip below), about 10 minutes. It must be at room temperature. Scrape down the inside of the bowl several times while beating.

8 · Beat in the butter at high speed in 2-tablespoon increments, occasionally scraping down the inside of the bowl. Continue beating for a couple of minutes until glossy. Beat in the cinnamon, vanilla extract, nutmeg, and cloves until uniform.

TO FROST THE CAKE

9 · Lay rectangles of wax paper on a cake plate or stand to protect it. Set one of the cake layers top side up in the center of the plate or stand. Dollop on about 1 cup buttercream in the center of the layer and smooth it to the edge, taking care that it doesn't mound at the center. Set the second layer of cake bottom side up (that is, the flatter side up) on top. Scoop up a little of the buttercream with a spatula and fill in at the edges between the two layers of cake.

10 · Dump the remainder of the buttercream on top of the cake. Using an offset spatula, spread the frosting, letting the excess ooze over the edges. Catch this excess and spread it along the sides, taking more off the top as necessary. Gently pull out the sheets of wax paper. Dust the top of the cake with grated nutmeg just before slicing. Store lightly covered in plastic wrap in the refrigerator for up to 2 days. Let the cake come back to room temperature before serving.

PRO TIP · To make a successful buttercream, the butter must be at room temperature, not even somewhat chilled. And the mixture in the bowl must have been beaten to room temperature, not a bit above it. To tell, hold the bowl in your palms. It cannot feel warm. Otherwise, the butter will solidify or break and the frosting will never come together.

BACIO ICE CREAM

· YIELD: A LITTLE MORE THAN 1 QUART ·

—— ◈ ——

Bacio (something like *BAHT-cho* in modern Italian) simply means "kiss" and has become a slang substitute for *baci di dama*, a chocolate and hazelnut confection. We use Nutella for the same ends to make a rich ice cream without enough egg yolks to be a true custard but with a silky, smooth finish. You can toast the hazelnuts in the oven, rub off the skins, and chop them up as we do in the Chocolate Chip Hazelnut Scones (see page 136). Or you can buy chopped, skinned hazelnuts and toast them in a dry skillet over medium-low heat until aromatic, about 4 minutes, stirring occasionally. Either way, make sure the nuts are cooled to room temperature.

2 cups heavy cream

1 cup whole milk

3 large egg yolks, at room temperature

1/3 cup granulated white sugar

1/2 cup Nutella or chocolate-hazelnut spread

1/2 teaspoon pure vanilla extract

1/2 cup chopped, toasted, skinned hazelnuts

TO START THE ICE CREAM

1 · Heat the cream and milk in a large saucepan set over medium-low heat until puffs of steam come off its surface. Meanwhile, beat the egg yolks and sugar in a large bowl with an electric mixer at medium speed until thick and pale yellow, until wide ribbons fall off the turned-off beaters, about 3 minutes. Beat in the Nutella and vanilla extract until smooth.

2 · Beat about half the hot cream mixture into the egg yolk mixture in a slow, steady stream until smooth; then beat this combined mixture into the remaining cream mixture until smooth. Set the pan over low heat and cook, stirring constantly, until the mixture thickly coats the back of a wooden spoon and temperature registers 170°F, 4 to 7 minutes.

3 · Strain the mixture through a fine-mesh sieve into a bowl; refrigerate for at least 4 hours or up to 2 days, covering once the mixture is cold.

TO FREEZE IT

4 · Prepare an ice-cream machine. Stir the ice-cream mixture and freeze it in the machine according to the manufacturer's instructions, until it mounds on a flatware spoon.

5 · Add the hazelnuts and let the machine's dasher stir them into the custard until uniform. Store in a sealed container in the freezer for up to 2 weeks.

À LA MODE IT · This is a luscious combo for sure but also pretty messy. Skip the white napkins. And maybe even the tablecloth.

ESPRESSO CREAM JELLY ROLL

MASCARPONE FROZEN CUSTARD

Here's our tiramisu fantasy: a light génoise, sort of like a cakey version of savoiardi (or ladyfinger cookies), rolled with a coffee-flavored filling and served with a frozen custard that includes lots of mascarpone. Tiramisu is supposed to be a "pick-me-up" in the afternoons. Save our combo for the evenings.

ESPRESSO CREAM JELLY ROLL

· YIELD: ONE 11-INCH-LONG FILLED JELLY ROLL ·

A jelly roll is a sheet cake that has been rolled up in a towel while warm, cooled into that tubelike shape, unwrapped, filled, and then rolled back up. We don't use a standard-size jelly roll pan here but rather the more standard sheet pan we've been using for sheet cakes and such in this book. You must let the espresso filling bubble in the pan. If you don't, the filling won't set but will instead be too liquid and ooze out of the roll. And don't stint when you dust the kitchen towel with the confectioners' sugar so the cake doesn't stick to that towel.

FOR THE CREAM FILLING

Unsalted butter, for greasing

2 cups whole milk (do not use low-fat or fat-free)

1 heaping tablespoon instant espresso powder

2/3 cup granulated white sugar

6 large egg yolks, at room temperature

1/2 cup all-purpose flour

FOR THE JELLY ROLL

6 large eggs, separated and at room temperature

1/4 teaspoon salt

1/2 cup granulated white sugar

1 tablespoon pure vanilla extract

2/3 cup all-purpose flour

Confectioners' sugar, for both dusting and garnishing

OVEN RACK · center | OVEN TEMPERATURE · 350°F
PREP · Line a rimmed 11 x 17-inch sheet pan with parchment paper. Butter both the parchment paper and the inside edges of the pan.

TO MAKE THE CREAM FILLING

1 · Mix the milk and espresso powder in a large saucepan and warm over medium heat until small bubbles fizz around the pan's inner perimeter.

2 · Meanwhile, beat the granulated white sugar and egg yolks in a large bowl with an electric mixer at medium speed until quite thick and pale yellow, until wide ribbons slide off the turned-off beaters, about 5 minutes. Add the flour and beat at low speed until combined. Then add the warmed milk mixture and beat until smooth.

3 · Pour and scrape this mixture back into the saucepan and set it over medium heat. Cook, stirring frequently (and more and more), until bubbling and thickened, about 4 minutes. Pour into a large bowl; cover with plastic wrap, pressing the wrap directly against the pudding. Refrigerate until cold, at least 6 hours or up to 2 days.

TO MAKE THE JELLY ROLL

4 · Use an electric mixer at high speed to beat the egg whites and salt in a large bowl until the whites can make soft, droopy peaks when the turned-off beaters are dipped into them, about 3 minutes. Set aside.

5 · Clean and dry the beaters. Beat the egg yolks and granulated white sugar in a second large

bowl at medium speed until thick and pale yellow, until wide ribbons slide off the turned-off beaters, about 4 minutes. Beat in the vanilla extract until smooth. Scrape down and remove the beaters. Add the flour; use a rubber spatula to fold it into the mixture, just until there are no dry specks of flour. Add the beaten egg whites and gently but efficiently fold them in, trying to keep as much of their loft as possible. Pour and spread the batter into the prepared pan.

6 · Bake until lightly browned and a bit puffed, until the cake feels firm and set, about 15 minutes. Transfer to a wire rack. Move immediately to the next step.

TO PUT IT ALL TOGETHER

7 · While the cake is still warm, spread a clean kitchen towel that is larger than the cake on your work surface; dust generously with confectioners' sugar. Invert the still hot baking sheet onto the towel; remove the baking sheet but not the parchment paper. Roll up the cake, parchment paper, and towel from the short end to form a log. Set aside to cool to room temperature, at least 45 minutes.

8 · Unroll the cake; remove the parchment paper. Spread the cake evenly with the cream filling. Roll it up from the short side again, this time leaving the towel behind. Transfer to a serving platter and dust with confectioners' sugar for garnish. Store lightly covered with plastic wrap at room temperature for up to 1 day or in the refrigerator for up to 2 days.

PRO TIP · Look for precut 11 x 17-inch parchment sheets that perfectly fit a sheet pan.

MASCARPONE FROZEN CUSTARD
· YIELD: ABOUT 1 QUART ·

We kept the vanilla extract out of this frozen custard. We wanted the mascarpone to have just a hint of honey, a more fragrant note to match the cream in the jelly roll.

1¼ cups whole milk

1 cup heavy cream

4 large egg yolks, at room temperature

6 tablespoons granulated white sugar

6 ounces mascarpone, at room temperature

1½ tablespoons honey

TO MAKE THE CUSTARD

1 · Warm the milk and cream in a large saucepan set over medium-low heat until puffs of steam rise off its surface. Meanwhile, use an electric mixer at medium speed to beat the egg yolks and sugar in a large bowl until very thick and pale yellow, until wide ribbons slide off the turned-off beaters, about 3 minutes.

2 · Beat about half the hot milk mixture into the egg yolk mixture in a slow, steady stream until smooth; then beat this combined mixture into the remaining milk mixture in the pan. Set over low heat and cook, stirring constantly, until the custard thickly coats the back of a wooden spoon and the temperature registers 170°F, 4 to 7 minutes.

3 · Pour the mixture through a fine-mesh sieve into a bowl. Whisk in the mascarpone and honey until smooth. Refrigerate for at least 4 hours or up to 2 days, covering once the custard is cold.

TO FREEZE IT

4 · Prepare an ice-cream machine. Stir the mascarpone mixture and freeze it in the machine according to the manufacturer's instructions, until you can spoon up a small mound with edges that do not instantly start melting. Store in a sealed container in the freezer for up to 2 weeks.

À LA MODE IT · Slice the jelly roll into 2-inch-thick pieces so that you've got enough cake on the plate to balance a big scoop.

PRO TIP · If the mascarpone is not at room temperature, it can leave small chunks in the custard.

WHITE CHOCOLATE VACHERIN

◆

BLACKBERRY SOUR CREAM SHERBET

With the exception of the Baklava Cups, we tried to make sure that the recipes in every pairing could stand on their own. But no one would make those cups or these meringue shells without the sherbet. We actually increased the sugar in these shells so they'd be delicately sweet, a good contrast to the much more sour frozen dessert.

WHITE CHOCOLATE VACHERIN

· YIELD: 6 MERINGUE SHELLS ·

◆

Our meringue shells are individual cups, painted with white chocolate, a little smooth sweetness to contrast the sherbet. A vacherin is notorious for its short shelf life: the meringue goes soft quickly, especially when it comes into contact with other ingredients. We've added a little cornstarch to draw moisture out of the beaten egg whites, helping the cups stay stable for a bit longer.

6 large egg whites, at room temperature

1/4 teaspoon cream of tartar

1/4 teaspoon salt

1 1/2 cups granulated white sugar

1 tablespoon cornstarch

6 ounces white chocolate, chopped, melted, and cooled

Confectioners' sugar for garnish, optional

OVEN RACK · center | OVEN TEMPERATURE · 200°F
PREP · Line an 11 x 17-inch rimmed baking sheet with parchment paper.

TO START THE MERINGUE SHELLS

1 · Beat the egg whites in a large bowl with an electric mixer at low speed until foamy. Add the cream of tartar and salt; continue beating at medium speed, then at high speed until you can form very soft, almost saucy, droopy peaks when you dip in the turned-off beaters into the mixture. Beat in the sugar in 1-tablespoon increments at high speed, then beat in the cornstarch. Continue beating at high speed until you can't feel any sugar graininess when you rub a little bit between your fingertips, about 7 minutes.

2 · Spoon this mixture into a large, 18-inch pastry bag fitted with a #7 plain, round tip (that is, a 7/16- to 9/16-inch tip). Pipe into six 4-inch circles on the prepared baking sheet. Pipe the bottom of each circle with some more of the beaten egg white mixture, then use a rubber spatula to smooth the bottom against the circular edge to create a fairly even, flat surface. Pipe a second ring on top of the outer edge of each circle to create a lip.

TO FINISH UP

3 · Bake the meringue shells until firm, about 90 minutes. Turn off the oven, set the door ajar, and leave the baking sheet in the oven for 30 minutes. The shells should be crunchy-crisp, a bit fragile, and not wet even in small spots.

4 · Transfer to a wire rack to cool for 15 minutes, then gently lift the meringues off the baking sheet with a thin metal spatula. Continue cooling them on the rack to room temperature, about 1 hour.

5 · Using a pastry brush, paint the inside of each shell with the white chocolate, creating an even but fairly thick coating across the interior. The meringue shells can be stored between sheets of wax paper in a sealed container at room temperature for up to 3 days before this step.

PRO TIP · The bigger the pastry bag, the easier the job. Refilling a pastry bag is a pain in the neck! To make even circles, turn the parchment paper over and trace six 4-inch circles with a pencil, using a heavy glass or even a drafting compass as your guide. Then turn the sheet over—the circles will be visible and you can easily outline them and fill them in.

BLACKBERRY SOUR CREAM SHERBET

· YIELD: I SCANT QUART ·

There's a distinct tartness to this sherbet, both from the blackberries and the sour cream. If you don't make the meringue shells, it's probably best as a pairing with the Big Soft Vanilla Bean Sugar Cookies (page 117) or the Cream Scones (page 133). We've added a little simple syrup (rather than gelatin) to smooth out its consistency. By the way, you can skip the whole blender-or-food-processor-and-sieve fandango by running the blackberries through a food mill.

2 cups granulated white sugar

I cup water

I pound fresh blackberries (about 2½ cups)

I¼ cups regular sour cream (do not use low-fat or fat-free)

2 tablespoons fresh lemon juice

I tablespoon pure vanilla extract

TO START THE SHERBET

1 · Stir the sugar and water in a medium saucepan set over medium heat until the sugar has dissolved. Bring to a simmer without stirring. Set aside off the heat and cool to room temperature, about 2 hours. (If desired, the sugar mixture can be made up to a month in advance; store in a covered glass container in the refrigerator.)

2 · Puree the blackberries in a covered blender or food processor until fairly smooth. Pour into a fine-mesh sieve set over a bowl; wipe the pulpy mass across the mesh with a rubber spatula to extract as much juice as possible, leaving the seeds and thickened pulp behind. (Discard these.) Stir in the sour cream, lemon juice, vanilla extract, and ½ cup of the cooled sugar mixture. (Reserve the rest of the sugar mixture in a sealed glass container in the refrigerator for up to 2 months.) Refrigerate the blackberry mixture for at least 3 hours or up to 2 days, covering once cold.

TO FINISH UP

3 · Prepare an ice-cream machine. Stir the blackberry mixture and freeze it in the machine according to the manufacturer's instructions, until you can scoop up a small mound with edges that do not instantly begin to melt. Store in a sealed container in the freezer for up to 1 month.

À LA MODE IT · Set a meringue shell on each plate and add a large scoop of the sherbet. Garnish with fresh blackberries and/or confectioners' sugar, if desired. And if you skip making the sherbet, substitute a high-quality, tart raspberry sorbet (not sherbet).

PRO TIP · The extra sugar syrup can be used to sweeten cocktails or in any recipe that calls for "simple syrup."

STEAMED HOLIDAY PUDDING

—◆—

FROZEN HARD SAUCE

We end with the end of the year: our version of a winter classic, served with a frozen version of its traditional boozy, buttery sauce. The resulting heavily spiced pudding (or cake, as it might be called on this side of the Atlantic pond) is quite crumbly: it won't cut into clean wedges and will in fact barely hold its shape on the plate with all that dried fruit in tow.

STEAMED HOLIDAY PUDDING

· YIELD: ONE 1½-QUART ROUND CAKE ·

—◆—

Unlike a traditional steamed pudding, there's no need to ripen this one in a closet or under your bed for months. We didn't use suet, so we're not looking to mellow its flavor. Instead, we use coconut oil, solid at room temperature. It gives the pudding a pleasing, slightly tropical flare. Note the tricky ingredient amounts: 1 cup chopped pitted dates (that is, measured after chopping) versus ½ cup dried cherries, chopped (that is, measured before chopping). Our decisions were about the easiest way to measure them yet maintain accuracy.

Unsalted butter, for greasing

I cup brandy

I cup chopped, stemmed dried figs

I cup chopped, pitted dates

½ cup dried cherries, chopped

¼ cup fresh orange juice (about 2 medium oranges)

2 teaspoons finely grated orange zest

3 large eggs, at room temperature and lightly beaten in a small bowl

I cup plus 2 tablespoons plain dried bread crumbs

¼ cup granulated white sugar

¼ cup packed dark brown sugar

¼ cup coconut oil, melted and cooled

2 teaspoons pure vanilla extract

½ teaspoon ground allspice

½ teaspoon ground cinnamon

½ teaspoon ground cloves

¼ teaspoon salt

PREP · Butter the inside of a I ½-quart round, high-sided soufflé or baking dish.

TO MAKE THE PUDDING

1 · Mix the brandy, figs, dates, cherries, orange juice, and zest in a large saucepan set over medium-high heat; bring to a simmer, stirring occasionally. Cover, reduce the heat to low, and simmer until the liquid has been absorbed, about 7 minutes. Set aside, uncovered, to cool to room temperature, for at least 1 hour or up to 3 hours.

2 · Stir the remaining ingredients into the saucepan with the dried fruit until uniform and well combined. Pour and pack this mixture into the prepared baking dish. Cover with parchment paper, then cover and seal tightly with aluminum foil.

TO STEAM IT

3 · Set up a steamer rack in a large pot with a lid. Put about 2 inches of water in the pot (but not enough to come up through the rack) and bring to a boil over high heat. Set the full, sealed baking dish in the rack, cover, reduce the heat to low, and steam for 1 hour 45 minutes, adding more water to the pot as necessary. Transfer the (very hot!) baking dish to a wire rack and cool for 30 minutes.

4 · Transfer the pudding to the refrigerator and store for at least 24 hours. Unmold the steamed pudding onto a platter and set aside at room temperature for at least 1 hour or up to 3 hours to take off the chill. Slice into wedges to serve. The pudding can be stored in its covered baking dish in the refrigerator for up to 1 week. To rewarm, steam, covered in its baking dish, over simmering water for at least 30 minutes or up to 45 minutes.

PRO TIP · Since coconut oil is solid at room temperature, you'll need to scrape it out of the jar with a fork. Pack the shreds in the measuring cup before you melt them over low heat (or in a bowl in the microwave on high in 10-second increments, stirring after each heating).

FROZEN HARD SAUCE
· YIELD: ABOUT 1 QUART ·

Hard sauce combines butter and a distilled spirit, often brandy. It's also often made with confectioners' sugar—and we kept that in the mix here to give the frozen confection a slightly grainy texture, to pull it away from the velvety feel of ice cream and gelato. We felt this texture was more in keeping with all the small crumbles in the steamed pudding.

1³/₄ cups heavy cream

1 cup whole milk

4 tablespoons (½ stick) unsalted butter, cut into small bits

4 large egg yolks, at room temperature

³/₄ cup confectioners' sugar

⅛ teaspoon salt

1 tablespoon cornstarch

6 tablespoons (3 ounces) brandy

TO MAKE THE CUSTARD

1 · Warm the cream, milk, and butter in a large saucepan over medium-low heat until the butter melts; do not bring to a simmer. Meanwhile, use an electric mixer at medium speed to beat the egg yolks, confectioners' sugar, and salt until quite thick and pale yellow, about 4 minutes. Scrape down the inside of the bowl, then beat in the cornstarch until smooth.

2 · Beat about half the hot cream mixture into the egg yolk mixture in a slow, steady stream until smooth; then beat this combined mixture into the remaining cream mixture in the pan. Set over low heat and cook, stirring constantly, until the custard thickly coats the back of a wooden spoon and the temperature registers 170°F, 4 to 7 minutes.

3 · Pour the mixture through a fine-mesh sieve into a bowl; refrigerate for at least 4 hours or up to 2 days, covering once the custard is cold.

TO FREEZE IT

4 · Prepare an ice-cream machine. Stir the brandy into the cold custard. Freeze it in the machine according to the manufacturer's instructions, until you can scoop up a small mound with edges that do not instantly begin to melt. Store in a sealed container in the freezer for up to 1 month.

À LA MODE IT · Because of the brandy, the frozen hard sauce may be a bit hard, even icy. Set it out at room temperature for 10 minutes before serving with slices of the pudding.

ACKNOWLEDGMENTS

—◆—

A cookbook is like an ice cream social: you have to have a lot of people. Ours included:

- Eric Medsker, one of the best photographers we know (and a terrific friend)

- Caroline Dorn, a spot-on eye for props to make the desserts look their best

- BJ Berti, a great editor who helped us craft the book into something better than we imagined

- Courtney Littler, always on top of things at the publisher, making our job so much easier

- Michelle McMillian, an art director who caught our vision for "hip but comfortable"

- Jan Derevjanik, a terrific book designer

- Danielle Fiorella, a great cover designer

- Marie Estrada, an on-the-ball marketer for cookbooks

- John Karle, a hardworking publicist in a fast-moving industry

- Leah Stewart, a copyeditor who made it seem all too easy

- Susan Ginsburg, our literary agent for (gulp) twenty-six cookbooks (and counting)

- Stacy Testa, our patient voice of reason at the agency

- Mary Rodgers and Ilona Gollinger at Cuisinart, who supplied the ice cream machines for recipe-testing and the photo shoot

- Kim Roman and Jill Sciuto at Digitas, who supplied ice cream attachments for the KitchenAid mixer as well as invaluable KitchenAid bakeware

- Gretchen Holt and her team at OXO, for more kitchen tools than we can ever count, including some pretty fine ice cream scoops

INDEX